CHICKEN SOUP FOR THE WRITER'S SOUL

Stories to Open the Heart and Rekindle the Spirit of Writers

Jack Canfield
Mark Victor Hansen
Bud Gardner

Health Communications, Inc.
Deerfield Beach, Florida

www.hci-online.com
www.chickensoup.com

We would like to acknowledge the following publishers and individuals for permission to reprint the following material. (Note: The stories that were penned anonymously, that are in the public domain, or that were written by Jack Canfield, Mark Victor Hansen or Bud Gardner are not included in this listing.)

Beginning passage of epigraph and *It Doesn't Matter What You Write*. Reprinted by permission of Elizabeth Engstrom. ©2000 Elizabeth Engstrom.

Excerpt from "Address Upon Receiving the Nobel Prize for Literature" by William Faulkner from *Essays, Speeches and Public Letters* (New York: Random House, Inc., 1966). ©1950 by William Faulkner. Reprinted by permission of Random House, Inc.

Ronny's Book and *Marriage and Metaphors: A Writer's Life On and Off the Pages*. Reprinted by permission of Judith A. Chance. ©1998 Judith A. Chance.

A Writer's Journey. Reprinted by permission of Ernest J. Gaines. ©1998 Ernest J. Gaines.

Vindication. Reprinted by permission of Ruben Navarrette Jr. © 1998 Ruben Navarrette Jr.

1,600 Articles Ago . . . Reprinted by permission of Gordon Burgett. ©1999 Gordon Burgett.

(Continued on page 403)

Library of Congress Cataloging-in-Publication Data

Chicken soup for the writer's soul: stories to open the heart and rekindle the spirit of writers / [compiled by] Jack Canfield, Mark Victor Hansen, Bud Gardner.

    p.   cm.

    ISBN 1-55874-770-2 (hardcover)—ISBN 1-55874-769-9 (trade paper)

    1. Authorship.   I. Canfield, Jack, date.   II. Hansen, Mark Victor, date.
III. Gardner, Bud, date.

PN137.C49 2000
808'.02—dc21   00-024342

Publisher: Health Communications, Inc.
               3201 S.W. 15th Street
               Deerfield Beach, FL 33442-8190

Cover art design by Akira Kikuchi
Cover redesign by Andrea Perrine Brower
Typesetting by Lawna Patterson Oldfield

I have come to believe that there are no new photos and few new stories, only unusual recombinations of things that have been told before. But what is new, and fresh and original is the author's lens through which these situations are viewed. Our gift, and consequently our responsibility as writers, is to view life situations in our naturally unique way and report the truth about their meanings and values to the reading public so they can have fresh insight into the human condition. We are each unique in the universe and, therefore, so are the stories we tell.

—Elizabeth Engstrom

I believe that man will not merely endure: he will prevail. He is immortal, not because he alone among creatures has an inexhaustible voice, but because he has a soul, a spirit capable of compassion and sacrifice and endurance. The poet's, the writer's, duty is to write about these things. It is his privilege to help man endure by lifting his heart, by reminding him of the courage and honor and hope and pride and compassion and pity and sacrifice which have been the glory of his past. The poet's voice need not merely be the record of man, it can be one of the props, the pillars to help him endure and prevail.

—William Faulkner
Excerpt from his Acceptance Speech
for the Nobel Prize for Literature
December 10, 1950, Stockholm, Sweden

RUBES. *Reprinted by permission of Leigh Rubin and Creators Syndicate.*

This book is dedicated to all the beginning and professional writers, journalists, novelists, freelancers, poets, screenwriters and cartoonists throughout the world who are striving, through their written work, to make the world a better place. Your heartfelt articles, poems, short stories, novels, nonfiction books, plays and cartoons enlighten, enthrall and entertain readers throughout the world.

We also dedicate this book to all the English, journalism, creative writing and reading teachers, at all levels in our educational system, who have dedicated their lives to inspiring our future generations to express themselves through the written word.

In addition, this book is dedicated to the Maui Writers Foundation, the sponsoring organization of the Maui Writers Conference and Maui Writers Retreat, annual writing programs that are changing the face of the publishing industry by bringing bestselling authors, agents, editors and publishers together with writers to produce quality literary properties.

Finally, this book is dedicated to all the readers everywhere, for without you, the great works of the world would lie dormant.

Thanks to all of you for keeping the spirit of writing alive.

Contents

6. MAKING A DIFFERENCE

7. OVERCOMING OBSTACLES

8. A WRITER'S LIFE

9. THE POWER OF PERSEVERANCE

10. INSIGHTS AND LESSONS

Acknowledgments

Chicken Soup for the Writer's Soul took three years to write, compile and edit. It has been a joyous—though often challenging—task, and we wish to thank the following people whose contributions have made it possible.

Our wives—Inga, Patty and Jennifer—who supported us by locating and reading many stories and sharing their lives with this project without complaint.

Our children—Oran, Kyle, Christopher, Travis, Riley, Elisabeth, Melanie, Lori, Jill and Cael—who have always been our inspirations and guiding lights.

Heather McNamara, our senior editor, who brought this book to its final stages of completeness. She was instrumental at every stage along the way, keeping the whole process on track in the midst of constant chaos.

Nancy Mitchell Autio, who oversaw the entire process of getting permission for all of the stories and cartoons we used.

Patty Aubery, who worked closely with us in the final editing phase of the book as well as oversaw the daily operation of The Canfield Training Group and Chicken Soup for the Soul Enterprises.

Deborah Hatchell, who typed stories, handled scheduling and oversaw the production and compilation of our final review manuscript. She did an awesome job under tremendous time pressures.

Leslie Riskin, who spent weeks helping with the permission process.

Ro Miller, who handled a lot of the correspondence and telephone calls associated with this process.

D'ette Corona, Veronica Romero and Teresa Esparza for typing stories and for holding down the office.

Patty Hansen, President of Legal and Licensing for Chicken Soup for the Soul Enterprises, for her expertise and continued support of this book project. Joy Pieterse, Patty's Executive Assistant, for her liaison efficiency.

Lisa Williams, Laurie Hartman and Laura Rush for operating Mark Victor Hansen's office.

Larry and Linda Price who, in addition to keeping Jack's Foundation for Self-Esteem operating smoothly, continue to administrate the Soup Kitchens for the Soul projects, which distributes thousands of *Chicken Soup for the Soul* books free each year to prisoners, halfway houses, homeless shelters, battered woman shelters and inner-city schools.

Peter Vegso, President of Health Communications, Inc., for his continuing support in the publication and distribution of the *Chicken Soup for the Soul* books all over the world.

Tom Sand, at Health Communications, Inc., who has worked so hard to get our books distributed more thoroughly around the globe.

Christine Belleris, Matthew Diener, Lisa Drucker, Allison Janse and Susan Tobias, our editors at Health Communications, Inc., for their generous efforts in bringing this book to its high state of excellence.

Randee Goldsmith, *Chicken Soup for the Soul* manager at Health Communications, Inc., for her masterful coordination and support of all the *Chicken Soup* projects.

Terry Burke, Irena Xanthos, Jane Barone, Lori Golden, Kelly Johnson Maragni, Karen Bailiff Ornstein, Kim Weiss, Larry Getlen, Kimberley Denney and Maria Konicki at Health Communications, Inc., for their incredible publicity and marketing efforts.

Akira Kikuchi for his original cover art design, Andrea Perrine Brower for her cover redesign, and Lawna Patterson Oldfield for her inside book design.

Claude Choquette who manages year after year to get each of our books translated into over twenty languages around the world.

John and Shannon Tullius, John Saul, Mike Sack, Dan Poynter, Bryce Courtenay, Terry Brooks, Jillian Manus, Patti Breitman, Sam Horn, Bill Brohaugh, Jeff Arch, Dave Barry, Ridley Pearson, Elizabeth George, Elizabeth Engstrom, Don McQuinn, Andy Cohen, Dan Millman, Jay Bonansinga, Ted and Diana Wentworth, Rhonda Bobst and all of our other friends at the Maui Writers Conference and Retreat who inspire and encourage us every year.

Everyone at Newman Communications for helping us with our public relations efforts.

Lois Sloane at Sloane Vision for aiding us with our licensing projects.

The following people who sent us cartoons we used: John Caldwell, Mort Gerberg, Johnny Hart, Michael Maslin, Tom Prisk, Leigh Rubin, Charles Schulz, Bob Thaves and Tom Wilson.

The following people who read and rated the 200 stories that were the finalists for inclusion in this book. Their evaluations, comments and suggestions for improvement were invaluable. We could never have come close to creating such a high quality book without all of them. They include: Maggie Bedrosian, Christine Belleris, Michael Berberich, Dianna Booher, Suzanne Caplan, Kathy Carpenter, Mary Croney, Tom Dayton, Lee Elliot, Jeannie

Esposito, Villa Fontana, Pat Gallant, Dr. Al Geritz, Margaret Goldsmith, Nancy Richard Guilford, Deborah Hatchell, Evelyn Hess, Sam Horn, Sondra Keeler, Carol Kline, Kathy Krape, Debbie Leibold, Barbara Lomonaco, Patricia Lorenz, Linda Mitchell, Nicole Petzott, Penny Porter, Greg Roadifer and Connie Shelton.

A special thanks to Lynn Pribus and Jackie Rogers for their expert copyediting.

We also wish to thank the more than 5,000 people who took the time to submit stories, poems and other pieces for consideration. You all know who you are. While many of the stories submitted were wonderful, most did not fit into the overall structure of the book. However, many will be used in future volumes of the *Chicken Soup for the Soul* series which includes *Chicken Soup for the Man's Soul, Gardener's Soul, Grieving Soul, Veteran's Soul, Grandparent's Soul, Artist's Soul, Laughing Soul, Rags to Riches Soul, Teacher's Soul* and *Fisherman's Soul.*

Because of the immensity of this project, we may have left out names of some people who helped us along the way. If so, we are sorry. Please know that we really appreciate all of you.

We are truly grateful for the many hands and many hearts that made this book possible. We love you all!

Introduction

Maybe once in a lifetime, along comes a book that makes a real difference in the life of a writer. *Chicken Soup for the Writer's Soul* is that book. The mission of this book— *to turn you, America and the world onto the value of writing*—has attracted some of the finest authors in the world to share their stories with you. You'll recognize many of their names because you have read their work before. However, you may not know how they began writing, struggled to get published, faced rejection, focused hard on their own work, and finally realized their dreams by becoming published authors. They have revealed their life stories here for you.

You'll learn how Sue Grafton wrote six unpublished novels before she sold *'A' Is for Alibi*, the first of fifteen best-selling mystery novels. Or read how Steve Allen, a TV personality and author of more than fifty books and 8,000 songs, was accused of plagiarism; how Catherine Lanigan overcame a university professor's cruelty to—after waiting fourteen years—publish bestsellers *Romancing the Stone* and *Jewel of the Nile*; how Ernest J. Gaines, who couldn't go into a public library until he was fifteen years of age, checked out his first book and declared "I'm going to be a writer" and is now an icon in American literature;

how Barnaby Conrad helped shape the young Alex Haley's writing career; how Gene Perret practiced writing hundreds of jokes for Bob Hope long before Bob Hope ever hired him; how Hugh Prather, frustrated with his writing career, began writing personal notes that became his bestseller *Notes to Myself*, eventually selling five million copies; how John Tullius's uncle mentored him toward a fulfilling writing career; and how Lois Duncan wrote her way through college, tripling her income as she learned.

These and many, many more great stories await you.

As you read these marvelous stories, you, too, will feel their passion and will be inspired to try your own hand at writing. You will begin to find your own writing voice, to experience value moments ("Ahas!") as you write, to overcome rejection, to gain the courage to persevere, and, by writing fine stories, you'll remake a world. We urge you to read these stories over and over again to capture the valuable lessons, insights and wisdom found within.

We believe this book will sustain you during times of challenge, frustration and failure, and will guide you to new levels of seeing, feeling, perceiving and being. We hope *Writer's Soul* will become your life-long companion, inspiring you to open your heart and rekindle your spirit again and again, motivating you to become the best writer you can possibly be. In short, let this legacy of heartfelt stories touch you deeply, enabling you to clearly understand, as writer Jennifer Martin puts it so well in this book, "how sacred is the written word that paints portraits on our souls."

Share with Us

We would love to hear your reactions to the stories in this book. Please let us know what your favorite stories were and how they affected you.

We also invite you to send us stories you would like to see published in future editions of *Chicken Soup for the Soul*. You can send us either stories you have written or stories written by others that you have liked.

Send submissions to:

Chicken Soup for the Soul
P.O. Box 30880-S
Santa Barbara, CA 93130
Fax: 805-563-2945
e-mail: *stories@canfieldgroup.com*
Web site: *www.chickensoup.com*

We hope you enjoy reading this book as much as we enjoyed compiling, editing and writing it.

You can also visit the *Chicken Soup for the Soul* site on America Online at keyword: chickensoup. The site offers news, chats, experts and contests.

1

HOW I BECAME A WRITER

When I want to read a good book,
I write one.

Benjamin Disraeli

Ronny's Book

At first glance, Ronny looked like every other kid in the first-grade classroom where I volunteered as the Reading Mom. Wind-blown hair, scuffed shoes, a little bit of dirt behind his ears, some kind of sandwich smear around his mouth.

On closer inspection, though, the layer of dirt on Ronny's face, the crusty nose, and the packed grime under his fingernails told me he didn't get dirty at school. He arrived that way.

His clothes were ragged and mismatched, his sneakers had string for laces, and his backpack was no more than a plastic shopping bag.

Along with his outward appearance, Ronny stood apart from his classmates in other ways, too. He had a speech impediment, wasn't reading or writing at grade-level, and had already been held back a year, making him eight years old in the first grade. His home life was a shambles with transient parents who uprooted him at their whim. He had yet to live a full year in any one place.

I quickly learned that beneath his grungy exterior, Ronny possessed a spark, a resilience that I'd never seen in a child who faced such tremendous odds.

I worked with all the students in Ronny's class on a one-on-one basis to improve their reading skills. Each day, Ronny's head twisted around as I came into the classroom, and his eyes followed me as I set up in a corner, imploring, "Pick me! Pick me!" Of course I couldn't pick him every day. Other kids needed my help, too.

On the days when it was Ronny's turn, I'd give him a silent nod, and he'd fly out of his chair and bound across the room in a blink. He sat awfully close—too close for me in the beginning, I must admit—and opened the book we were tackling as if he were unearthing a treasure the world had never seen.

I watched his dirt-caked fingers move slowly under each letter as he struggled to sound out "Bud the Sub." It sounded more like "Baw Daw Saw" when he said it because of his speech impediment and his difficulty with the alphabet.

Each word offered a challenge and a triumph wrapped as one; Ronny painstakingly sounded out each letter, then tried to put them together to form a word. Regardless if "ball" ended up as "Bah-lah" or "bow," the biggest grin would spread across his face, and his eyes would twinkle and overflow with pride. It broke my heart each and every time. I just wanted to whisk him out of his life, take him home, clean him up and love him.

Many nights, after I'd tucked my own children into bed, I'd sit and think about Ronny. Where was he? Was he safe? Was he reading a book by flashlight under the blankets? Did he even have blankets?

The year passed quickly and Ronny had made some progress but hardly enough to bring him up to grade level. He was the only one who didn't know that, though. As far as he knew, he read just fine.

A few weeks before the school year ended, I held an awards ceremony. I had treats, gifts and certificates of achievement for everyone: Best Sounder-Outer, Most Expressive, Loudest Reader, Fastest Page-Turner.

It took me awhile to figure out where Ronny fit; I needed something positive, but there wasn't really much. I finally decided on "Most Improved Reader"—quite a stretch, but I thought it would do him a world of good to hear.

I presented Ronny with his certificate and a book—one of those Little Golden Books that cost forty-nine cents at the grocery store checkout. Tears rolled down his cheeks, streaking the ever-permanent layer of dirt as he clutched the book to his chest and floated back to his seat. I choked back the lump that rose in my throat.

I stayed with the class for most of the day; Ronny never let go of the book, not once. It never left his hands.

A few days later, I returned to the school to visit. I noticed Ronny on a bench near the playground, the book open in his lap. I could see his lips move as he read to himself.

His teacher appeared beside me. "He hasn't put that book down since you gave it to him. He wears it like a shirt, close to his heart. Did you know that's the first book he's ever actually owned?"

Fighting back tears, I approached Ronny and watched over his shoulder as his grimy finger moved slowly across the page. I placed my hand on his shoulder and asked, "Will you read me your book, Ronny?" He glanced up, squinted into the sun, and scooted over on the bench to make room for me.

And then, for the next few minutes, he read to me with more expression, clarity, and ease than I'd ever thought possible from him. The pages were already dog-eared, like the book had been read thousands of times already.

When he finished reading, Ronny closed his book, stroked the cover with his grubby hand and said with great satisfaction, "Good book."

A quiet pride settled over us as we sat on that playground bench, Ronny's hand now in mine. I at once wept and marveled at the young boy beside me. What a powerful contribution the author of that Little Golden Book had made in the life of a disadvantaged child.

At that moment, I knew I would get serious about my own writing career and do what that author had done, and probably still does—care enough to write a story that changes a child's life, care enough to make a difference.

I strive to be that author.

Judith A. Chance

A Writer's Journey

For a long time when I was asked how I started writing, I would say that I started writing in that Andrew Carnegie library in Vallejo, California, 1949. But for the last few years, I have come to realize that my apprenticeship as a writer happened many years earlier. Until I was fifteen years old, I lived on a sugarcane plantation in south Louisiana. Many of the old people on that plantation had never gone to school a day in their life. My aunt who raised me told me that I should write letters for the old people who could not write, and read their letters for them when they received mail. Writing the letters was a task that I did not look forward to doing, because the old people had little to say after, "Dear So and So, how are you? I am well and hope you are the same." After that they became quiet, and it was my duty to create the letter by asking them questions, and then adding some observations of my own. They always wanted you to write on both sides of the sheet of paper, but they had not said enough to fill even half the page on one side. So if you wanted to go out and shoot marbles or play baseball with your friends, you had to think, and think fast, which I did. I wrote about the weather, about the vegetable gardens in the backyard, and any other little thing that seemed important—but quickly as I could, so I could be free to play with my other brother and my friends who were not required to do this kind of work. The old people would pay me a nickel or maybe tea cakes and milk. I did not realize that, at the time I was sitting on the floor near their chairs, I was training to be a writer. I was between twelve and fourteen years old at the time, and I was as educated as anyone else on that plantation except for the schoolteacher.

I came to California at the age of fifteen in 1948. My mother got a job in one of the military plants, my stepfather enlisted into the merchant marines, and I was sent to school.

But like any fifteen or sixteen year old, I wanted to be with my friends after school. If we did not play football, we would hang around on the street corners, until my stepfather came in from one of his trips in the merchant marines and told me I had better find something to do with my free time.

I had three choices, the movies, the YMCA, or the library. I didn't have any money, so movies were out. That left the library and the YMCA. I chose the YMCA because I had never been inside one before. I had never been inside a library before either, but YMCA sounded more exciting. There was a basketball court, a swimming pool, a weight lifting room, and a dance hall with a piano. I did not know how to play basketball, I could not swim, I did not know how to shoot pool, or play a piano. But I hung around and watched others do these things.

One day someone asked me if I would like to put on some boxing gloves. I had put on boxing gloves once or twice before, but I knew nothing about the art of boxing. I had nothing else to do that day, and I wanted to be accepted; so I put on the gloves and got into the ring. I was to find out later that my opponent was a sparring partner for a professional fighter. But no one had to tell me that—I found out for myself by the second round. Between the first round and half way through the second, my opponent had hit me everywhere that it was legal to hit someone. Midway through the second round, I turned my back on him and leaning back against the ropes, I began removing the gloves, using my teeth to hurry the process, while everyone in the gym stood around laughing. Next day or a couple days later, I went to the library.

This was the first time I had ever gone into a library, because the one in town nearby where I lived in Louisiana was for Whites only. I can still remember the day I first went into that Carnegie Library in Vallejo, California. I had to go up a set of marble steps, through double doors, through a foyer, into the main room of the library. I saw two or three women behind a counter, and other people reading magazines and newspapers at tables. These people were of different races and different ages, so I felt it was all right for me to be there too. I approached the magazine rack, took a magazine at random, and sat down at the table. No one paid me any attention. But I watched everything around me. I spent more time looking over the top of the magazine than I did reading it. For the next few days I must have done the same thing, taken a magazine or a newspaper off the rack, sat down at the table and looked around more than I did reading.

I noticed that some people left the library carrying books under their arms. One day I got up enough courage to ask one of the women behind the counter how does one take books from the library. She gave me a form and told me to have my parents fill it out and I would receive a library card. About the time I received the card, I noticed a set of stairs leading up to a second floor. It took me a while to build up the courage to go up there, and it was like taking a trip into a foreign country. There were racks and racks and racks of books, more books than I could have imagined existed. I walked down every aisle that was not occupied by someone else, looking at the books, the titles, the authors' names, but never removing the books from the shelves. I know I did not check a book out that day, and maybe it was several more days before I took a book home. But whether I was taking a book home or reading it at the library, I became aware that I was choosing books with certain titles without really knowing why. If the title had *road* in it, or *water* or *tree* or *land* or *field* or *country* or *farm*, I would take that book from the shelf. Later I realized that I chose those titles because I was looking for something about my background, southern and rural. During my first fifteen and a half years, I had lived on a plantation where I had worked in the fields from the time I was eight years old. I had fished in the bayous and the rivers at about that same age, and I had gone into the swamps to pull the end of a hand saw when I was no more than eleven. So when *tree* came up in a title, or *earth* in the title, *land* or *water* in the title, my interest perked up as well.

But many of these books left me with a feeling of disappointment. Though they spoke of earth, land, water, trees, and the people who lived and worked there, they were not describing *my people*, the people I had left in the South—my aunt who raised me, and the old people who visited her and for whom I wrote letters. They were not describing my brothers and my uncles; they were not talking about my friends with whom I had played ball and shot marbles. They were talking about others, and I did not see me there.

In 1949, my mother had a baby boy—Michael. That summer, it was my duty to look after Michael while my mother was at work. I thought this would give me an opportunity to write a novel. Novel writing couldn't be very hard; look how many books there were in the library. My big problem was to keep Michael quiet and not disturb me while I wrote. That was accomplished by both of us lying on the floor, and while I wrote in longhand on a notebook, the other hand was held lightly over Michael's eyes. When he got tired of that, he would eventually give up trying to stay awake and go to sleep.

When I finished my book in longhand, I got my mother to rent me a typewriter. I knew nothing at all about typing, just as I would find out that I knew nothing about writing a novel. I would spend hours on hours pecking on the typewriter with one finger, while I kept my other hand over Michael's eyes until he went to sleep.

Since books are printed on sheets about half the size of the average sheet of paper, I decided to cut my sheets of paper in halves. Since books are printed on both sides of the page, I did that as well. Since books are printed in single space, I did that too. I wanted to make it easy for the publishers.

I finished my novel sometime during the spring or summer of 1950. I found some brown wrapping paper in the kitchen and some strings somewhere in a drawer, and I wrapped and tied up my manuscript and sent it to New York. A month or so later it came back accompanied by one of those patented rejection slips: "Sorry. But keep us in mind." I took the manuscript outside and burned it in the incinerator. That was the end of my initial attempt at writing—because I had been neglecting my school work and falling further and further back in my classes.

After graduating from high school and spending two years in junior college, I enlisted into the army. On being discharged, I enrolled at San Francisco State to study writing and American Literature. Later I would win a fellowship to Stanford University. Both at State and Stanford I had wonderful teachers who encouraged me to write about the things I knew—to write about that Louisiana I had come from, and the lives of the people who lived there. They told me to write about my aunt and about the old people who could not read and write, and to write about my brother and my friends and the way we lived and the way we played. They assigned me books to read, and they showed me how other writers had put their experiences into writing.

For seven years, I wrote and supported myself with a variety of menial jobs before my first book, *Catherine Carmier*, was published. It was another three years before my work began to be recognized when *Of Love and Dust* was published in 1967. Since then, most of my books have been translated into many foreign languages. The best-sellers, *Autobiography of Miss Jane Pittman* and *A Lesson Before Dying*, won Emmy Awards for their film adaptations. Because of my work, I have received the MacArthur Foundation Award for a lifetime of literary achievement, have been named Chevalier of the Order of Arts and Letters by France and have been elected to the American Academy of Arts and Letters.

When I look back on this long journey, I feel that I'm still writing those letters for the old people, and not only for the old, but for the young as well. And not only for those whom I knew as a child, but for those who lived many generations before. They were not given a chance to read and write, and I was. But without their voices, had I not sat on that porch and wrote those letters fifty years ago, I doubt that there would be any book or films, or awards. I am certain that I would not be where I am today.

Ernest J. Gaines

Vindication

Q: Confronted with a world of new possibilities and towering expectations, what is a Mexican-American Harvard graduate most likely to do in life?

A: Disappoint.

And, despite a résumé which is unusually long and distinguished for a thirty-one-year-old, I have always been most terrified of disappointing my parents. For all that my mother and father were unable to accomplish in their own lives, growing up as they did surrounded by poverty and discrimination, the accomplishments of my brother, sister and me have somehow been expected to compensate.

And for me, attending and graduating from the most prestigious university in the country was a fine start. Trouble is, the career path I chose after that went in a totally different direction from the one that they would have chosen for me. They had always expected me to simply become a lawyer, an option that now seems to me terribly unimaginative. My father, in particular, had, as a career cop, always held lawyers in high regard and had always prompted me in that direction, force-feeding me his ambitions like a plate of vegetables.

But now, years later, I have arrived, by fits and starts and against the grain of my proud parents' ambitions, at a place that I never dreamed existed.

I'm a writer.

That path has been, at times, fraught with discomfort, anxiety and doubt. I was often tempted to turn back. One reason that I didn't was that I realized, along the way, that the choice had never really been mine in the first place, but that my journey, however difficult, had been pre-determined by fate.

The precise moment of my liberation came at the point at which I admitted to myself that, despite the culture of achievement in which I had been raised, I'd rather be a struggling writer than a successful lawyer. And now that the road is clear, my heart is filled with the satisfaction of knowing that I am finally able to scratch out a comfortable living doing what I dearly love doing, and I know what I am supposed to be doing.

But, it is also scarred by the clear memory of those turbulent and uncertain days, days which are behind me for now, but not far and maybe not for long.

I remember, for instance, that an argument with my father two years ago was an especially vicious one. The shouting, the cursing, the flaring of tempers on opposite ends of the phone line, each party striving to be heard over the recriminations of the other. The drama—which used to play itself out, on cue, two or three times a year—would inevitably begin with a dose of parental concern. The old man's words were chosen carefully and intended to soften the blow of the lecture to follow.

"We worry about you, your mother and me. It's hard for you, we know."

Yes, it was hard. It had been hard since the beginning—harder than I could ever have imagined, years ago, when I first decided to make a full-blown profession out of something that many others, of perhaps sounder judgment, are content to delve into only as a hobby.

It was excruciatingly hard making a living at it, to be sure. As a freelancer, I'd write nearly every day, faxing out unsolicited essays and editorials to a stable of newspapers and magazines. Sometimes, checks would arrive in the mail. But never as dependably as bills did. And so, I was living back in my native San Joaquin Valley, nestled in the center of California. I was seeking shelter under my girlfriend's roof and occasionally working, for seventy-five dollars a day as a substitute teacher in poor, rural, elementary and secondary schools to help support my writing habit. I'd also lecture, when invited to, on college campuses, collecting speaking fees and honorariums whenever possible. And, since I had once been employed as a radio talk show host in Los Angeles, I would occasionally hire myself out to sit in for a local radio personality. And it was all to support my writing.

Apart from the immediate scramble to survive, I would also peck away, whenever possible, on long-term book projects. Having already written and published one book at a young age—I was twenty-five—I spent several hours a week coming up with new ideas and drafting new book proposals so that I might duplicate the feat. And then, I'd wait and wait and wait. Then the wait would end in a stream of rejection letters from unconvinced publishers. And so, I'd flip on my computer and start again.

"How long do you expect to keep this up? You're not making it. You're struggling. Your mother and I want to see you successful."

And I wanted to see my parents proud of me again. After nine years as a freelance writer, an author, a lecturer, a contributor to major newspapers and national magazines, a radio talk show host and part-time teacher, I was still struggling to pay my bills and meet my responsibilities.

Finally, in the spring of last year, I had had enough. Not of the writing but of where I had been doing it. Determined as I had been to be a writer, I had been just as determined to be one in my hometown. But one goal seemed to work against the other. I had always chalked up the desire to remain close to my roots to a sense of guilt over my classmates and I having, as ambitious teenagers, so eagerly abandoned my hometown in the sort of brain drain common to small towns of limited opportunity. The difficulty came with the simple truth that the San Joaquin Valley could support only a limited number of professions and mine was, apparently, not one of them.

Suddenly, I knew that I could not accomplish both goals. I had to choose. And I chose the writing.

And so, reluctantly and with a sad heart, I began to look again beyond its borders, spreading the word to editors at various newspapers that I was ready to leave the valley if anyone was interested in making me an offer. Within ten days, I was sent a plane ticket and hotel accommodations for a two-day interview with the *Arizona Republic* in Phoenix. Two months later, I had a lucrative offer, complete with moving expenses. More importantly, in hiring me as both a reporter and a columnist, those who hired me were challenging the rules of conventional journalism and allowing me to do what other newspapers had been reluctant to—maintain my own voice.

I remember the exact day that I accepted the offer. Standing in the shower, my mind wandered to all that I had endured over nine years—all the mistakes, all the tortured prose, all the rejection letters and collection notices and I felt proud, somehow, that I had found the strength and courage to keep the faith. Then, in a mixture of relief and pride and joy, tears streamed down my face. And I was overwhelmed.

Now I spend my days in a newsroom, surrounded by others who make their living wrestling with the written word. We have cell phones and pagers and expense accounts. My salary is five times what it was last year. I don't have to teach anymore—my stints of "bus duty" are over. But I still lecture and host radio shows. And I'll write more books.

But none of that is as satisfying as the knowledge that my parents are sleeping better these days, that they are proud of me again.

And even if success is the best revenge, it cannot be as sweet as the words that my father spoke one afternoon recently. We were back home, driving in the mountains near the spot where we'd gone fishing when I was a boy. We stopped at an old general store, where my father struck up a neighborly conversation with an old man stacking canned goods behind the counter.

"We just came up here for the afternoon," my father said. "Thought we'd see how high the water was, maybe do some fishing later.

"That's my boy there," he said, pointing to me.

"He's a writer."

Ruben Navarrette Jr.

1,600 Articles Ago . . .

A professional writer is an amateur who didn't quit.

Richard Bach

It began innocently enough, a many-mile bike ride to the Des Plaines Theater to see a Saturday afternoon Roy Rogers movie. My fate was sealed when Dick Bauer walked by and asked me if I knew how to type.

Mind you, I was a sophomore in high school and about half as tall as a human. Dick Bauer was a junior and loomed like a giant.

"Why?" I asked at such a weird request, as the line started to move toward the door.

"Because if you can, go over to the *Suburban Times* office before four and talk with Floyd Fulle, an old guy, who needs somebody to write the high school sports for the paper."

Forget that I'd never touched a typewriter—I'd cross that bridge if I came to it. I saw Roy, Gabby Hayes and Trigger win again, then peddled across town to find the old man Fulle, who was every bit of thirty-five.

"Can you type?" Fulle asked.

"Sure, why?" I replied, too scared to be diplomatic or coy.

"Because my last sportswriter handwrote everything, and he couldn't spell either. He'd put a person in three times with three different spellings. If you can type, it's ten dollars a week. Fill up the page and have it here Tuesday morning before school. For God's sake, ask people how they spell their name." He waved me away like a hired gnat.

"You need something this Tuesday?" I asked.

"Aren't you still on vacation? No, start next Tuesday. Go talk to the football coach. Check cross-country. You're the sports editor, you figure it out. Just give me a full page."

There I was, an instant sports editor, suddenly rich, and he never once asked if I could even finish a sentence! So much for playing for the Cubs or buying a man's hat and becoming some kind of an executive after high school: I was a journalist!

You can imagine the surprise back home when I shared the news. Gordon got a job! You'd think they were announcing the sinking of the *Titanic* or Liberace's marriage. And a journalist! My mother was certain they had hired the wrong Gordon. My twin brother couldn't stop laughing. My kid brother looked at me like I'd contracted a disease. Only my dad had his wits about him. "You can type? What are you going to use, Guttenberg blocks?"

I'd come to the bridge.

"Well, I can't really type, but how hard can it be? You just hunt around until you find each letter, hit it and keep going. It'd be a little slow in the beginning . . ."

"Yeh," my twin added, "like the football season will be over by the time you finish your first article."

"So I get the information on Saturday, write the stuff on Sunday, and type Monday after school. Big deal." I wasn't about to go back to Floyd Fulle and lose my weekly windfall.

"Dad, you've got parts of every mechanical contraption ever thrown out down at your place. Don't you have a typewriter—or two halves we could stitch together?"

He laughed. "I'll dig around and see what I can find." The following Monday my father brought home a huge monstrosity coated in dust, the keys obscured by machine oil and sweat. He owned a job shop and was an inventor—a "perfector," he called it: "They tell me, or bring it in, and I make it work." He was vague about the origin of this machine. I suspect he'd paid three dollars to one of his buddies who found it in some storage bin.

"It works," he announced. "I wrote a letter, and it was as smooth as butter!" That brought instant dismay, then laughter since my father had cut off his typing finger in a punch press and couldn't spell. He was as likely to type a letter as he was to dance in *The Nutcracker*. Not a ringing testimonial.

We dusted it off, got out the turpentine, and cleaned off the keys and their arms. It sparkled when we were done. But nobody actually tried it, other than to bat at a few random keys to see if we could read the result. We could. I'd keep it pure until I really needed it.

Getting the information was simple enough. Everybody liked to talk about themselves, including the coaches, particularly if they would read about it later. Put it all in some order, get the schedules for the fall sports, and I was ready for my debut. It seemed like robbery taking ten whole dollars for just that.

I read the entire *Chicago Daily News* sports section the next Sunday morning looking for clues. Keep it to two sentences per paragraph, no jawbreaking words, don't use "I," and let somebody talk every few paragraphs, preferably the coach or the stars. Duck soup.

I wrote two articles that afternoon.

An interview with the football coach and a few of the better players about the coming year. In retrospect, they all sounded the same. The coach either said nothing or talked like a machine gun, but to write it that way made him sound like he had an IQ of forty-five. The players, who probably weren't that smart, rambled on, fumbling their verbs and mismatching their pronouns. So I converted their incoherence into complete sentences that finished in the same direction they had started. Their girlfriends must have been impressed. Nothing to sportswriting that a dictionary, thesaurus, imagination and a pencil couldn't correct.

The article about boys' cross-country (girls were still considered too delicate to run that far in public) was easier. The coach was a regular teacher, English or history or something requiring articulation. He gave me yards of prose which I pruned to feet. I didn't call any of the runners. It didn't matter. Who cared about cross-country?

And lots of schedules with opponents, times and places. Page fillers, bless them.

All that was missing was putting this text and the schedules into typed form. I rushed home on Monday, ate a sandwich, cleared off the table in the basement, found a tall chair, inserted paper and started the hunt for the letters.

Simple as poking a pig, except when I got to the letter "e," which was the second letter I needed. The key went down, the arm made noise, something flew up paperward, but nothing printed. I checked the renegade type arm: There was no font attached to it!

A mean internal voice asked, how many other keys have nothing at the end of them? I banged every key— qwertyuiop, and so on—and only the "e" had fled. It could have been worse.

So I typed as if the "e" was replete and brilliant, the star of the pack, except that I put tape on the key itself to send my finger to the space bar. I'd write in the "e's" later. I began at about five, expecting to finish in time to do some homework, hear a radio show, and go to bed by ten. At 5:15 the next morning I finished typing my copy. Then I wrote in the missing "e's," just in time to survive a fried egg, throw the copy and my untouched books in my bike basket, and pedal like the wind into town, drop off the text and rush to school, with one minute to spare. Forget about sleep, I had six classes, each good for a short nap. Beating the deadline was what counted.

That afternoon I called Floyd Fulle to see if what I wrote was okay.

"What happened to the 'e' on that typewriter? Get it fixed. Don't use the word 'and' so often. Get your check every Tuesday morning."

My dad took the typewriter to work and brought it back a few days later. He'd purloined an "e" from another typewriter and welded it to mine. It looked ugly, required twice the punching power, was the wrong font, and listed about fifteen degrees to the right. But it lasted three full years, 120 weeks times ten dollars. I was too young and dumb to know what I was doing touching all those athletes and their families with stories still sitting yellowed, in albums in attics. But I did spell the names right, and it was a lot of fun. The only problem: It was so much fun it prevented me from making something of myself. I could be a plumbing wizard or a yodeler or even a hypnotist, but for the joy of tweaking words. Being a journalist was duck soup.

Gordon Burgett

At Aunt Jennie's Knee

*The Native American voice was once a mighty
    roar across this land.*

*But just as the vast buffalo herds once thundered
    across the plains*

*and are no more, the voice of the American
    Indian has faded to a whisper.*

*The powerful voice and the age-old wisdom of
    the Native American—carried in drumbeat
    and passed from tongue to tongue as the
    evening fires met the twilight—still live.*

*The timeless philosophy and principles for living
    await those who choose to—Catch the Whisper
    of the Wind.*

Cheewa James

When we were young children in the 1940s, my
brother, sister and I would pile into the back seat of our
car every Sunday for the ride to visit my great-great-great
aunt Jennie Clinton, who lived on the Klamath Indian
Reservation in Oregon.

She was the last survivor of the Modoc War of 1872 to 1873, fought in what is today the Lava Beds National Monument, California. The Modoc War was the only American Indian war ever fought on California soil. Considering the number of Indians involved, it was one of the most expensive American Indian battles, in loss of money and lives. Fifty Modoc warriors, who had their women and children with them in a natural lava fortress, held off a military force that by the end of the war numbered one thousand U.S. military soldiers. Jennie was a young woman during the war and would pull needed clothes and ammunition from the bodies of fallen soldiers. She hated her job. Jennie died in 1950 somewhere around one hundred years of age.

As we would leave to visit Jennie and some of the other Indian women on the reservation, my mother would turn around to the three of us in the back seat and admonish us not to admire any of the possessions of the older people—especially jewelry. If we expressed admiration for something, chances were, it would be given to us. It was something we three kids picked up on very quickly—and something my mother was very swift to squelch.

As it turned out, the unimagined gift I received from Aunt Jennie proved to be much more valuable than jewelry. As I sat listening to Aunt Jennie tell stories, I knew something special was happening—but at my young age I couldn't comprehend its full significance. Yet deep down I felt a stirring, an emotional bonding with Jennie, a seed being planted that would ultimately shape my life. But what was this thing that I felt so deeply?

I have often thought back on that early lesson in Native American generosity and lack of emphasis on material possessions. For a little girl just learning about life, I saw the priority the elders gave to the act of sharing. Children do not do what you say; they do what you do. I had my role models early on.

Aunt Jennie was my first and greatest role model as a storyteller, which ultimately shaped my writing life. On those Sundays we would visit Jennie in her old house made of lumber that had long ago peeled to a weather-beaten gray. We three children would sit on her front porch, gathered at her feet.

That put me right at eye-level with her hands. At first they frightened me and reminded me of a bird's claws. But Sunday by Sunday, I got used to them. They were part of her. To this day, when I see the bony, aging hands of elderly people, I feel tenderness.

Jennie often read to us from the Bible. She was totally blind. Like most of the Modoc, she had become a Quaker after her arrival in Oklahoma Indian Territory, where the Modoc exiles were sent as prisoners of war after the Modoc War. In 1907, the Modocs were allowed to return to the Oregon/California area. Although most did not return because the land of exile had become home, Jennie still remembered the homeland, where her people had resided for many thousands of years, and went back. Knowing she was losing her eyesight, she had memorized great portions of the Bible. With the three of us grouped at her feet, she would open her Bible to a prescribed page and "read."

Jennie was a master storyteller in the tradition of Native American people. Where written language does not exist, passing information down orally, in an accurate way, becomes an art form, made famous by Alex Haley in *Roots*. It was also a means of survival. Medicinal cures, theology, food gathering and preparing techniques, geographical directions, herbology—all facets of life were passed down by word of mouth. It was indeed the transferral of a culture.

Jennie Clinton would tell wonderful stories that often had to do with the core of life itself. Into many of her stories, she would weave a message or lesson for us. Because it was all in the framework of meaningful, exciting stories, we did not easily forget the moral.

Jennie taught the beauty of sharing time with words. We have so many substitutes today. Television, computers and video often replace sitting at an elder's knee. People now have no idea how their parents met, what their grandparents did as young people, or even what happened on the day they were born.

But in those periods of time I spent with Jennie, there was something even more important than the passing of information. I don't remember everything Jennie said. I was only a small girl at the time. But what I do clearly remember is the emotion—the bonding and the incredible feeling of being part of a continuing circle of love. When I think of her rusty old voice drifting through the air on those lazy Sundays, I feel a warmth, a flood of human caring.

As I wandered through life, attending college, getting married and raising a family, my mind kept drifting back to Aunt Jennie. What was it that felt so incomplete—something missing in my life?

Then one day, it hit me like a bolt of lightning out of the blue: *Aunt Jennie's true gift to me was not jewelry, but the art of storytelling.*

At that moment, my future became clear: I, too, would become a storyteller—a professional writer. With a burst of energy over the next few years, I wrote and sold 150 articles and, eventually, two books.

Since I'd married a man who likes birds, snakes and bats, I found my greatest stories in my own life, right under my own nose. I sold my first story to the *Kansas City Star* on what it was like to be a birdwatcher's wife. More of my articles appeared in *Smithsonian* and *National Wildlife* on rare bats, stories that read just as I would speak them.

Most of the articles I published, I was able to share initially in verbal story form with my two sons, David and Todd. As a writer, I discovered very quickly that adult readers are just grown-up children.

Life is a series of stories—and everyone has one. It was only right that my first book, *Catch the Whisper of the Wind*, be a compilation of stories about Native North Americans. Where did I find these people? They sat next to me on planes, pumped my gas, sold me jewelry. In other words, any Native American that I chanced to run into in the course of a day was great material for the book. Although many people started their stories by telling me they really didn't have a story, they all had a story to tell.

Later, writing—and storytelling—helped me find a niche as a television talk show host, news anchor, and finally a professional speaker.

I learned well at Aunt Jennie's knee. Even though she never put it into words and would probably be astonished at what she has passed on to me, Jennie taught me a lot about writing and life.

Jennie taught me that the human heart and mind are boundless and amazing. She taught me that the greatest tool a writer has is not the pen, paper, typewriter or computer. It isn't even the command of grammar, composition and word formation. It is the ability to listen.

Aunt Jennie's voice, once a strong force across this land, is long gone now. But her spirit—who she was, what she stood for, and what she taught me—lives on. Even today, I can hear her voice—if I'll only catch the whisper of the wind.

Cheewa James

The Writer's Song

Growing up, I was among the forgotten. I was battered, beaten, emotionally and sexually abused. For over ten years my father invaded my life, attaching himself like a barnacle, unwanted and feared. The names he hurled at me eroded my self-esteem. I was called "the girl with no mouth." I rarely spoke to or answered anyone. Between my father and me was my mother, silent and unmovable. The Sphinx factor who cast a long, dark shadow over me. With fists and switches, she made the bruises and welts that hid beneath my skirts. I was the Cinderella of the family, stripped of emotional ties.

For years I went through life bandaging deep, bleeding wounds that wouldn't heal. I read books and articles about the abuse but kept the secret sealed within. I joined (at forty-three) a church support group: Incest Survivors Anonymous. The hurt I listened to strained like toxic puree through me. It was then I learned the value of my writing. We were asked to write a paragraph about the abuse. Instead, I brought in a letter I had written to my father. In clear tones, struggling to keep my composure, I read what I had written. When I looked up, a sea of crying faces looked back at me—with compassion, with understanding.

It had taken me an hour to write that letter. It had taken me my whole life to form the words.

After the meeting, the women stopped to talk to me. "Your letter was wonderful," one said. "I wish I had the courage to write it." I had forgotten the power of words: how they speak to the heart, vindicate the spirit. I thanked her and hurried on.

Months later, I made my first appointment to see a psychologist. In the reception room, on the walls, hung tropical plant pictures in muted shades of turquoise and peach. On the small desk was a calendar, set on yesterday's date. It didn't matter what the time or date. It had taken me forty-three years to get here from nowhere. Destination blurred, I was a ship meandering the channels of a haphazard life.

In her office the psychologist read the patient history I'd filled out. She said to me: "You've answered all the questions like a psychologist would. What brings you here so late in life? You seem to have managed well enough by yourself."

The truth was, I hadn't. I was a circuit board riddled with fears and anxieties. And was an anomaly even to myself. I am an incest survivor whose baggage had become too heavy to carry by myself. She drew me out, offering, at times, tissues from a box. I shredded and rolled the bits and pieces of them as I talked.

"It's okay to cry," she murmured, seeing the shame on my face.

We picked our way through sessions guardedly. Then, one day, she asked: "If you could do anything you wanted, what would it be?"

Without hesitation, I answered: "Write."

"Then let's do it," she said. "Let's make you a writer." She sent me home with an assignment: Write a two-page letter to my father about the abuse. No excuses, just do it.

I returned with six pages, more than she'd asked.

"You wrote all this?" she said holding it up.

Then quietly she leaned back in her chair and read it—not in a hurry—but thoughtfully. When finished, she took off her glasses and looked at me: "Your writing is powerful," she said, tears in her eyes. "What would you like to write?"

"Something to help others like me," I said. "A book"—I wasn't sure.

"I want to read it when you're done," she said. When, not if. "The only impediment I see is you. Believe in you!"

I remember her words. I remember the song of my childhood. The inner drive to put words to paper. No—not just words—but heart and soul. When the kids in school complained about book reports and essays, I was already halfway through them. My imagination blazed an ink-blurred trail across the paper. When I graduated valedictorian from high school, I wrote my own speech. I remember still the hush of the audience, the sudden roar of applause.

Discouraged by my parents, whose abuse strangled me, I gave up writing, except for classes. "Writers never amount to anything," they told me. "You will be a teacher." Inside, the embers still glowed.

I am a writer and a poet now. My poetry has been published in three anthologies. It isn't standard poetry. It whistles a different tune. Its words are coated with the echoes of abuse. I write from the heart—to the heart of incest survivors everywhere. Mine is a universal voice. I've listened to my heart and let it sing.

Sometimes I write silly things. For two years I wrote a column for the *Frog Pond* newsletter. It's dedicated to frog collectors like me. I also write articles for *Florida Gardening* magazine. In the past I've been a copywriter for three radio stations.

But always, I return to the book. It's what defines me. It is my symphony. I write it for the child in me who never knew love. I write it for the children of our yesterdays. For the children of our tomorrows. I hear them calling me. I know so well the patterns of their lives. The trail of tears they follow. In them—in me—I've found the answer to my psychologist's question: "What will you write?"

I must write the words that tell. I must break the silent code that binds us, that others, like me, will know they're not alone, that, despite the darkness, they (like me) may sing again.

Josie Willis

Write—To Conquer Your Fear

*Every accomplishment large and small begins
with the same decision: I'll try.*

Ted Key

It was finally time to face my deepest fears. I was standing outside the second-floor classroom in Davies Hall at American River College (ARC) in Sacramento, California, with my knees knocking, my palms sweaty and my confidence at an all-time low. After all, what right did I have to be taking a writing for publication class anyway? Let's face it: Jocks don't write.

In 1967, I was in my seventh year as an athletic coach at ARC, and I had finally mustered enough courage to sign up for Duane Newcomb's "Writing and Selling Magazine Articles" class. I was petrified. I nervously slipped into a seat on the back row, hoping nobody would recognize me among the sixty or so eager students. I've never felt more insecure in my life.

I had been wanting to try my hand at selling my writing for the past ten years, but I wouldn't even try—because I didn't think I could meet my own high standards. I longed to be a published writer, but fear and doubts had blocked me all this time. I had no way of knowing that my decision to face up to my fears by taking this class would change my life forever.

Duane Newcomb was the catalyst. He opened the class by slamming down a stack of magazines onto the desk and said, "Here's your new Cadillac. There's no reason why these writers should earn big money from their writing instead of you. Just picture your byline—your name—in these magazines and you're on your way." That really got my attention.

Then something stirred deep within me when he added, "To sell your writing today, you need 90 percent desire and 10 percent talent." *Wow!* I thought. *Only 10 percent talent. Hey, that's my category. And I can get excited!* Just then the inspirational words of Gustave Flaubert, the great French writer, danced across my mind, "Talent is long patience."

As Newcomb explained the process of selling our writing, I began to tingle all over. For the first time in my life, I began to believe I might be able to do this. A rush came over me as I stood in line to talk to Newcomb at the end of the class. Connecting instantly, we enjoyed a beer in a local pizza parlor; then we talked the night through. As I left his home at three o'clock the next morning, convinced I had just met my Messiah, Ted Key's words echoed in my head. I decided to try.

A few weeks later, Newcomb, in front of class, challenged me: "Now that you all know how to write a query letter, Bud will you write one to read to the class next week?" My throat tightened as I nodded. Later, I kicked myself for agreeing to such a foolish stunt. I just knew I was going to embarrass myself in front of the class. I agonized over that query for a week, writing it five times. It was about Vic Leach, a three-time national professional archery champion, who had recently demonstrated his skill in my archery class.

When I nervously read my first-ever query in the writing class, I was stunned by the students' reaction: They gave me an instant ovation. Grinning, Newcomb said, "It's ready. Fire it off to the magazine." I dropped it off at the post office on my way home that night.

Four days later, I got a second shock: a reply from the editor of *Archery World* magazine stating, "Can't wait for your article for publication." After struggling through five drafts of "Aim of a Champion," I reluctantly sent off the manuscript with fifty-six black-and-white pictures. Eight months later, I got a check for seventy-five dollars and a copy of *Archery World* with my article as the centerfold story, which extended over seven pages. I was even in one of the pictures! I couldn't hold back my tears of joy. I wept for a long while. I had finally made it; I was now a published writer.

Adrenaline flowed for months as I wrote and sold fourteen articles to little-known, low-circulation magazines without a single rejection. I was getting a bit "swolled up" with myself, as my wise dad used to say.

Then my bubble burst. I was so happy to be in print that I eagerly showed off my published articles to my family and all of my friends. One dear friend, while looking at my latest published article, got a funny look on his face. "Oh wow," he said without much enthusiasm, "this is r-e-a-l-l-y something." His bitterness was unmistakable. I had just learned a valuable lesson: Be careful whom you show your published work to; some close friends will be jealous of your success.

My first of many rejections caught me off guard. When I drove the editor of *New West* (a higher-paying upscale magazine, now defunct) to the airport after she had spoken to the California Writers Club of Sacramento one evening, I suggested an article idea to her. She not only liked it but asked me to send her a query letter right away. Receiving my query, she promptly gave me a go-ahead. I was ecstatic. Visions of my fifteenth straight sale—this one to a quality, high-circulation magazine—danced in my head. When the *New West* editor got my manuscript, she wasted no time in rejecting it. I can still feel the pain of that rejection. Duane Newcomb's words helped some, "There is no such thing as a rejection, just an article that hasn't sold yet." But my confidence began to wane. My fears surfaced again. *I guess I'm not good enough,* I thought, *to sell to the higher-paying markets. I'm not a real writer after all.*

That's when I made a career decision: I would put writing on hold and take a position as a college administrator at Sacramento's Cosumnes River College (CRC). During this time, Duane Newcomb and I co-founded the Sierra Writing Camp (SWC), a summer getaway for writers in the Sierras near Pollock Pines, California. At the camp I had so much fun teaching writing that, after a seven-year stint as an assistant dean, I returned to teaching in the English department at ARC.

Because I had let fear keep me from writing for ten years, I was determined to motivate my students to try at all costs. For a dozen years, I dedicated myself to being a top-notch teacher. Even though my students were selling well, I still felt hollow. *How could I teach writing and not be writing myself?* scolded the voice in my head. *I'm not walking my talk. I'm a fraud!*

After a few agonizing weeks, I decided to try writing again. That decision paid off. I began selling my stuff right away. It felt so good to be writing again. Oh, how I had missed it. Because I couldn't find a good inspirational book for my writing students, I combined teaching with writing when I teamed with Carol O'Hara, an award-winning writer and editor, who published *Write to $1,000,000—Turn Your Dreams into Dollars* through her company, Cat*Tale Press. This book, featuring personal stories from twenty-four of my students who collectively had earned a million dollars from their writing, made a Tower Books bestseller list. A second truism became crystal clear to me: When we put words on paper, the world takes notice.

I had published sixty articles when I wrote "Write Articles to Boost Your Speaking Career" for *Professional Speaker*, the magazine of the National Speakers Association. Because of that article, I was asked to give the opening keynote address for the Maui Writers Conference. I've been on the Maui Writers Conference teaching staff for seven years now, and Dan Poynter and I served as co-captains of the nonfiction segment of the Maui Writers Retreat.

Writing has been awfully good to me. It has given me the opportunity to meet or connect with celebrity authors such as Steve Allen, Maya Angelou, Dave Barry, Ray Bradbury, Terry Brooks, Jack Canfield, Barbara Cartland, Barnaby Conrad, Ernest J. Gaines, Sue Grafton, John Gray, Alex Haley, Elmore Leonard, Art Linkletter, Garry K. Marshall, Dan Millman, Ridley Pearson, Gene Perret, Ann Rule, seasoned editors like Phil Osborne, formerly of the *Reader's Digest*, dozens of outstanding literary agents and many, many other great writers who have also written stories for *Writer's Soul*.

I'm glad I faced my fears and began writing. Otherwise, I would have led a pretty boring life. And you know what: I've even gained a bit of confidence along the way.

Bud Gardner

From an Abyss to the Mountain Top

One thing all successful writers have in common: a stomach for failing.

Repeatedly. Perhaps years on end. A true professional has a wastebasket full of paper, a drawer (or more) full of rejections, and, of course, another work in progress.

Like all creative souls, writers learn over time that while they may be failing, they are not failures. They learn from their mistakes, and they keep on going. When it seems they've hit a stone wall, they find a way to move ahead. Even if it takes them down a radically different path.

Looking back on my checkered career, one lesson stands out. Failure is opportunity in disguise. I started out to be a stand-up comedian. "The World's Greatest Entertainer" to be precise. If the goal sounds a bit lofty, consider that I was seventeen and had just garnered my first laughs in front of the Lincoln High School assembly. From that flukey initial performance, I figured that my dream was a piece of cake. Easily achievable by age twenty—twenty-five max. But by age thirty, I was still struggling to pay the rent. I wasn't getting anywhere, and, swift learner that I was, it finally dawned on me that I must be doing something wrong.

How was I going to afford a one-bedroom apartment, much less become The World's Greatest Entertainer? Clearly, I needed help. Career advice and counsel. But from whom? Certainly not my family. They wanted me to forget my crazy show-biz notions and go into the dry goods business, become the world's greatest Jockey shorts salesman.

I decided to go to the pros. Talk to great comedians. Ask how they achieved stardom making people laugh. But for a no-name struggling comic, interviewing comedy stars was another nearly impossible dream.

My first celebrity interview was a happy coincidence. Through a friend of a friend I was introduced to Ed Wynn, known for his lovable and brilliant comic character as The Perfect Fool. He agreed to answer my questions, and I eagerly recorded his wise comedic insights on a machine the size of a Buick.

What I learned talking to that dear man helped shed new light on my career. Among his philosophical gems was sagacious advice that has stayed with me for a lifetime. "Larry, always remember," he counseled, "you can be a failure twenty times and still be a tremendous success."

A fellow performer read the transcript and agreed it was gold. "You ought to have this published," he said. A light went off (not the one in my moldy refrigerator). If somehow I could interview top comedians, not only would it help with my stand-up, it might make a good book. Right away, I leaped to thinking hardcover bestseller.

In between nightclub gigs and one-nighters, with no funds or inside connections, I spent the next three years trying to make it happen. I researched the great laughmakers, made endless phone calls, wrote stacks of letters and schlepped my hernia-producing tape recorder on planes whose coast-to-coast fares I could ill afford. Eventually, I talked to sixteen of the most distinguished comedy talents of the times: Woody Allen, Milton Berle,

Shelley Berman, Jack Benny, Joey Bishop, George Burns, Johnny Carson, Maurice Chevalier, Phyllis Diller, Jimmy Durante, Dick Gregory, Bob Hope, George Jessel, Jerry Lewis, Danny Thomas and Ed Wynn.

Each interview was a gem. I figured the publishing world would see the project as I did—a phenomenal work, the only one of its kind, destined for the bestseller list.

After twenty-six rejections, *The Great Comedians Talk About Comedy* was published. Critical acclaim helped counterbalance the rough start. The book went on to enjoy a long life in hardcover and softcover editions. You'd have thought the sequel would have been easier. But no. It took two trying years to complete and sell *How the Great Comedy Writers Create Laughter,* which included interviews with Goodman Ace, Mel Brooks, Art Buchwald, Abe Burrows, Bill Dana, Selma Diamond, Jack Douglas, Hal Kanter, Norman Lear, Carl Reiner and Neil Simon.

Those books elevated my career as a comedian and helped me hone my skills—a priceless education for a performer. But I had been bitten by the writing bug. And I was hopelessly addicted to having a few bucks in my pocket. (I now had a two-bedroom pad in Hollywood I wanted to keep.) Relishing my new life as a comedian-slash-author, I got really optimistic and wrote a novel. Semi-autobiographical, the humorous account of a struggling comic.

One night, I button-holed an editor at a cocktail party and gave him my verbal synopsis. Out of self-defense, he agreed to read the novel. (I just happened to have a copy in the trunk of my car.) He carted the manuscript back to New York. Three weeks later it was returned with a note: "Funny book. Well written. Should be published. Unfortunately, not by us. Good luck."

A few weeks later he left a message on my answering machine. Wow! He had changed his mind. I wasted no time returning his call, thinking I'd ask six figures. Another six for foreign rights and double that for the movies. He said, "Larry, your novel showed me you really know how to handle humor. So we'd like you to do a book of Polish and Italian jokes." I nearly dropped the phone. This was not the break I had envisioned.

I didn't tell ethnic gags on stage. Though I didn't know one Polish or Italian joke, something told me to take a chance. The specter of the rent, I imagine. We signed a contract for considerably less than six figures. With my generous advance, I got fifty dollars worth of quarters, a tape recorder, and made up a big sign that said: "I'll pay twenty-five cents for each Polish or Italian joke." I stood in front of the student union building at UCLA. By the end of the day, I had the raw material for a first draft.

That double-sided little paperback—Polish jokes on one side, Italian jokes on the other—sold 1,600,000 copies in thirty-six printings. The largest selling humor collection in history. Now, a couple of decades later, I have fifty-three books on my résumé covering every aspect of comedy, magnifying the humorous side of the human condition. Hardcover and paperback, serious and silly, for speakers, writers, performers, students of comedy and folks who simply want to laugh.

A framed quote on my office wall says, "America's Best-selling Humorist"—*The New York Times*. The closest I ever came to The World's Greatest Entertainer. Still, had I not been a failing young comedian—who talked to Ed Wynn who set me dreaming of doing a book about comedians and then comedy writers, and wrote a novel that never got published but took a chance writing a joke book and ended up a motivational humorist fifty-three books later—who knows what would have happened?

There's an old saying: If you fail, it's because you took a chance. If you succeed, it's because you grasped an opportunity. My opportunities have come in disguise. Fortunately, their false noses and Groucho glasses didn't throw me off the track.

Larry Wilde

Why I Write

I never wanted to be a writer. As a kid, all I ever dreamed of was living in a house with central air and heat and a toilet that flushed. My mother told me I was going to college: no ifs, ands and buts about it, and that I need not be concerned with "having anybody's babies until after I had a degree in my hand." As a result, I was too scared to have sex during high school (all my friends were), so I took to reading. Got my first job shelving books at our local library and spent much of $1.25 per hour hiding in the 700 and 900 sections on the floor.

This is where my dreams began to turn outward. I started traveling all over the world. I flew with Amelia Earhart. Sat with the Brontës. Rode on a sleigh in the snow with Robert Frost. Touched and smelled green with Thoreau. John Steinbeck fooled me with that story that had no mice in it. I thought he could've been black. James Baldwin frightened me when I saw his dark face on his book jacket. When did black people start writing books, I wondered? And then there was *Bartlett's Quotations*, which blew my young mind because it was like this dictionary of thoughts on all kinds of topics that I used to lie awake at night and ponder over but never had anybody to talk to about. I didn't know then that I was already lonely. Because I couldn't share my feelings, or maybe because I knew no one really cared what I felt or thought.

But then I go to college and my reading became a little broader, and one day this guy whose name I still can't remember breaks a major portion of my heart, and I find myself sitting on my twin-sized bed in this tiny college apartment, and I'm in a coma for like four hours because I am unable to move (though I don't try), and finally when I feel the blood flowing through my body again, it hits my brain and explodes, and I jump up without knowing where I'm going or what I'm about to do, and I grab a pen and a steno pad and begin to write these words down one, two, three, ten at a time, and I'm not even thinking about what I'm doing because it is happening so fast, and I don't realize until I'm out of breath, and four whole pages are filled with these words, and I sigh a deep sigh of relief and exhaustion, but I suddenly feel better, but then I panic because when I look at these words it sounds and looks like a poem, but I know damn well I didn't write this stuff because I have never written anything before in my life.

And that's how it started.

This writing stuff has saved me. It has become my way of responding to and dealing with things I find too disturbing or distressing or painful to handle in any other way. It's safe.

Writing is my shelter. I don't hide behind the words; I use them to dig inside my heart to find the truth. Plus, writing seems to be the only way I've been able to garner any real control over a situation or at least try to understand it. I guess I can say, honestly, that writing also offers me a kind of patience I don't have in my ordinary day-to-day life. It makes me stop. It makes me take note. It affords me a kind of sanctuary that I can't get in my hurried and full-to-the-brim-with-activity life.

Besides that, I'm selfish, and self-absorbed. But I discovered that writing makes me less so. It has made me more compassionate. In fact, it's what I've always prayed for: to have more compassion. For everybody. I've learned that every human being has feelings despite the fact that sometimes I have my doubts and everybody thinks no one understands how they feel and that no one could possibly feel what they feel. It's simply not true. Shock, shock, shock.

I'm also nosey, and I want to understand why I do some of the things I do and why we're so stupid, and in order to come close to empathizing, I had to learn how to get under someone else's skin. Writing has become my in and out.

If I understood half of what I do or feel, I probably wouldn't waste my time writing. But I like that probing. I like being scared sometimes. I like worrying about folks. I want to know if everything's gonna turn out okay for these folks. I want to show what can happen when we err, and when we "do the right thing" because as they say, no matter what you do sometimes, "sh-- happens." I like how we handle the sh-- when it does hit the fan—especially when we throw it into the blades ourselves.

I just want to pay attention to the details of everyday life. I want to be a better person. I want to feel good more often. I want to know when I don't, why I don't. Writing gives me this.

Chekhov said, "Man will become better only when you make him see what he is like." This is what I'm trying to do when I portray African-American men and women behaving "badly."

Painting as accurate a picture as I can of our behavior as I see it. I'm not trying to "air dirty laundry" at all; I'm just trying to get us to hold up a mirror and take a long look. Most of us don't think about what we do; we just act and react. Many of us don't reflect or wonder what larger issues are really at stake.

Writing is helping me mature as long as I'm not bullsh---ing myself, the act itself forces me to face and understand my flaws and weaknesses and strengths, and if I'm honest—really honest—then writing is like a wake-up call. I become my own therapist. Because nobody knows me better than me, and if I do my job, I can ease my heart inside another character's until I feel what they feel, think the way they think, and when I'm able to become—say, a chronic liar and begin to lie, and as the writer come to know and understand why this person uses lies as a way to defend him- or herself, then I know I'm on the right track because I cannot write about someone I do not in real life respect or admire but whom I've come to understand. Writing has taught me not to be judgmental. I usually write about people I don't necessarily favor, who do things I would either never dream of doing, and, therefore, I sort of have to make myself undo my own sense of thinking and being. It can be exhilarating, freeing, a real eye-opener, and painful as hell.

Maybe I'm weird, but I want to know what it feels like to die. To have your heart broken. Why do people hurt each other intentionally? Why do folks lie? And cheat? What kind of person can kill another person and sleep at night? What does a man feel when he beats his wife? Why does she stay? How do women like this tolerate the pain alone? How do children learn to hate? Their parents? What is a good parent? What does it feel like to discover that you are gay and you're twelve? Why do some people not have the capacity to forgive? How long can I hold a grudge? And why are some people nicer and more likable, more responsible than others?

I could go on and on—but the bottom line is that I didn't make a conscious decision to become a writer. I never did it for the money. I never did it for fame. Who knew? Who ever knows? I think somehow that the craft chose me. The words have given me ownership and a sense of security. Writing is the only place I can be myself and not feel judged. And I like it there.

Terry McMillan

We Were All Beginners Once

One of the first things a writer is asked by a new acquaintance is if he or she has ever had anything published. There was a time when this irked me, until I saw it as a natural enough way of establishing one's professional status or lack thereof. One may be a painter without being hung or a traitor without being hanged; similarly, one may be a writer without being published, but one cannot be a *real* writer, so, er, ahem, *have* you had anything published, Mr. Block?

Indeed I have, I'll assure my new friend. I've been supporting myself with my typewriter ever since college. I've made, certainly, a better living in some years than in others, but I've always scraped by. And as for being published, I was still in college when my first books and stories saw print.

My conversational partner will nod at this, grateful to know he is not in the presence of an impostor, a writer *manqué.* Then a sullen glaze will come into his eyes.

"You read about the struggle writers have to get published. The years of heartbreak. The endless rounds of rejection slips. The poverty, the menial jobs. But you, you never had any of that, did you?"

Didn't I? "Oh, it was all ages ago," I'll say. "Back around the time of Columbus' second voyage. So it's really pretty hard to remember."

Hard to remember? It might have been yesterday.

All I wanted during my first year at college was to be published. I'd decided a couple of years earlier that I intended to become a writer. How was one to manage that? By majoring in English, I supposed, and by reading everything I could lay my eyes on, and, finally, by sitting down at the typewriter and actually writing something.

And then submitting it, whatever it might be. Poems, sketches, three- and four-page short stories. I'd blush to recall the adolescent tripe I had the gall to submit for publication, but for the arrogance implicit in such a blush. Publishers, I now know, are forever inundated with unsuitable, amateurish submissions. My efforts were not even outstanding in their unsuitability, in their amateurishness. I'm sure they were examined and rejected and returned in short order, leaving no impression on the poor slush reader's mind once they'd left his hands.

I remember one of those stories. It was about two feral children in a scientific experiment. There's a global war or some comparable calamity and only those two infants survive. So they grow up and mate and have two children, and they call one Cain and the other Abel.

Oh, dear. I was to learn that every magazine gets that story two or three times a week. And even if that weren't the case, what I'd written wasn't a story. It was a gimmick afloat on a thousand-word ocean.

And where did I send it? *Harper's, The Atlantic, The New Yorker.* Places like that.

In an autobiography, *Call It Experience,* Erskine Caldwell tells of his first sale. The future author of *God's Little Acre* and *Tobacco Road* had written some earthy stories about poor folks in red-dirt Georgia. He sent them around and got a letter from Maxwell Perkins at *Scribner's Magazine*. Could Caldwell come to New York to discuss two of his stories?

Caldwell rode up on a bus and Perkins took him to lunch, where they talked about everything but the two stories the young Georgian had sent in. Over coffee the editor said: "About those two stories. I'd like to publish them. I thought we might pay you two-fifty for the short one and three-fifty for the longer one."

Caldwell looked unhappy. Perkins asked if something was wrong.

"Well, I suppose it's all right," Caldwell allowed, "but I thought I'd be getting more than six dollars for two stories."

The first money I ever got from a publisher was two dollars from a magazine called *Ranch Romances*. Pines Publications issued *Ranch Romances,* and at the time it was the last survivor of a whole string of western pulps. It was, editorially speaking, a bizarre hybrid, featuring love stories on horseback, as it were.

In the summer of 1956, I spent three months working as a mail boy at Pines Publications. When I got back to college, I clipped *Ranch Romances.* The editor bought it as a filler and sent me a check for two bucks, along with a note of encouragement. I don't know if she'd have bought it if she hadn't remembered me. Oh, well. It's not what you know; it's who you know. Right?

It was money from a publisher, and that was something. But it wasn't for anything I'd written.

There was something almost schizoid in my attitude, it seems to me. On the one hand, I believed (or thought I believed) that one ought to be prepared to starve for one's art, that a writer's artistic integrity was his most precious possession.

One the other hand, I would have done anything to get published. *Anything.*

It's hard to remember the urgency of my need to see my words in print. I can see now that what a beginner really needs is not to be published but to grow as a writer. The writing I did was valuable to me, but why did I have to send off all my poems and stories?

I suppose the whole process helped me to take myself and my ambitions seriously. Even the rejection slips, tacked neatly to my dorm-room wall, seemed to validate what I was doing. They were visible proof that I was engaged in a process aimed at eventual publication.

If I hadn't been submitting things, if I hadn't been trying to get into print, I'm not sure I'd have kept writing.

The first money I received for writing of my own was seven dollars from a religious magazine. A friend and I wandered into a Bowery mission one night and watched the down-and-outers endure the service so they could get the meal that followed it. I went home and turned the experience into a seven-hundred-word article. "We Found God on the Bowery," I called it, and I told how what began as a lark ended in a conversion experience. "We came to scoff," I wrote, "but we stayed to pray."

That wasn't what happened. Cynical sophomoric wretches that we were, we came to scoff and scoffed our way home. But, as I told you, I would have done anything to get published. I submitted my story to a magazine published by the denomination that sponsored the mission. They bought it, printed it, paid for it.

They even used my title.

While I was working as a mail clerk in Pines Publications, I wrote a story about a wise-guy crook who works at a drugstore and steals from his boss, then moves on to mail fraud. The mood was pretty good, but it didn't really make a story. Back at school, I polished the story and sent it to *Manhunt*.

It came back with a note from the editor. He liked it, but

it needed a snapper for an ending. If I could think of something, he'd like to look at it again.

I couldn't believe it. I ran out, bought a copy of *Manhunt*, read every story in it, then rewrote mine with a new ending in which the narrator is hoist on his own petard, investing his ill-gotten gains in what the reader can tell is phony uranium mine stock. It was a hokey notion, and the story came back with another nice note, saying it didn't really work and better luck next time. I wasn't surprised. I hadn't really expected to sell it.

Meanwhile, I had a couple of poems accepted here and there. And I was producing stories regularly for a fiction workshop class. And one day I thought of a way to redo my *Manhunt* story. I had the narrator move up another rung and become a contract killer. I was pretty sure it worked this time, and I sent it off, and the editor bought it.

A hundred bucks. It was months before I got the money, more months before the magazine was on the stands. I couldn't wait; I wanted the story to be on sale the day after I got the letter of acceptance.

I'm still like that. I want to type THE END, take the last page out of the typewriter, then walk around the corner and see the book on sale in the stores. My publisher seems to be similarly inclined. He has listed books of mine in his catalog before I've gotten any further than the title, has had covers printed before I've finished the manuscript, and gets the book on the shelves in a fraction of the time most publishers take.

A man after my own heart.

You know what? I'm still a beginner. I've written more books than anyone should have to read, yet every time I hold a new book in my hand, I get a thrill not unlike the one I received when I picked up a copy of *Manhunt*. I still try new things, and sometimes they're as ill-advised as my Adam-and-Eve story. I still take chances, and sometimes they work and sometimes they don't. On some level, I still look to publication as a form of validation of who I am and what I do.

In *Cup of Gold,* John Steinbeck's first novel, an old sage said something along these lines to the earnest young hero: "You are young, and want the moon to drink from as a cup of gold. Reaching and straining to catch the moon, you may catch a firefly. But if you grow up you will realize that you cannot have the moon, and would not want it if you could. And you will catch no fireflies."

That's paraphrase; I don't have the book at hand, and it was twenty-five years ago that I read it. There's been a lot of water under the bridge since then, or over the dam, or wherever it goes.

A lot of fireflies, too. Aren't they pretty? And don't they cast a lovely light?

Lawrence Block

"I don't have a title yet, or even a subject. All I have is the price: twenty-three ninety-five in hardcover."

2

LIVING YOUR DREAM

It took me fifteen years to discover that I had no talent for writing, but I couldn't give it up because by that time I was too famous.

Robert Benchley

Alex Haley—A Writer of Destiny

"I'm going to be a writer if it kills me!" said one of the first customers in my saloon. He wasn't a star then. Unknown and unpublished, Alex Haley was destined to be a writer who would command the attention of the world.

I first met Alex in 1951 when I was teaching creative writing in an adult education program at the Marina High School in San Francisco. He was a cook in the Coast Guard and had achieved considerable success in a strange branch of writing: While at sea, he would write imaginative love letters at a dollar a pop for his shipmates, who would subsequently reap fine rewards on shore from the objects of their affections. He was a steady customer at El Matador, my restaurant and bar. He didn't drink, but he hung around the bar, always hoping to meet people in the writing game who could help him achieve his lifelong ambition of being a writer. He had little natural talent, but he was a good storyteller, worked hard at writing every day, read everything about writing and never gave up. He finally sold a little piece about the Coast Guard to the Sunday newspaper supplement "This Week." He said, "They paid me one hundred dollars. I went and got it cashed into one hundred one-dollar bills. I had fifty in one pocket and fifty in the other, and I walked down the street squeezing them—oh, that tactile feeling." In the Matador that night, we broke out a bottle of champagne to celebrate.

One night the author Budd Schulberg flew in from New York and came to the Matador; I phoned Alex in Oakland and he sped over the bridge to San Francisco in record time. Alex's favorite books happened to be *Waterfront* and *What Makes Sammy Run,* and he was thrilled to meet the author of them. They sat in the bar and talked until four in the morning. Budd encouraged Alex's writing, and in a few months *Reader's Digest* published "My Most Unforgettable Character," an essay by Alex on his Pullman porter father. His career, while not exactly soaring, was beginning to take off. He did countless articles for many different magazines such as *True, Argosy* and *True Confessions.* He always said the confession magazines were a great training ground for learning the importance of conflict and characterization. Then he had a great breakthrough: He created a question and answer format while writing an article on trumpeter Miles Davis, and this became the style for the *Playboy* interview. Alex had been given six weeks to write six thousand words. Halfway through, he realized he didn't have enough to write the article.

"Miles was monosyllabic," he said. "If you're a friend of Miles Davis, around 6:30 in the afternoon the phone might ring and a voice would come on and say, 'Chili,' and hang up. The translation was that he had cooked up a mess of chili, and you should come over and partake.

"So what I did, because I was desperate to get into that magazine, I took a gamble. I took half of that six thousand words and did the best I could—rewrote and rewrote—an essay about his world. Then I took the other three thousand words, took every utterance he'd made, and made up questions to make it seem he'd answered them. I took it to the editors and the readers liked the style."

That style for the *Playboy* interview still exists today.

He did many such interviews for that magazine, including one with the infamous neo-Nazi and racist George Lincoln Rockwell. Alex's bizarre encounter with the self-styled führer occurred at Rockwell's extensive headquarters in Arlington, Virginia. When *Playboy* called Rockwell to set up the interview, the neo-Nazi agreed "as long as you don't send down one of your Jews."

When Alex called to tell Rockwell when he was arriving, the man said, "Now you're sure you're not a Jew?"

"Uh, no," Alex assured him. "No, uh, I am definitely not a Jew."

"Okay then," said Rockwell. "I'll give you one hour."

Once he arrived, Alex was escorted by burly, uniformed men past Nazi flags and portraits of Hitler to Rockwell's office. *"Sieg heil!"* the guards said, as they opened the door. Rockwell's jaw dropped when he saw that Alex was black.

"Jesus Christ," he said. Still, he reluctantly agreed to go ahead with the interview.

"But let's get this one thing straight!" growled Rockwell, leaning back in his chair. "I regard you and your people as no better than chimpanzees."

"That's fine," said the unflappable Haley. "You're welcome to your opinion." As they started the interview, Alex spotted an electric typewriter on a stand by the desk.

"Mr. Rockwell, I generally take notes on a typewriter. May I use that one?"

Rockwell looked at him and exclaimed pointedly, "But it's electric!"

Alex smiled back. "I think I can manage, sir."

Alex began the questioning and typed the answers as Rockwell gave them with exaggerated slowness.

"Sir, you may speak faster," said Alex, who once won a championship speed-typing contest in California.

"Well, when I was born . . ."

"You may talk faster, sir."

Rockwell went a little faster, at normal speed, and Alex recorded the words almost as they were spoken. Rockwell speeded up, and Alex kept up with him. Faster and faster Rockwell spoke, and Alex's typing went right along with him. Rockwell stopped and gazed at Haley in unfeigned amazement. Alex looked back, shrugged and said modestly, à la Stepin Fetchit, "Pretty good for a chimpanzee, eh man?"

Later, Alex wrote the successful biography of Malcolm X, which has sold over six million copies. But he had an even bigger book inside of him, begging to get out: The story of his origins, his roots, told in the form of his own family's oral history, which had been passed down to him by his grandmother and aunts on the front porch of their house in Henning, Tennessee—a story that could be that of virtually every black American. At first he called it *Before This Anger*, and he wrote part of it in my studio while I was living in Tahiti. Upon my return, I was so moved as he told me the story that, even before he had finished writing it, I sent him to Hollywood to see my agent, lawyer Louis Blau. Blau is highly successful, tough and always frantically busy with clients, who include many famous stars, directors and writers.

"I'll give you fifteen minutes to tell your story, Mr. Haley," he said. "That's all the time I have."

Alex began to recount in his quiet way the saga of Kunta Kinte, his ancestor, who was captured in the rain forest of the upper Gambia River in Africa. Kinte was brought in chains to America and sold to Dr. William Waller of Spotsylvania County, Virginia. Alex began to tell the story of Chicken George, of Tizzy and of the entire larger-than-life family—the great tapestry of characters that would eventually be known throughout the world of literature and television as *Roots*.

At the end of fifteen minutes, Blau told his secretary to cancel all his appointments and telephone calls and sat riveted for two hours as Alex told the entire tumultuous story of all the generations that had preceded his birth. Blau said not a word until Alex had finished with the last sentence: "And that little baby was me."

Then Blau stood up slowly, extended his hand and said huskily, "Mr. Haley, if you can write that story the way you just told it, you will change the world!"

Alex could, and Alex did.

And before that day with Blau ended, Alex had a deal to make the TV series that more people in the world would see than any other in history.

After *Roots* became a runaway bestseller and won both the Pulitzer Prize and a National Book Award, Alex Haley was in great demand as a speaker. He gave one talk at Simpson College in the little town of Indianola, Iowa, to a crowd of one thousand people, and afterward, while autographing books, he noticed one man, a patrician-looking person, who seemed to want to speak to him but was hanging back diffidently. Alex finally said, "Sir, did you wish to say something to me?"

The man cleared his throat and said, "Mr. Haley, I'm the academic dean here, and I read your book, and I checked my family records. I'm a genealogy buff like you."

"Yes?" said Alex.

"Well, I'm not sure how to put this delicately."

"Yes, go on."

"Well, it would appear, Mr. Haley, that Dr. William Waller, my great-great-great-great-grandfather owned your great-great-great-great-grandfather, Kunta Kinte."

Alex told me later, "There we stood, staring at each other, the mutually great-great-great-great-grandsons of the late-1760s master and slave. In Dr. Waller Wiser's home, we exchanged lineages into the wee hours and became friends for life."

Not all of Alex's stories about his family are in *Roots*. He told me one about his father, which directly shaped Alex's and his siblings' lives.

Simon Haley, the son of a former slave and share-cropper from Savannah, Tennessee, was determined not to end his days as a field hand. He worked his way through high school and struggled partially through A & T College in Greensboro, North Carolina. However, he began to feel he'd have to give up his dream of an education because of the double burden of earning both his living and the tuition fee. He took a job as a Pullman porter while deciding whether or not to return home to sharecropping. On one of his trips, he waited on R.S.M. Boyce, a retired executive of the Curtis Publishing Company, who took an interest in the polite, alert young man. Boyce asked him about his life and his ambitions. Later, he sent Simon five hundred dollars, enough for full living expenses and tuition for a year at college. This enabled Simon to graduate, first in his class, and win a scholarship to Cornell University for his master's degree.

Thus Alex, instead of growing up on a farm in bleak sharecropping poverty, was reared in an atmosphere of books and the love of learning, and he became a writer; his brother George is chairman of the U.S. Postal Rate Commission; his brother Julius is an architect; and his sister, Lois, is a music teacher. All because of one man's generosity on a train way back in 1918.

Alex was always the storyteller; one he told us in El Matador reflected the kind of simple man of great values that he was. He described a cousin from his hometown, an arrogant and conceited young man who flaunted his education. He never left home without his Phi Beta Kappa key dangling from a gold chain around his neck. One day,

an elderly aunt took a close look at the cousin's Phi Beta
key, wrinkled her old brow, and said: "Ver' nice, boy, ver'
nice, but what do it open?"

Alex is gone now, and I will simply say, in the words of
George Bernard Shaw, "I can lose a friend like that by *my*
death but not by his."

Barnaby Conrad

Dreams Do Come True

From the time I was a young girl, I had dreamt of becoming an author. Throughout my youth I cherished creative writing assignments, and upon entering college, even majored for a brief period in journalism.

Circumstances forced an abrupt end to my college education and reality set in quickly as I was forced to find a "real job" in the middle of my junior year. Through perseverance, luck and timing, my career led me on a path which far surpassed my wildest expectations, and over time I rose to the level of Senior Executive Vice President of an international marketing company.

My writing skills were left to training manuals, memos, minutes and the occasional "white paper," but whenever people would read anything I wrote (thank-you notes were my specialty), they would always say, "Christine, you should be a writer."

I heard the phrase so frequently that I thought long and hard about why I had never pursued my passion. The same answer always floated to the top of my list: I couldn't think of a subject that I felt I knew enough about to put a pen to paper.

The year was 1994, and I was on top of the world. I had

just signed the largest contract in the history of the retail service industry! I had just turned forty; my husband and I were coming up on our twentieth wedding anniversary; I had two healthy, happy sons; we were buying the house of our dreams; life was great! It came to a screeching halt in a day.

I found a lump in my right breast during a routine self-examination. Having lost my mother to breast cancer at the tender age of forty-two, I had been very cognizant of my family history. The lump proved to be cancerous, and I began what would turn into a twelve-month journey of surgery, aggressive chemotherapy, radiation, and a loss of my best asset: my long, thick, curly, luxurious brown hair.

Following my mother's radical mastectomy some twenty-eight years prior, my mother had sunk into a deep, clinical depression. She stopped washing her hair, shaving her legs, or even brushing her teeth. In the months that followed her surgery, my father—a physician, unable to deal with my mother's depression—left my mother.

Having witnessed this atrocity as a child, I could only imagine upon hearing the words, "Christine, I'm so sorry. You have cancer," that my fate would be the same as my mother's. Anger, fear, denial, and grief set in, and my surgery was scheduled for New Year's Eve.

Four weeks after my surgery, I awoke in the middle of the night with a vision: cartoons. I made my way in the dark downstairs to our family room, and as I sat down at my desk, fifty cancer-related cartoons started flowing into my head. I scribbled madly, sketching and writing punchlines, until exhausted. I crept back up to bed, pulled the covers up to my chin and thought to myself, *"What was that?"*

The next day I got up, dressed, and went to both the public library and a Barnes & Noble bookstore. I strode into the bookstore first, walked up to the information counter, and announced, "I'd like to see all of your humorous books about cancer, please." The clerk behind the counter squinted his eye as he looked at me disdainfully and pronounced, "You're sick." *Aha!* I chuckled to myself as I pulled a notepad out of my purse, scribbling down his very words: another cartoon for my book!

I proceeded across the street to the library where I was guided to one book classified under Humor and Cancer: Erma Bombeck's *I Want to Go to Boise, I Want to Grow Up, I Want to Grow Hair.* "I think I'm on to something," I thought gleefully as I pulled out of the parking lot and headed toward my daily radiation therapy.

Days, weeks, months passed by as I trudged on through my treatments. My cartoons and "my book" became my focus as I searched for signs of humor in my predicament. The harder I looked the more I found, and my first book *Not Now . . . I'm Having a No Hair Day!* was born.

Exactly one year from the day I sat in the hospital recovering from cancer surgery, I sat in my publisher's office and signed a contract for not one, but two books about using humor as a tool to deal with a diagnosis of cancer. Both of my books—*Not Now . . . I'm Having a No Hair Day* and *Our Family Has Cancer, Too!*—written especially for children, have won awards and received international acclaim and media attention.

I look back on the many roles I have played in my life: daughter, sister, student, wife, mother, businesswoman, entrepreneur, professional speaker, friend, cancer survivor.

But the role that I hold dearest to my heart and fills me with pride is that of "author."

Today is the perfect time to dream.

Christine Clifford

Dreams Lost and Found

When I was a very young girl, my mother took me to see *Swan Lake*. It was our maiden voyage into what would become a shared, lifelong tradition. I'd never seen ballet before, and afterward, all I could dream of was becoming a ballerina. A prima ballerina, of course, with an internationally-renowned company, the kind of company where the mere mention of the name brings looks of wonder to people's faces. I hadn't the slightest idea what kind of lifestyle this would require, nor did I care. I only knew, with a child's unwavering certainty, that I had to be part of the vibrance and passion we saw there on the stage, part of this beauty that had the power to move even grown-ups to tears.

Though I loved school throughout my early years, and was particularly fond of reading and writing, I was equally inclined toward athletics. I eagerly looked forward to playground recesses when, flying past my playmates in foot races or swinging energetically across the monkey bars, I would imagine myself in tights and leotard, time and space in my grasp as I soared effortlessly through the air in some achingly beautiful *pas de deux*.

My father, a self-made businessman who had enormous faith in what he saw as the unlimited potential of each of his children, had drilled into my brothers and me from early on the belief that we each had the ability to achieve any and all of our dreams, as long as we kept them firmly in our sights. I believed with all my heart that he was right and spent part of every day *seeing* the reality of my becoming a ballerina in my mind.

When, in about the fifth grade, I began tripping over my own feet more and more frequently, the sublime childhood assumption that everything will always remain the same prevented me, at first, from realizing that something might be wrong. But when my older brother, who had been experiencing similar problems, was diagnosed with muscular dystrophy, it was a short path to follow that I had it, as well. Even so, the fact that muscular dystrophy can be a slow-moving disease, caused my initial symptoms to be minor enough that, with the enviable ignorance of youth, the possibility that it would completely change my dream never occurred to me.

It wasn't until my middle school years, when my legs looked undeveloped, different, somehow, from other girls in their first stockings, and my first grown-up pumps had to be replaced with orthopedic shoes, followed by leg braces, that I finally became conscious of some hard facts.

At that time, my parents' property had a huge old oak tree in a secluded corner that I'd always loved climbing. I'd sit up there and daydream, as young teen girls are wont to do, fantasizing about this or that or camping out for a good long cry when things were particularly melodramatic. It was the automatic choice for me to run to at a time like this, but at the same time, it was becoming more difficult to do so. I went there anyway, though, clumsily hoisting myself up to hide among the branches, trying desperately to will away all fears.

One of my most profound fears, of course, was that the day would soon come when I would no longer be physically able to perform the simple act of climbing a favorite tree—clearly, ballet was out of the question. While I didn't want to face it, I rarely thought about anything else. On one particularly tough day, I went to my hideout straight off the school bus, book pack on my back and all. I was especially miserable that day. I'd tripped, again, and had a spectacular fall at school, this time right in front of the boy I'd had a secret crush on during the last year. Though those schoolmates that witnessed my disgrace had not laughed, had been kind, even, all I could think about was that this was my fate for the rest of my life.

I'd been crying hard, and I wanted a little moment to myself before going into the kitchen and letting Mom see my tear-streaked face. Desperate to calm down, I grabbed my notebook out of my backpack and started writing a poem about the feelings I was experiencing. We'd been studying haiku that semester in class, and I was taken by the simple purity of words that could bring forth strong images with great economy.

The writing calmed me, setting free the harmful thoughts that had had me in their grip such a short time ago. Having achieved this relatively tranquil state, I decided to try another poem describing my agonizing fears of my physical deterioration. Once again, it worked; it was as though the simple act of writing set free the demons that seemed to have taken up permanent residency, allowing me to step outside those thoughts and see them in a different, more detached perspective.

The next afternoon, I went straight to my tree, wanting to see if what had worked once would work again. As soon as I'd climbed to my perch, however, it seemed that all I could focus on was the fact that this hideaway was physically slipping out of my grasp. As if to hang onto the mental imagery of these moments, I began listing every detail I could think of, describing the rough bark against my back, the creaking sound of heavy limbs swaying in the breeze, the dappled afternoon sun splaying across my hands as it worked its way through rustling leaves. I wanted to capture the feel of it, somehow, to commit these things I would miss to some fail-safe, retrievable memory bank. By writing it all down, I felt I'd be able to keep these feelings close to my heart always, regardless of whether my memory or my body failed me.

What began that long-ago afternoon was to become a lifelong love affair with words, both spoken and written. I realized, as early as that first time I sat in my wooded perch and began to record, that the power of those words would help me remember the things I'd been lucky enough to experience and to keep them safe within me for as long as I needed it. It was much later when I realized that those same words would help me let go, help me put one well-lived experience behind me in order that I might move on to something new and equally important.

Now, that I'm well beyond those youthful years and a full-time freelance writer, it seems that those long-ago afternoons will always stand out in my memory. The act of writing always takes me back to that initial, willful act of faith, a way to look, touch, and savor all life's moments while they are happening, to make each of them count and not to take any of them for granted. It is a prayer, of sorts, that continues to help me attain and conquer my life without, in the end, being conquered by it. When I put thought on paper today, whether it be for a particularly compelling piece of fiction or a more mundane news piece, there is always the memory of that first thrill of capturing each moment as it happens, of knowing that, no matter how far distant it becomes in memory, the simple act of writing will keep it forever safe, forever authentic.

Kate M. Brausen

Dreams Have a Price

More people have talent than discipline.
That's why discipline pays better.

Mike Price

Each writer's career begins with a dream, a fantasy, a goal that looms on the distant horizon. "I want to write a novel." "I'd love to publish poetry." "I want to see my name on the screen as the author of a movie."

My career began with a dream. I wanted to make people laugh. I wanted to write comedy.

But each writer must realize, too, that every goal has a price tag. Admission to a fantasy is never free. There's research to be done, studying to do, and practice, practice, practice. The cheapest, and usually the quickest, way to attain any desire is to pay the full price. Do the work.

When I decided to become a comedy writer, I wanted to study the profession. Bob Hope, I thought, had the most readable and useful material for analytical purposes. His comedy material was funny on paper, pure humor. Of course, Bob Hope's expert timing and delivery enhanced any joke he was telling, but it was still a joke that could be read and analyzed. Other comics, like Jerry Lewis could be funny, but it was more their antics that created the hilarity. On paper, the material was not as useful to a student as Hope's.

So, I studied Bob Hope. I would audio tape his television monologues and then type out a transcript. I'd analyze the joke forms, wording, rhythm, the arrangement of gags in a routine, and so on. Then I'd put that monologue away for awhile.

In a few weeks, I'd select new topics from the newspaper and try to write new jokes using the techniques I'd learned from Hope's latest monologue. With this technique, Bob Hope and his writers became my mentors.

It worked. I began writing for local comics, then national comics, then landed a spot on a television variety show staff.

Then it worked even better. Bob Hope called me.

"I've heard about your writing and wonder if you'd like to do some gags for me for the Academy Awards. I'm the host this year, you know, and I'd like to see if some of your jokes would work for me."

This was a part of my dream that I didn't dare dream, but here it was happening nonetheless. I took a pad and pen out to my backyard and wrote a few hundred gags about current movies, celebrities, anything that would apply to the Oscars. Naturally, I used the tricks that I had learned from years of studying Bob Hope's comedy style.

Mr. Hope did ten of my jokes on the telecast and I was thrilled. The following day he called me again and said, "I loved your material. It looks like you've been writing for me all your life."

"I have, Mr. Hope," I said. "Only you didn't know about it."

I've been writing for Bob Hope ever since.

There were two valuable lessons in this experience that all writers can learn and draw inspiration from:

The first is that there is effort involved in making any dream come true. Dreams are powerful, but only when they're reinforced by research, study, and effort.

The second is that if you do the work, you'll reach your goals.

Gene Perret

Frank and Ernest

© 1999 Thaves/Reprinted with permission

FRANK & ERNEST. *Reprinted by permission of Newspaper Enterprise Association, Inc.*

For Love or Money

When I was a struggling writer I drove a taxicab, as a struggling writer should. I wrote three or four scripts a year, mostly at night when a normal guy would have been dating. I became overloaded with frustration, fear and demoralization. I remember sitting alone in my small apartment after yet another script had gone unsold, the last one, the straw on the camel's back, the script that was going to sell, or I was going to have to face the fact that I was wasting my time. I sat in the dark and I wept, and I had a long conversation with myself. I'm sure I drank. The next day, I started a new script.

In retrospect, this was not a bad experience. Sometimes frustration, fear and demoralization are the only familiar faces in a writer's life. Accept them. Embrace them and learn from them. And then write something new.

When I finally did sell a script, it was more than a relief, it was a revelation. I had been managing to live in Los Angeles, an expensive city, for a little under $20,000 a year. Suddenly, Warner Brothers handed me a check for $400,000. More money in one check than my grandparents had earned in their long lives of back-breaking labor. Do the math; I could live for twenty years!

But first, I had struggled for a long time. I deserved some nice things. A better apartment, one with sunlight. A nicer car. That old TV was awfully small. Don't forget taxes, and the agents and the lawyers' 15 percent, 1 percent plus 1/2 more to the Writers Guild. Okay, maybe I could live for five years.

Suddenly I found myself employable. I did originals and rewrites. My price kept going up. In time, I got a picture made—sole credit—and my price soared. That first check from Warners started to seem quaint. In fact, after five years, the studio lured me to rewrite that original spec script, and paid me more for the rewrite than they had paid me to buy the script in the first place. My wife and I bought a nice house in a nice neighborhood. The good times were here.

As the money kept rolling in and my name kept appearing in the trades, it occurred to me that I needed a house where I could have Wendy Finerman or Jon Peters or Joel Schumacher over for dinner. We sold our little house in the nice neighborhood and bought one in Brentwood at six times the price. The cars got faster. I employed an army of gardeners and maids. We dug a pool on the side of a hill. We planned an extensive remodel. We took limos to the airport and rented houses on the beach on Maui.

And the headaches got worse. I gained a lot of weight and my back went out. My wife and I weren't talking as much, but that was understandable; there was a lot to manage between the house and the grounds and the new baby. At least the work kept coming. I agreed to write a *Superman* movie, not because I was dying to spend my precious writing time with Clark Kent, but because the residuals on a project like that would put my grandkids through college. I agreed to rewrite another script, which I hated, for an exorbitant price because how do you turn down money like that for eight weeks of work? I put off my dream of directing my own work because I was making too much money writing. I had more than I ever dreamed I would have, and I was spending it all, and I was miserable.

Then, one day I did something I will remember on my deathbed. I sat down at my computer in the morning and turned it on, and while I was waiting for Scriptware to open, I reached for my calculator. Instead of thinking about what my characters were going to do that day, what they would talk about, where they would go, I was thinking, "If I deliver this draft by the end or the month, I can get the commencement check for project X by mid-July, and that will pay for the guest house." My life's purpose was no longer to write; my writing was a way to make money.

It came to me in a rush that I had not enjoyed writing in some time. I did not believe in all of the projects I was taking on, and even the ones I felt passionate about were suffering. Life had given way to lifestyle. The joy and the love that kept me writing at night after twelve hours behind the wheel of a taxi were gone. I dreaded the keyboard. And there they were my old friends: fear, frustration and demoralization.

I woke my wife up at three the next morning, after lying awake for hours, and told her that I wanted to sell her dream house. The house she had cried over when she first found it. And what do you think she said? "Oh, thank God." And thank God for her.

It was as if an anvil was lifted from my shoulders. Literally, within hours, writing became a joy again. I sat down each morning filled with anticipation at what my characters would do that day. I laughed with them, cried over their mistakes, and applauded when they said something I didn't see coming. Over the next six weeks I had twelve-page days and half-page days. I soared, I gnashed my teeth, I wrote laughable first-draft dialogue and found meanings in things I didn't suspect. Good God, I had fun! And I wrote one of the best drafts of my life, a draft that was subsequently greenlit. You see, I am not a banker. This is what I do. I write.

Please don't misunderstand me; money is great. I love it. And the great truth is, since I stopped worshipping it, I make more of it than I ever did before. But the money to me is a wonderful by-product of writing; it is not the reason to write. There are plenty of writers in Hollywood who only care about the money, I know; I rewrite them every day. And sometimes they rewrite me. And if their sports car is faster than mine is, God bless them. Over the years you will have to write things you are not proud of. That's okay. It's even admirable. The goal is to buy the freedom to write what you love.

My advice to aspiring writers is always the same: If there is anything else you can see yourself doing with your life, then please, go and do that thing. This is not a road to take if you have any doubts. But if this is it for you, if this is what feeds your soul, then jump in and work hard. Struggle and cry and sweat it out onto the page. And don't forget to love it, even when it starts paying off.

Gregory Poirier

Take That Chance!

If one advances confidently in the direction of his dreams and endeavors to live the life which he has imagined, he will meet with success unexpected in common hours.

Henry David Thoreau

They called it the "mud dive." You went down to fifty feet in the black, icy water in front of the Bayonne, New Jersey, U.S. Naval School and sank deep into the mud—and if you didn't panic, you could complete the rest of the rigorous course.

"You really don't have to make this dive," said Dan Crawford, the Chief Petty Officer in charge, as I sat on the diving stool in my deep-sea suit. "You're just writing it up. We'll fill you in on how it is."

I already knew something about how it was by reading the diving manual. "Bolt the helmet on, Chief," I said, "before I change my mind."

In moments like that, one is inclined to wonder how he finds himself in such a situation. Six months before, I'd been sitting on a padded chair in an advertising agency with a steady salary and an expense account. Then the little painless lesion on my cheek was tested and turned out to be malignant. In the depths of my terror, I found resolve.

"Christine," I said to my wife, "all my life I've wanted to try my hand at freelance writing. Now I'm going to give it a whirl—while I still have most of my face."

"I was wondering what it would take," she said.

I quit my job, and we put $5,000—all our savings—down on a huge, decrepit old stone farmhouse in northern New Jersey. We bought a jeep for the family car and enrolled our three children in the local schools. We painted, caulked, roofed, glazed, dug and mowed our four acres of field.

Out back, attached to the barn, was an old chicken coop which, to my enchanted eye, had the makings of a writer's studio. With hammer and nails, I replaced the planks that had fallen askew. I cut back the blackberry bushes that were curling through the cracks and carted half a ton of well-seasoned chicken droppings off to the vegetable garden. I made my desk from a square of plywood which I set on saw horses, and we scrounged a rusty old coal stove from a neighbor's basement. I moved in an old captain's chair and my typewriter and was ready for business. This assignment—about the life of a Navy diving student—was one of my first stories.

I backed down into the water and, keeping a tight grip on the descending line, let myself sink into the gloomy depths. The ear pains began at once. In the dark I could feel the current washing my bulky diving suit against the pilings. The ear pains became excruciating—like two red-hot needles. I tried to clear my ears by swallowing. No luck. When my diving glove slipped on the slimy line, I began to sink fast, and one of my heavy diving boots jammed in a piling. Red wheels of panic revved up in my head. "Bring me up!" I yelled into the helmet microphone.

Dan Crawford was chuckling when he lifted off the helmet. Something had been collecting in the back of my throat. I spat it out—bright red blood.

"You broke some blood vessels in your eustachian tubes," Crawford said. "It happens all the time. But you did okay—you got to forty feet."

A national publication bought the story, and I was able to pay a lot of bills that had been backing up. But, most important, I had finally put into action the working philosophy that I had adopted for my new career: Pick the most demanding mission, go through it myself, then tell what happened. Henry David Thoreau wrote:

"The cost of a thing is the amount of what I will call life which is required to be exchanged for it, immediately or in the long run."

To me, this translated out: When a chance is offered, take it.

I've been doing this now for twenty-six years, and my chicken-coop studio is filled with mementos—trivial, even foolish, maybe, but all of them earned by Thoreau's kind of coin. There is the little blue-woolen diver's cap I wore for the mud dive. Those police handcuffs on the bookcase were used when I was writing a story about a boy who'd been kidnapped, tied up, and eventually driven and knocked out at high speed over back roads to a river. I wrote it nine times. Flat as stale beer. I asked Christine to tie me up, gag, handcuff and blindfold me and drive me over rough back roads on Schooleys Mountain and down to the Musconetcong River. She drove so fast that I was black and blue from bouncing around in the springless jeep. At one point, I thought I was going to swallow the gag. I was weak with relief when we stopped. But the exercise paid off. The kidnap sequence wrote itself; the story was published and, later, anthologized.

Then there is that lump of coal on the shelf I brought home as a souvenir of a mining story assignment in

Hellier, Kentucky. Appalachian hospitality is as warm as a cherry-red stove, or it comes from the muzzle of a 32.20—depending on what you do. So when my truck was suddenly surrounded one night by a group of grim-faced men with rifles leveled, I didn't do anything but sit still and pray. My companion, a fellow I knew only as the Preacher, motioned me to keep quiet, climbed down, walked over to the moonshiners and talked with them. I don't know what he said, but I have a solid hunch he saved our lives. The men backed off and let us pass.

"Nightmare County," my story about the Kentucky mining country, sold in the United States and Great Britain, and once again we caught up on our bills.

These were a few high points in our new life. But there is another side to Thoreau's coin. It involves not only the acceptance of risk but, very often, considerable belt-tightening. As author-critic Joseph Wood Krutch comments, "Security depends not so much upon how much you have as upon how much you can do without." One summer, for lack of funds, we did without a new pump and hauled our water by hand from the spring. We robbed the piggy bank when there was anything in it, and we froze so many string beans even the neighbors wouldn't have them. Twice I took pedestrian jobs to keep us going—once as a fund raiser, another time as a real estate salesman—but always, somehow, one more writing assignment came up, and I got back to the chicken coop.

And so my chicken coop is an incredible clutter of disreputable furniture, files full of research material and knickknacks from various corners of the earth. I write in my bare feet, wriggling my toes in a thick lambskin rug from Kenya. Scattered about the room in plain view are a jaguar skull from Ecuador, a bronze statue of Shiva from India and a chunk of lava I picked up one day when it was 115 degrees in the Rift Valley of East Africa. On bitter nights when the wind shrieks past the windows, I throw photographic slides on a screen that rolls down over the bookcase, and I am transported instantly to the Arctic, the Congo, the Pacific Islands. When I am beset by those ever-recurring moments of frustration and self-doubt, I lock the barn door, pick up my .22 caliber pistol and blast away at a target propped in front of a huge heap of firewood forty feet away through the open office door. I use the two-handed police grip, lock my extended arms and squeeze down on the trigger as delicately as a safe cracker feeling for the combination. After all these years and nearly 12,000 rounds of ammunition, I can cluster six shots in a five-inch circle. Beats Valium!

Often at night, sitting in my office, I think of the greatest chance-taker I know. Christine deals in subtler areas of peril. For her it is not diving into chilly depths or facing gun-toting mountaineers. It is the much riskier business of bucking up the flagging spirit of another person—me. One morning after we moved to New Jersey, I looked at all the spendid homes along our road and an appalling thought hit me. "What," I said, "will all these people think if I fail?" Christine laughed. "Well, they don't know our names," she replied. "They'll probably say, 'Hey, know what happened to that new family on the road? They starved to death.'"

Then there was the terrible moment when a publisher asked for changes in my first novel on which I'd been working for eight years—he wanted material taken out that was basic to what I was trying to say in the story. My first instinct was to protect the integrity of my work. On the other hand, I desperately wanted to see it in print. What to do? Christine told me. The next day I went back and, through gritted teeth, said to the publisher, "The book goes as is, or I'll try it elsewhere." It went, and *The Lion Pit* put our children through college.

Finally, there is one memento in my studio that has nothing to do with writing. It is a lucky nut, the fruit of a tree that grows along the Amazon. These nuts fall into the river, float out into the ocean and are eventually washed up in places like Daytona Beach, which is where I found mine. I value it because it reminds me of the retired philosophy professor who gave me the best tip on chance-taking of all. On a rough day when the surf was making the dunes shake, he would wade out into the fury, duck under a big roller and swim out to sea.

One morning I could stand it no longer. I asked him why.

"Big waves have always terrified me," he replied. "What you see me do now is something I've wanted to do all my life—but couldn't. Then I decided I would have to try it if it killed me. I waded out, watched one of those monsters gather itself until it towered up like a cliff and ducked under. When I surfaced behind it, I was king of the world!"

His eyes twinkled, "No man can hope to control his destiny. The best he can hope for is to control himself—one single act at a time. Those acts are like bricks in a wall. A wall made of such bricks is a man's character."

I believe this because, shortly afterward, I put it to the test. Driving up our road one winter night, I saw a tongue of fire billowing out of the back of the chicken coop. My first thought was for the one and only copy of a lengthy manuscript, which at that time, was nearly completed. I floored the accelerator, skidded into the driveway, left the car on the dead run, and a moment later was staring into a wall of flames floating between me and the desk where the manuscript lay in a plastic box. I realized in one of those rare flashes of insight, the chance we all must take once in our lives. I took a deep breath, squinted my eyes, lunged through the fire, grabbed the box and got out—all in one breath. Only then did I feel the pain in my hands from the nearly molten plastic.

The burn scars that I still carry probably make the best brick I'll ever put in my wall.

But I find I keep coming back to the words of Henry Thoreau concerning the true cost of a thing—anything. It is still basic to my writing career, and it is more; it has become the structure of my day-to-day existence. I have seen it work for others. When I see a person, young or old, rich or poor, who has a realizable dream for which he is willing to exchange a piece of his life, I know that person is building toward the highest goal he can attain. He is rising to a new level of being, using precious moments to mature and grow, to become stronger, braver, maybe even kinder and wiser.

I do not advocate rashness. Always look before you leap. But once the move is made, be bold, take that chance! Never curse the dark. Light a candle, a match, anything, always remembering that the finest helping hand you are ever likely to find is the one attached to the end of your own arm.

Frank Harvey

$\overline{3}$

DEFINING MOMENTS

There's a difference between writing for a living and writing for life. If you write for a living, you make enormous compromises, and you might not even be able to uncompromise yourself. If you write for life, you'll work hard; you'll do what's honest, not what pays.

Toni Morrison

A Serendipitous Visit to Revelation Island

I'd been hanging out in the West Indies for the better part of two years, writing, painting, surfing, and hobnobbing my way through the expat culture of sunstruck Americans, British, and assorted South Americans that had found the languid pace of the islands relaxing. Now, alas, the time had come for my return to California, so I had conveniently managed to hop a ride to Miami, Florida, aboard a friend's private plane.

Two days later we were lifting off in a Queen Air plane from Barbados' Grantly Adams Airport. Once airborne I discovered there would be only one stop on our flight to Miami, in the British Virgin Islands.

It was well into midday when we put down at the Reef Island airport, then took a taxi to the Virgin Gorda residence of the pilot's business associate.

At the top of a ridiculously steep hill sat the sprawling estate that was our destination. Once at the top I was mesmerized by the astounding view. The sculpted postcard-perfect coastline rolled out before us like a prime-time advertisement for packaged trips to paradise.

After introductions to our congenial host and his wife, my pilot and the owner of this opulent hilltop hacienda retreated to a poolside cabaña to discuss their affairs. This left me sitting in a spacious living room enjoying an exotic imported cigarette, and chatting up the attractive lady of the house, a charming young woman indeed.

After a few moments, I began to notice in detail the rich and tasteful decor of the room, particularly what appeared to be a pair of original Matisse portraits.

Upon inquiring about the paintings, the woman gladly walked me through the room and the adjacent corridor, guiding me on a tour of their impressive art collection. Now this was a privilege to see. They were indeed real Matisse paintings, and there were also a Degas, three Dali's, and a Chagall. We took our time viewing the works, and they were all impressive, but what finally stopped me in my tracks was an unusually ornate gold gilt frame showcasing a large piece of richly crafted calligraphic poetry.

The penmanship was exquisite, looking so much like an illuminated manuscript from Fourteenth Century Firenze, only in English. We both stood gazing in a reverent silence as I read the work, which now held my total attention.

By the tenth line, it dawned on me that I was somehow familiar with the piece. The more I read, the more familiar it seemed. By the last stanza, I realized I knew the author very well indeed. My surprised expression caught the notice of my hostess's sharp eye.

"It's special, isn't it?" she exclaimed.

"Why yes. Very." I replied. "Where did you get it. . . . Who did this?"

"There's a bit of a story attached to it . . . ," she said. "Sadly enough. I don't know who the author is."

I turned to look at her, my eyes smiling, and I said, "Well, I do. Would you like to meet him?"

She looked at me with an expression of mildly humorous disbelief.

"You're kidding, of course . . ." But with her gaze riveted on my face, she quickly realized that I was entirely serious. "Would I ever! You don't know what this poem means to me."

"Why don't you tell me where it came from, and I'll tell you who wrote it. Agreed?" I replied, burning with my own curiosity about how she came to have this work of art.

And tell me she did, in brief, explaining that the antique frame had come from a friend who had found it in the Amsterdam flea market, and that a pair of artists in New York City had done the calligraphy and the artwork at her request from a poem she had found on a restaurant bus tray, tossed out with the dirty dishes and silverware.

Her face fell when I asked, "Did you find this poem in Ford's Café at Victoria Cove in Laguna Beach, California, sometime in the late summer of 1976? Probably written on a paper placemat?"

After a stunned pause she blurted out, in a genuinely suspicious state of awestruck wonder, "How on earth could you possibly know that? . . . where I found this poem? How . . .?"

I may have left behind hundreds of poems on forgotten topics on an equal amount of tabletops, but this one I knew only too well.

It was written the week I separated from my then-greatest paramour. Ford's Café was my regular stop-off on the way home from surfing Salt Creek Beach. Now the site of the Laguna Nigel Ritz-Carlton Hotel, Salt Creek was then a pristine stretch of coastline, a virgin beach, great surf below, a wild watermelon patch above.

The subject of the poem that I now stood before was one of loss, redemption, and the wholehearted embracing of dramatic change. It was one that held a prominent place in my personal history and was the first page of one of my poetry chapbooks. I remembered the poem being dated September 1976. I knew the work in all certainty to be mine. I must have left a raw draft of the poem on a Ford's Café placemat—shortly after dreaming it up while soothing my lovesick heart in the cool and comforting arms of the blue Pacific surf.

"How could I know that? Simply because . . . I am the author of this poem!"

I don't know who was more shocked by this revelation, she or I, for we both stood stock-still, frozen for an infinite moment by the sheer strangeness of our shared discovery.

"This is beyond belief," she said, and took my hand and led me across the room to a long white linen sofa where we sat, still holding hands. "I can't believe this is happening." She continued, searching my eyes for some sign of a trick, for confirmation of the truth of my confident pronouncement. We just stared at each other until we both broke into ridiculous grins. It was true, and we both knew it.

"What do you say we—" She rose, moved to an elegant adjacent bar, and returned with a cold bottle of Cristal champagne and two long-stemmed glasses. "This is a special moment. Will you share a glass with me?"

Naturally, I accepted, opened the bottle for her, and poured out what instantly took on the air of a ceremonial toast. As I watched the tiny bubbles streaming up from the bottom of my tapered wineglass, she began to unfurl the colorful details of how she came to have my poem, and the dramatic results of her reading it.

With an innocent sense of real intimacy, this lovely woman told me a tale of how she had been a struggling waitress who was, at the time, dealing with the tragic loss of her fiancé in a fatal car crash. Despondent, repeatedly harangued by her boss, and drifting on the verge of an emotional implosion, she had found my poem sticking out from a pile of dirty dishes in a red plastic dishroom tray. For no logical reason she set down the food order she was carrying, fished the crumpled paper out of the muck, smoothed it out and read the darn thing.

Finally, after rereading the coffee-stained thirty-line sonnet for the fifth time, she realized she was half sobbing, half laughing while a flood of fat, sad tears streamed down her face. Having something of an epiphany, she ran to the dining room of the café shouting at the startled customers, demanding, pleading, to know who had written this poem. All she got were blank, somewhat frightened stares, and her boss was so bent out of shape by this emotional outburst he promised to dock her a week's pay.

Apparently, that was all it took. She quit her job on the spot. Within a week, after hawking her furniture in a yard sale, she left southern California and its sad ghosts, setting out for San Francisco in a beat-up Volvo, her cat at her side, and all of her worldly possessions piled on the back seat.

After only one day in the Bay Area, knowing no one, and with little money, her luck took a sudden positive swing. She met a young couple in a city bakery who offered her a free apartment and a job. The place was across the bay in Oakland and was part of a project to build a temple for a remarkable man from India, who was identified only as Baba. The pay wasn't much and the neighborhood was a little dodgey, but it was a nice apartment, and the people were absurdly friendly, and it was a fresh start.

She fell in with the temple project people, helping cook for the building crews, answering phones, and helping other newcomers feel their way around. It was there, two weeks into her new adventure, that she met the kind-hearted man who would become her husband.

He was an architect who was donating time to the

building project. One afternoon she served him some peppermint tea, and the rest, as they say, is history. Extremely happy together, they were married within three months. Less than a year later, he had moved his practice to New York City. They first came to love the Caribbean Islands when he was commissioned to design a luxury resort in the region.

When his grandfather left him a fortune, they decided to move to the Caribbean and raise their first child out of the big city.

She had the poem laid out by a renowned calligraphic penman, then had it turned into an "Illuminated" page in the style of the Florentine Renaissance by a top museum restoration artist. And that was her story.

Entranced by this amazing saga, I then recounted to her how I had written the poem, and why, and how, through my habit of penning public poetry, she had come to find it.

She confided that she considered my poem the key to her current happy fortunes, that this cast-off piece of scribbling had been the catalyst to the most dramatic change in her life, and for this reason she had enshrined it here, among their collected masterworks.

With both the bottle and our revelations spent, we were again rendered speechless, mostly by the true oddity of our chance meeting, and for her, I assume, the "mystery of the poem" being finally revealed.

There came a shift in the mood, and a bit of embarrassment, and some explaining, when at the exact moment that she decided to hug me, her husband and my friend entered the room. They both found the story of the poem, and my being there, a tale that defied all probability.

My friend's business now concluded, it was time for a quick but excellent seafood meal, during which we all agreed that the odds of us ever meeting at all, five-thousand miles from where we once crossed paths, and three years later, were somewhere around 10 billion to one, or greater.

I was given an open invitation to visit their home again, and after kind farewells and a comfortable ride to the airport in their white Range Rover, I found myself winging my way through a brilliant Bahamian sunset, en route to an unknown future of my own.

Throughout that flight, and over the many years since, I have always been amazed at the lesson I was given that day: That we are all inexplicably bound together, and that to commit ourselves to both the act of writing, and to the free sharing of our ideas and efforts, provides us with a secret wealth that we should never doubt the value of.

How could I feel sad about the challenges of my chosen path knowing that something so simple as that abandoned poem would be the source of such amazing inspiration to a total stranger? Now I know the truth.

Noel Phillip Rodriguez

Writing Can Be Magic

My second marriage was tearing apart. Troubled, I walked the path under the blue oaks along the Cosumnes River, a little light remaining at the end of the hot day. Since we had acquired the ranch ten years ago, my husband and I had commuted the twenty-five miles from the California gold country to Sacramento. But like many people, I lived in the fast lane—in airplanes, on asphalt and concrete. A former college professor, I consulted for industrial corporations. I felt rootless.

I was walking where the Miwok people had lived for 5,000 years, trying to imagine how life had been before the Forty-niners massacred them and drove the stragglers away. The heat was losing its grip on the land. With the cooler air came the aroma of moss in the backwaters. Every leaf was still—a magical time.

A rustle came from above. I looked up through dark branches against the fading sky but saw no bird. A friendly welcoming feeling settled over me as I breathed the good scent of oak, hundreds of green acorns ripening in the branches. Life was fecund. Gradually, I became aware of a sort of gentle communication raining down on me, softening the crusts of my urban life.

I sensed a human presence, Miwok I was sure, a mother. I felt a woman-to-woman intimacy, as if I were sharing this time with a dear friend. I didn't want to leave; the feeling of connection was intense. "Tell the story of my family," she urged.

In the darkening twilight I stood in awe. The Miwok people didn't speak of their deceased family members; therefore, little of their history had been told. Research would be difficult. I had written freelance articles and many academic and government-related papers, but what form of writing would this be? Whatever, I wasn't one to do things halfway; it would be full-time work. How would my husband feel about assuming sole financial responsibility for all our commitments? It could end our marriage, force us to sell the ranch. Could I keep writing somewhere else? Would the inspiration of this evening keep me going? Maybe I was losing my mind to think of quitting work. But the gentle bond held me.

Stop driving in the thickening traffic and worsening air? A weight seemed to lift from my shoulders. Yes. Research ethnologies and historic papers. Interview old-timers. Yes. Stop being a dilettante writer, go the whole way. Yes. Yes.

The longer I stayed there accepting the challenge and honor, the more joyful I felt. Fear dissolved. The path was dark when I finally hurried home. I ran upstairs, turned on my computer, and the narrator's voice flowed through my fingers:

> *Once I was Eagle Woman. Now I am an oak tree.*
> *When I walked these paths the nights came often,*
> *and life in the village hurled past like the river in the*
> *time of early flowers.*

That was the summer of 1990. By early 1996 I had written two "history novels," the first about the narrator's son, who helped fight the Mexican presidios, the second, *River of Red Gold,* about his daughter, "Indian Mary," in historic journals. Every day I had walked the beautiful land, and the magic of the tree never abandoned me, nor did the sly coyote who watched from his hiding places. My own roots had taken hold; I would never move from this place. Perhaps due to my new calm, my marriage had mended; my husband worked long hours to keep up the payments, encouraging me every step of the way.

We decided to issue *River of Red Gold* first, because it told of the Gold Rush and the Donner Party, and this was the 150th anniversary of those events. ("Indian Mary," about fourteen, and Elitha Donner, fourteen, had married the same settler on the ranch—I'd discovered the Donner Party connection after I started to write.) This book was timely as well as big.

Heartwarming reviews had arrived, but I worried how the Miwok people would receive it. I had sent a review copy to Chaw-se Grinding Rocks State Park and crossed my fingers. Had I properly represented their culture? Months later I hadn't heard from them. I phoned, but park rangers said to wait, there was a committee. Weeks passed. No one returned my voice mail. I feared the worst. It was late September, and the docent who answered said everyone was outside preparing for the Big Time. She knew nothing about the book.

The Big Time was a spiritual gathering of the people. I had longed to see a ceremony inside the dancehouse, but hadn't wanted to attend uninvited, though outsiders and tourists were allowed. The sociological observer part of my life was over. Instead I had researched, consulted with a very wise old headman, and written from my heart. Besides, today I had a book fair on schedule.

At the end of the day, a profitable one for *River,* I looked toward the Sierras, knowing the first dances would begin at dusk. Judging by the sun, I had time to get to the park. I might find the person who had read my book. I headed the car eastward, perhaps toward severe disappointment.

The park grounds were bustling with milling people, colorful tents, strings of feathers and vending booths. I found a park ranger and asked where the docent was who reviewed books. She didn't know. Hundreds of people were preparing to camp. It would be like finding a needle in a haystack. Venison was slow-cooking in a pit, and Indian food would be sold in the small building, the ranger said, near the structures roofed over with willow branches. I went there and asked a man with long braids if he knew the person who reviewed books.

A woman turned. "That's me."

Amazed, I braced myself. "I'm the author of this book." I held it up.

"Oh," she said. "I read half of it,"—only half?—"but it disappeared from my office. Vanished. I keep hoping some-body will return it. It was wonderful! Incredible research. I hope I get to read the rest!"

Six years of pent-up emotion released with my breath. I couldn't stop the big smile from stretching my face as I promised her another copy.

"Come with me," she said. "You've got to meet Mary."

Inside the shack where jars of mustard and other condi-ments lined the shelves, a woman stood facing the other way, a fall of black hair against a red blouse. She turned. While the docent briefly explained who I was and left, I saw that Mary was a very attractive young woman with the soft features of the California natives.

"Did you see my book?" I said, holding it up.

"No, I don't know anything about it. It's about Miwok people?"

"Yes, their experiences with John Sutter and the gold miners 150 years ago. A Miwok girl is a major character.

It's about power and place and the meaning of home, as your people knew it."

She seemed to be absorbing me along with my words. "Sutter was bad."

I nodded. "The girl's name was Mary. She went to Sutter's Fort. All the events in the novel really happened. Sutter mentioned her in his diary." Feeling about as articulate as a stick of wood, I extended the book to her.

She took and opened it. I barely breathed as she read the prologue. She stared at the mustard jars, then turned the page to the first chapter, read a few minutes and looked up at me, the black pools of her eyes glistening. "Pedro?"

"Yes, he's another major character."

"How did you know?"

"Know?"

"About the tree? And Pedro?"

I stuttered something about the tree, the spirit, and said the people I interviewed had forgotten the name of the man, so I named him Pedro.

She looked at me in amazement, read more, then fanned the 624 pages.

I showed her the end notes and sources, and told her diarist Heinrich Lienhard had written about a beautiful Indian girl named Mary who bamboozled John Sutter out of $2000 worth of gold.

She laughed and said, "I'm glad she did that. I never heard that story."

"Take this book," I said. "Here, I'll sign it for you." Seeing her smile, I wrote a note to another beautiful Indian girl named Mary.

"Where exactly did Mary live? The one you wrote about?"

"Bridge House," I said, handing her the book. Most people had never heard of the Gold Rush town, now wiped off the map. "I live there on the twelve-acre remnant of the old ranch. Most of it was developed and is now called Rancho Murieta."

Quietly she said, "My family came from Bridge House."

I felt prickles on the backs of my arms. We stood looking at each other in the darkening shadows, women of two cultures, neither given to shows of emotion, she and her people justifiably wary, I the outsider. Yet suddenly we were hugging. She felt wonderful in my arms, solid, clean, real.

"Come to the Big Time," she said when we pulled to arm's length, her face as wet as mine. "My husband is an elder. Dance with us in the roundhouse."

Naida West

PEANUTS. *Reprinted by permission of United Feature Syndicate, Inc.*

Papa's Gift

Papa wasn't smiling that night. He'd been very quiet lately—not his usual jolly self at all. I was only six, but I knew his thoughts were far away from our bedroom where we both sat on Mama and Papa's bed with our backs against the bed pillows. He was reading me a chapter from *Wind in the Willows,* but he didn't even laugh at the funny places. The chapter over, he sat without speaking for a long time. Finally his mind wandered back through the mists to join me.

"Cookie," he said, "I've read or told you a story almost every night for six years. Now it's your turn. You tell me a story and I'll write it down."

"Okay," I said after a few minutes. "I think I got one. When I was a little kid about four years old," I began, "Mama and I visited Grandma Cook's farm. Mama and Grandma went into the house, but I stayed out in the yard. It was a very hot day. I was barefoot and liked to feel the cool grass between my toes. All of a sudden I heard a loud 'cock a doodle do.' I turned around and a big red rooster almost as tall as I was stood next to me. He was looking at my feet. He must have thought my toes were something to eat because all of a sudden he stabbed my big toe with his beak. Ouch, it hurt like anything. It felt like a sharp knife had cut me. He got ready to do it again, but I started running. He chased me pecking at my heels. 'Mama, Mama,' I yelled. She heard me and came out of the house. She snatched me up in her arms just as the rooster was going to stab me again. Grandma grabbed a broom and chased him away. I was sure glad I was safe. Mama put medicine on my toes. It stung, but it didn't hurt as much as that rooster's beak, thank goodness."

Papa was writing furiously. "Did you get it all?" I asked.

"Every bit," he said. "That was a fine story—very scary. What a mean rooster! I'm glad he didn't eat you."

"I thought he was going to," I said.

Three weeks went by. Papa read to me or told me a story every night, but he still didn't seem as happy as he used to be. One night, as we sat on the bed again, he seemed like his old self. "Have I got a surprise for you?" he said giving me a hug. "Close your eyes."

I did, but when I opened them all I saw was a newspaper.

"Look closer," he said. I did and there in black letters I recognized my name: Myrtle Cook.

"It's your story," said Papa. "This page is called the *Junior Page*, and it has stories written by children. I sent your story to the editor, Mother Hubbard, and she printed it so other girls and boys could read it."

"Honest?" I said. I couldn't believe my eyes. My own story in the paper with my name at the top. I was never so thrilled in all my life. A good thing too, because the following months were very sad. A few days after Papa showed me my story, he didn't come home. Not that day or the next or the next.

"Where's Papa?" I'd ask every night. After a few weeks Mama told me. "Papa and I are getting a divorce," she said. "That means he isn't going to live here anymore. He got a new job in a place called Chicago, far away. He loves you very much and wanted to get a job near here, so he could see you all the time, but there weren't any jobs around here. He had to take this job because he needed money to send us for food and clothes."

I was heartbroken. How could Papa do this to me? Who would read me stories now? Not Mama. She was too busy working. Even though Papa and I exchanged cards and letters over the years, I never saw him again. I would have grown up thinking Papa didn't love me except for that wonderful thing he did—sending my story to get published. That was the beginning because soon after that I started school, learned to write, and began sending stories myself to the *Junior Club* page. Almost always they were printed. How could I stay mad at Papa? He gave me the best good-bye gift imaginable. It opened the door for me to enjoy a lifetime of happiness, brought me wonderful excitement, magnified all my days, colored my whole life. I'm eighty-four years old now. I've spent countless marvelous hours, dreaming, composing, plotting, then spending the checks my editors send me. Writing has been my hobby, my vocation, nourishment for my soul. Thank you, Papa, wherever you are.

Cookie Potter

You Can't Afford to Doubt Yourself

The fear of rejection is worse than rejection itself.

Nora Profit

On a spring evening some years ago, while living in New York, I decided to take in an off-Broadway musical where I heard Salome Bey sing for the first time. I was enthralled. I believed I had just discovered the next Sarah Vaughn.

The moment was magical. Even though half the seats were empty, Salome's voice filled the room and brought the theater to life. I had never witnessed anything quite like it. I was so moved by Salome's performance, yet disappointed about the sparse audience, I decided to write an article to help promote her.

Struggling to contain my excitement, the next day I phoned the theater where Salome Bey was appearing and unabashedly acted like a professional writer:

"May I speak with Salome Bey, please?"

"Just one moment, please."

"Hello, this is Salome."

"Miss Bey, this is Nora Profit. I'm writing an article for

Essence magazine, spotlighting your singing achievements. Is it possible for us to meet so that we might talk about your career?"

Did I say that? Essence *is going to have me arrested,* I thought. *I don't know a thing about her singing achievements.* My inner voice shouted, *You have really done it this time!*

"Why, of course," said Salome. "I'm cutting my fourth album next Tuesday. Why don't you meet me at the studio? And bring along your photographer."

Bring my photographer! I thought, my confidence fading rapidly. *I've really tied myself in a noose this time. I don't even know anyone who owns a camera.*

"While I'm thinking about it," continued Salome, "Galt McDermot, producer of *Hair, Dude* and *Highway Life* will be performing a benefit with me at the Staten Island Church-on-the-Hill. So why don't you plan to come to that, too, and I'll introduce you to him."

"Umm—of course," I said, trying to sound professional. "That will add an extra dimension to the article."

An extra dimension? How would you know? snapped the nagging voice in my head.

"Thank you, Miss Bey," I said, bringing the inquiry to a close. "I'll see you next Tuesday."

When I hung up, I was scared out of my mind. I felt as though I had jumped into a pool of quicksand and was about to be swallowed up with no chance at salvaging my dignity.

The next few days flashed by quickly. I made an emergency run to the library. *Who is this Galt McDermot anyway?* And I frantically searched for anyone with a 35mm camera. A real photographer was out of the question. After all, I had spent all my extra cash on the Broadway theater ticket.

Then I lucked out. I learned my friend Barbara had become quite an accomplished photographer, so after I begged and pleaded, Barbara agreed to accompany me to the interview.

At both the recording session and the church benefit, Barbara clicked away, while I, a bundle of nerves, sat there looking very pensive, taking notes on a yellow pad, asking questions that all began with, "Can you tell me . . . "

Soon it was all over, and once outside the church, I ran frantically down the street, wanting to hail an ambulance because I thought I was going to die from the stress. I hailed a taxi instead.

Safe at home, I calmed down and began writing. But with every word I wrote, a small, stern voice inside me kept scolding: *You lied! You're no writer! You haven't written anything. Why, you've never even written a good grocery list. You'll never pull this off!*

I soon realized that fooling Salome Bey was one thing, but faking a story for *Essence,* a national magazine, was impossible. The pressure was almost unbearable.

Putting my heart into it, I struggled for days with draft after draft—rewriting and reediting my manuscript countless times. Finally, I stuffed my neatly typed, double-spaced manuscript into a large envelope, added my SASE (self-addressed stamped envelope), and dropped the package into a mailbox. As the mailman drove away, I wondered how long it would take before I'd get the *Essence* editor's unqualified "YUCK!" reply.

It didn't take long. Three weeks later there it was, my manuscript—returned in an envelope with my own handwriting. *What an insult!* I thought. *How could I have ever thought that I could compete in a world of professional writers who make their living writing? How stupid of me!*

Knowing I couldn't face the rejection letter with all the reasons why the editor hated my manuscript, I threw the unopened envelope into the nearest closet and promptly forgot about it, chalking up the whole ordeal as a bad experience.

Five years later, while cleaning out my apartment

preparing to move to Sacramento, California, to take a job in sales, I came across an unopened envelope addressed to me in my own handwriting. *Why would I send myself a package?* I thought. To clear up the mystery, I quickly opened the envelope and read the editor's letter in disbelief:

> *Dear Ms. Profit,*
>
> *Your story on Salome Bey is fantastic. We need some additional quotes. Please add those and return the article immediately. We would like to publish your story in the next issue.*

Shocked, it took me a long time to recover. Fear of rejection cost me dearly. I lost at least five hundred dollars and having my article appear in a major magazine—proof I could be a professional writer. More importantly, fear cost me years of enjoyable and productive writing. Today, I am celebrating my sixth year as a full-time freelance writer with more than one hundred articles sold. Looking back on this experience, I learned a very important lesson: You can't afford to doubt yourself.

Nora Profit

A Perfect Night to Die

When I was little, my mother delighted in telling me the story she was going to write someday, in her book. She was going to use all her experiences, and everything she'd learned about all the people she knew, and write a novel. I always loved when she'd start telling me about it, because somehow just talking about it seemed to make her happy. What a wonderful thing it must be, I thought, to write something so beautiful! We were all going to be famous and rich, she'd promise. And I believed it; just talking about it made her so happy. I couldn't even imagine how happy we'd all be when it came true.

As I got older, I would get impatient if she began talking about her book. After all, even then I knew that if you were going to be a writer, you had to write, not talk about it. Somehow, she never did.

But I did.

A couple of miracles started my writing career. The first, my newborn daughter, only weighed about three and a half kilograms. If I hadn't lived through the unique experience of having my first baby in Japan, I would never have written—and sold—my first article about that experience.

But she was only the catalyst; ten more years of "ifs" would happen before the birth of my first book. After that first miracle, if we'd chosen to vacation closer to Japan instead of coming back to California, where I happened to go to a writers' conference . . . If the editor I met there hadn't been a friend of a woman who, many years later, heard about the orchestra I conducted . . . If she hadn't happened to be too busy that day to make it to her own interview with the publisher, and if I hadn't just happened to call her that day, and she hadn't offered me her interview spot . . .

. . . years and years of "ifs" . . .

. . . then I never would have written and published that first book.

Which became the second book, then the third . . .

The list of "ifs" is so long that I can't think about it without amazement. Surely there's another explanation, more reasonable, rational, I always tell myself whenever I think about how I got started on this strange path of sharing my written words with strangers.

I've always believed, in a nebulous way, that we all inhabit circles that move about in the universe, bumping into each other once in a while. And when these circles touch, things happen. Sparks fly from one circle to the other, linking our lives and our selves in ways we could never dream of. If I invented such events in my fiction, people would tell me, "Real life doesn't work that way!"

Can it all be coincidence?

The circles collided, and I was going to be published. A company I'd never heard of before, three thousand miles away, was going to publish my first book. And then, before I had a chance to break out the champagne—the publisher went bankrupt.

I knew it was a salable book, since I'd done a lot of the regional pre-marketing research for the publisher. But the book had just died with the company that was going to give it—and me—life. I was furious. I was bitter. It was obviously not meant to be. But unbeknownst to me, my defining moment was there, daring me to take the next step. So I did.

My turning point was more of a leap—into the deep-end-scary world of independent publishing. If I'd been just a little less knowledgeable then, or if I'd known a little more of what I know now, I might not have done it. But instead, at just that moment, that turning point, I was just stupid enough and daring enough and naive enough . . . And here I sit, holding my fifth book.

If I'd known, then, that once I became a publisher I'd be a businessperson first and foremost (anathema, to a writer-type), that my days would be filled with phone calls and business letters instead of creative writing, that my *free* time from then on would be filled with speaking engagements . . . But I didn't. So I jumped in with both feet—and now have nine awards, a foreign contract, hundreds of articles and two novels.

A few years ago, my father called; it was time for my brother and me to go see our mother one last time, just in case. We both had to fly from the West Coast to the East. John arrived earlier in the day; my plane landed in Pennsylvania almost at midnight. That cloudy, numbingly cold winter night, he met me at the airport, and we drove directly to the hospital to see our mother. It was almost too late. She was unconscious.

Later, around two o'clock in the morning, before I slipped into bed in the front room of my parents' home, I knelt to look out the window. As I gazed unseeing across the empty, dark street at the fir trees and the statue of Mary on the church grounds, it began to snow. It was beautiful. Without a sound, slowly, the fir trees turned white, and the street lamp was surrounded by a silvery haze. Snow fell on the lumps of car-blackened slush that already lay in the gutters of the street, turning them pure white. It was perfect.

A perfect night to die, I thought. *Take her now,* I prayed.

She died before morning.

And her book died with her.

It would have been a wonderful book. Its story had warmed me, comforted me, cheered me and made the two of us closer while I was a child. It had sustained my mother's dreams and hopes, and given her something to yearn for.

It died that night.

A writer must write. That is my mother's legacy to me. That lesson, learned so profoundly over years of disdain, of impatience with her, has driven me to produce more writing than any class I've taken, than any article I've read, than any advice I've ever heard.

How I've wanted to read my mother's story!

I must see to it that my own children never feel such remorse, such yearning to know their mother. I must see to it that the words in me have a voice that can be shared. I will write. And on the night when I die, my children will know me. They'll know that I loved them and why. They'll know what I loved about life, and that I was a writer.

Then it will be a perfect night to die.

Dierdre W. Honnold

A Chat with Alex Haley

The chief glory of every people arises from its authors.

Dr. Samuel Johnson

On December 8, 1980, as a writing conference director, I sent a letter to Alex Haley, the renowned author—not really expecting a response. My letter began this way:

> *Dear Alex,*
>
> *A can of sardines and a few pennies left to your name—wow, that's a scary thought. Thanks for hanging in there and eventually bringing us* Roots, *Alex, because you and your story have become an inspiration to struggling writers everywhere. That's my purpose in writing you.*

Then, realizing this was a very long shot, I asked him if he would deliver a conference keynote address for me:

> *Since there are many other scared, aspiring writers out there who need all the encouragement they can get, would*

*you please take time out of your very busy schedule to share
your personal story with 400 beginning and advanced writers at the 20th California Writers Club Conference to be held
at Mills College in Oakland, California, on June 27, 1981, at
8:00 P.M.?*

Then I appealed to his emotional side.

*We need you, Alex, as our keynote speaker—to infuse us,
to enlighten us, to inspire us, to guide us. You are more than
just a writer, you are legend.*

I could hardly believe it; my persuasive letter worked.
Three weeks later, Alex called me.

"Hi, Buuuuuuud. Your letter got me, man. I'm yours.
Tell me what you want me to do, and I'll do it."

"Wow, Alex, you've given me the greatest Christmas
present possible. Thank you, thank you, thank you!"

We talked for nearly an hour about the details of the conference and a variety of other things. Then I got an idea.

"Alex, my daughter Lori is home for the holidays from
the University of California at Davis, California, where
she's a pre-med student. In the spirit of Christmas, would
you mind saying 'Hi' to her?"

"Sure. I'd love to, Buuuuuuud. Put her on."

I left my home office and found Lori watching TV in the
family room.

"Telephone, Lori. Take it on my office phone."

"Who is it, Dad?"

"It's Alex Haley, the author of *Roots*. He wants to talk to
you."

"Yeah, right, Dad."

"I'm serious, Lori. Come on, Mr. Haley is waiting."

Still not believing me, she barked into my phone, "Who
is this?"

I watched her eyes grow wider and her face turn beet red the instant she recognized his famous voice.

"Oh, Mr. Haley, I'm so sorry. I thought my dad was playing a trick on me."

They talked for a few minutes, Lori sputtering and blinking. When I came back on the line, she silently mouthed "I'm sorry," then tore down the hall to tell her mother what had happened.

I was really touched by his graciousness. "Thanks, Alex, for talking to Lori and for agreeing to be our keynote speaker. I think I love you."

"I love you too, Buuuuuuud."

When I got the word out that the great Alex Haley had agreed to be our CWC Conference keynoter, the registration soared. In fact, we had to cut it off at 425 registered participants, the largest group ever assembled for a CWC Conference in forty years. I was on cloud nine all spring and into June.

Then about a week before the conference, I got the bad news that the airline controllers were threatening to strike any day. If they did strike, Alex, Eve Bunting, Lois Duncan, Walt Morey, Robert Silverberg and many other top author/teachers would not make it to the conference. I was on pins and needles and got very little sleep during this time.

By June 26, the day the conference began, I was feeling somewhat better. All my author/teachers had arrived— except Alex. I had my fingers crossed. If the controllers could hold off just one more day, Alex would be here.

Then I got a phone call that shattered my hopes.

Jackie Niapo, Alex's office manager, called me at Mills College to report that Alex had flown to New York to meet with a *GEO* editor and wouldn't be flying into Oakland from Los Angeles as planned, but coming into San Francisco International Airport about 3:00 P.M. the next day.

I was devastated. When I hung up, I felt like I'd just been stabbed in the gut. I feared the worst: that the controllers would strike or that Alex would get hung up and not arrive on time to address our sold-out conference crowd, which had now swelled to more than 500 participants, teachers and guests.

I felt sick. What would I tell the conferees, many of whom had traveled a couple thousand miles to hear Alex speak? I was literally a basket case.

The next day, Mac McCall and Ivan Hafstrom, staff assistants, and I nervously waited at the San Francisco airport as 279 passengers departed from the airplane Alex was supposed to be aboard. When the last passenger walked by, I panicked. Alex had missed his plane!

I slowly turned toward Mac and Ivan in total disbelief. "What are we going to do now?" I asked in a weak voice.

Just then Mac smiled and pointed toward the off ramp. I couldn't believe my eyes. There, standing in the doorway, was one of the most beautiful sights I'd ever seen: It was Alex Haley, wearing a tan suit, enveloped in sunlight like some god.

"Fooled ya, didn't I Buuuuuuud?" He'd planned to be the last to deplane just to bug me.

I fought back tears of relief. "Yep, you got me good, Alex."

We embraced, quickly jumped into Mac's car, and raced back to Mills College.

"Hey, Buuuuuuud, I'm beat," said Alex as we left the airport. "I need a nap, man."

Alex explained that he had flown to New York to meet with the *GEO* editor the day before under the pretense of fine-tuning the overdue article he was writing for them. The truth was, Alex hadn't even started the piece and flew to New York to buy some time. He had lunch with the editor, then dashed to his hotel room and wrote all night long. The next morning, he grabbed a cab, delivered his finished article to the *GEO* office and made a mad dash to the airport. He was the last passenger to board; the stewardess literally slammed the airplane door on his heels.

"Buuuuuud, you didn't answer me. I said I need a nap bad, Buuuuuuud."

"Alex, I hate to break this to you, but the minute we arrive back at Mills College about 5:00 P.M., we have 100-plus media folks, including two TV stations, all set to interview you. Then, at 6:00 P.M., we have 110 copies of *Roots* for you to autograph. We eat dinner at 7:00 P.M., and your speech is scheduled at 8:00 P.M. sharp."

I held my breath.

"Okay, Buuuuuuud. You're the boss. Then I'll just have to gear down."

The press conference went well. Alex, standing in front of the old administration building that had been moved to Mills College in the 1800s on log rollers, was magnificent. *Where did he find the energy?* I thought.

During the book signing, Alex delighted everyone by signing more than 107 copies of *Roots*. "I've done so many book signings of late," he said jokingly, "that you'll have a tough time finding a copy of *Roots* in America *without* my signature in it."

Just then the unexpected happened. Alex was down to the last three books when the lawn sprinklers came on. Alex and the few remaining participants scattered, avoiding the spewing water.

On our way to dinner a few moments later, Alex couldn't resist.

"What a stroke of genius, Buuuuuuud," he said, pulling my leg. "That was brilliant."

"I didn't do that, Alex. I had nothing to do with the sprinklers coming on."

"Sure you did, Buuuuuuud. You saw how tired I was

and got me out of there. You're a genius, man. Good job!"

All through dinner, my efforts to convince him of my innocence fell on deaf ears.

Promptly at 8:00 P.M. in the theater, Alex Haley delivered the greatest speech—"A Chat with Alex Haley"—I've ever heard. In the fifteen years I've been a member of the National Speakers Association (NSA), a worldwide group of professional speakers, I've heard the best of the best: Zig Ziglar, Norman Vincent Peale, Anthony Robbins, Brian Tracy, Jack Canfield, Mark Victor Hansen, Jim Rohn, and hundreds of other great speakers. But this night, Alex, as the kids say today, was *totally awesome.*

After I introduced him, you could hear a pin drop as Alex began telling how as a starving writer, he'd hopped apartments in Greenwich Village, New York, because he couldn't pay his rent. Then he hit the jackpot:

He got a $20,000 advance to write *The Autobiography of Malcolm X,* which freed him to write books full-time.

Then he launched into his famous story of Kunta Kinte, his ancient ancestor, how he researched and wrote *Roots* for twelve years, how it was turned down by many publishers, and how his life drastically changed when *Roots* finally came out.

I sat there mesmerized as Alex unfolded story after story. I was so engrossed, I almost missed my cue. Because Alex was so exhausted from being up all night and a full day more, he'd commanded me earlier: "Don't leave me out there." He insisted that I let him know when he'd spoken for an hour and a half by tugging on his coat. I agreed.

He'd been talking for exactly ninety-two minutes, when I reached over and tugged his coat. He stopped speaking, looked down at me (we were the only two people on the stage), waved me off, then began speaking again. I waited about ten more minutes and then tugged his coat a second time. This time he not only stopped speaking, he smiled at me, then put on a serious face and turned to the audience.

"Buuuuuuud's trying to get me to stop. Do you want me to stop?"

The audience exploded! "Booooooo! Let him talk! Leave Alex alone!" Imagine the sound of 500 people screaming at you. I got the picture fast. Alex was having a ball. I didn't tug his coat again. He spoke for two and a half hours with no break. He finished to a standing ovation that was deafening. Then he bowed and made a quick exit out the back door to get some well-deserved sleep. The audience kept cheering after he'd gone.

Looking back on this exciting experience, I feel blessed to have met and enjoyed the late Alex Haley, one of the truly great authors of our time. And I learned a great lesson from him: A positive attitude determines a positive result. I'd almost driven myself crazy worrying about what could go wrong, instead of focusing on what I wanted to go right. Since then, I've followed Alex's sage advice: "Your attitude is everything. Believe in yourself and trust your material. To be a successful writer, write every single day whether you feel like it or not. Never, never give up, and the world will reward you beyond your wildest dreams."

Bud Gardner

Cash Rewards

The student intern hovered around my desk. Deep into the process of sending out résumés and developing a portfolio, Lisa wanted to see my clippings. She was determined to find the perfect presentation and most effective samples to get her a high-powered public relations job with big cash rewards.

As I flipped through the pages of ads, annual reports and news releases, a yellowed news clipping slipped out of the lining of my portfolio. The weathered paper was a relic from my own student intern days, over a quarter century ago. I had kept it as a reminder to myself that no matter how important the cash rewards seemed, there were other, more important benefits to a writing life. In this case, it was the ability of my writing to draw me closer to someone I love.

That summer of 1971, most of my assignments were the routine stuff a rookie in the newsroom would expect to be doing: proofreading endless columns of type, pounding out obituaries of local businessmen or matrons, and crafting cookie cutter "bridals." Those were the days when we announced weddings with a good twenty inches of type: *The bride carried stephanotis and baby's breath. The bridesmaids*

*wore Empire-style gowns of lavender voile, the sleeves trimmed
with broomstick lace.*

One of the choicest assignments was reviewing shows
at the nearby Saratoga Performing Arts Center, with a free
pair of tickets going to the reviewer. Seniority determined
who got their pick of the tickets, but since the only other
person in the newsroom under thirty was the police
reporter, he and I divvied up the coolest groups. He'd
take Chuck Mangione and Joe Cocker; I got Arlo Guthrie
and Judy Collins. The older staff snapped up the crooners,
big bands and symphony orchestra.

But in June 1971, one pair of tickets was making the
rounds of the newsroom without any takers—*The Johnny
Cash Show*. The managing editor was getting nervous. The
unspoken agreement with the arts center was they provided a season's worth of tickets, and we delivered a season worth of reviews. How could we miss one of the
opening acts?

I knew my father would love to go. *The Johnny Cash Show*
was his new favorite television program, edging out the
Lawrence Welk Hour and *Hee Haw* for his loyalty. Still, I hesitated to ask for the tickets. I was only a summer intern,
after all, and I did have Arlo and Judy already tucked under
my desk blotter and dates for both shows.

I had other reasons to drag my feet. I was twenty-one,
cool, a college junior. Not the type who fancied herself at
a cowboy concert, even for Dear Ol' Dad.

Then there was my dad himself to consider. In younger
days he was eager to trip the light fantastic to the likes of
Tommy Dorsey and Glenn Miller, but of late he'd taken to
finding his entertainment in quietly hoeing his garden or
welding parts for the army surplus Jeeps he loved to
restore. He had become a bit of a homebody.

There were other tensions, too. A man who left school
after the sixth grade to support his immigrant parents, he

was now struggling to put his child through journalism school. A proud veteran of World War II, he was troubled by my generation's opposition to the war in Vietnam. I sensed that the father who wanted me to get a good education and fulfill my dreams was also a weary worker and a loyal American, who couldn't help but sometimes wonder if it was all worth it.

I mulled over these things as Father's Day approached. Then, since I had no budget for a gift, I got those tickets and slipped them into a homemade card with a silly handwritten verse.

As we headed to the concert, I began to have my doubts again. Would my tie-dye and jeans fit in with the cowboy-shirt-and-boots crowd? Would my VW Beetle look out of place among the pickup trucks in the parking lot? Would I be the only person under fifty there? I was surprised to see as many young hippies as I did older country-western types in the audience. It turned out that Cash was against the Vietnam War, too, and that had earned him a young following I hadn't known about.

When Johnny Cash came roaring onto the stage with all the force of a locomotive engine, I surprised myself again by being caught up in the energy and power of his performance. In fact, the locomotive image would become my lead for a powerful and positive review.

My Dad and I had a great time that night and left knowing we would both remember the concert for years. He bought me a souvenir music book, and I regaled him with my organ versions of "Folsom Prison Blues" and "I Walk The Line."

But the biggest thrill of all—and my surprise "Cash" reward—came the next day when the paper hit our doorstep. My review, pulsing with the energy I felt in Johnny Cash's performance and painting a colorful word picture of the crowd and performers, struck a note with my dad. At that moment, I think he finally understood me. He now knew why I just *had* to be a writer. Dad had shared in the experience that created the piece, and it made the concert live again for him. He smiled. "Very nice, Doll" was all he said; then he solemnly cut out the review and folded it to fit into his lunchbox. He took it to the rug mill the next day to share with his friends.

I've published a lot of writing since then, getting paid for most and honored for some. But no paycheck or award I ever get can make me feel better than my father's simple show of pride in my story.

I still have my copy of the Johnny Cash review, but I don't still have my Dad. Yet the memory of his love for me, and his pride in my work carries me away—like a roaring locomotive—every time I reread it.

Michele Bazan Reed

Why I Keep Writing

One of my many jobs as a writer was writing a weekly column for a very small, very local paper. The column work was part-time; my full-time job was raising two small boys. Life was filled with juice, the park, the Discovery Museum, the park, cartoons and writing column notes on the back of checkbook receipts at the park.

Column subjects ranged from pregnancy to carpet-cleaning commercials, from nursery school evaluations to the time Michael dragged a garden hose into the living room and doused the television and VCR with a nurturing shower of water. I wrote about what I knew, the political, the commercial and the amusing parts of being a modern mother, which, in the eighties, was not an easy thing to be.

While I spent the better part of an afternoon cleaning off dried banana and rice cereal from the table with a belt sander, most of my peers were running laps on the fast track. A woman was supposed to be a lawyer, a stockbroker, a wearer of gray suits. I had stopped running the race about seven years too soon. My lifestyle wouldn't become vogue until my children outgrew it.

Enter my best friend. A woman with a degree in theatre

arts and a wicked sense of humor. She read my column every week and not only liked it, but agreed with me. But more important than that, she had no ambivalence about being home full-time with her own two boys; she had no desire to own a gray suit and drive a BMW. It was an attitude I basked in, a friendship that confirmed my own choices and became one of my lifelines to sanity.

When she moved to a town three hours away, I was devastated, and, of course, wrote about it:

> *Most of us are focused on the large. The big deal, the big tragedy, the big story. The small everyday things that take up more hours and days of living are often ignored.*
>
> *Mothers at home are often ignored because mothers never seem to do anything big. If a mother does a good job, you will never read about it in the news. Say the word "mothers," as in a group of mothers, and there still lingers that image of women sitting around a cheerful, spotless kitchen drinking coffee while their children tear around the house dressed in nothing but underwear and Teenage Ninja Turtle masks.*
>
> *The image remains because it's still true.*

At least one afternoon a week the boys and I visited my friend Susan and her two boys. We didn't drink coffee (keeps us up at night), and we didn't eat cookies (too fattening). It looked like the typical suburban experience: mothers talking, children racing around and isn't this a pleasant, easy life?

Not really. The friendship mothers form are born of need, sometimes desperation. We need to communicate to another adult, to use polysyllabic words and long sentences. We need to talk about the frustrations of child raising, of husbands, of being so alone in a society that doesn't seem to value motherhood very much anymore. We talk about our own mothers.

Both Susan and I had stories, long, drawn-out epics involving casts composed of mutual friends and relatives. We shared these weekly, keeping track of who's who. She was glad my brother finally called. I was glad her nieces caused a scene during Thanksgiving dinner.

And we'd see each other around town. Every morning our cars passed as we ushered our boys to different preschools. Each time we passed we waved, me in my mini-van, she in her red station wagon. Every day I made it a point to look for her car. Reassurance? A friendly face during an unfriendly morning? I don't know why it was important, but the sight of her car, of someone else doing what I did, boosted my own self-esteem. It reminded me to call in a couple of hours and ask if her sister-in-law ever got a job.

The day after she moved away, I automatically scanned the street, looking for her car. It took a minute of searching before I realized that I'd never see it again. I cried all the way to preschool that morning.

Susan and I had known each other for five years. I have friends who I've known longer, but not any friends who have lived closer. She was my first real neighbor, the kind of neighbor you borrow from and give to. The kind to invite to Tupperware parties because I knew she'd always show up. The kind of neighbor who took care of my oldest child the morning I went to the hospital to deliver my youngest. We've been close friends for longer than the lifetimes of our children.

I liked that it was easy to see her, that we communicated so well. I liked hearing her stories and telling her mine. I appreciated her reassurance that my oldest will indeed become toilet-trained within this decade and that some day the boys will give up wrapping Dad's socks around their head for that fashionable Ninja look and yelling "Cowabunga Dude!" as they hurl themselves from the couch to inches from the fireplace edge.

We don't, I don't, miss great big grand gestures. We don't pine away wishing for more spectacular moments. What breaks the heart is one small missing link in the chain of everyday events.

Every day at 8:15 in the morning, I miss waving to the woman in the red station wagon.

I wrote the column, published it in the paper and didn't think much about it except for genuinely missing my friend. It took weeks before I stopped looking for her car.

About the time I was recovering from my loss, a woman hailed me in the produce section, between the Crane melons and the Gravenstein apples.

"You write for the paper, don't you?" she asked.

"Yes." I eyed my cart filled with a jumble of stuff and reached for the organic apples. I figured she either had something to say about my nutritional choices for my family, or she hated last week's column.

"Thank you," she whispered instead. "My best friend just moved away, and you said what I felt, but I didn't have the words."

I was lucky; someone actually confronted me with the power of my work. It made me realize that in the end, writing is not about the money. Money is that big event, the grand gesture that while good, doesn't last very long in the heart. Writing is about memorable phrases, evocative descriptions. It's about being a link in someone else's understanding of the world.

That morning I learned that writing is about giving a single person, one reader, the right words.

Catharine Bramkamp

4

FINDING YOUR VOICE

*F*ind *a subject you care about and which in*
your heart you feel others should care about.
It is the genuine caring, and not your games
with language, which will be the most com-
pelling and seductive element in your style.

Kurt Vonnegut

It Doesn't Matter What You Write

Do the thing and you'll have the power.

Ralph Waldo Emerson

When I was young, the only thing I ever wanted to be was a writer. I always knew that some day I'd see my name on the spine of a book, but it wasn't until I had a little life under my belt, a few gray hairs, a few credits from the school of hard knocks, a little life experience and something to say about the hope for mankind, that I was ready to sit down at the keyboard and pour out my mystifications. The "message" that burdens every writer had finally floated to the top of my psyche. My "message" had gelled. It was time to write.

But everything I wrote sounded pompous or opinionated or biased. I couldn't make good fiction out of my message for mankind.

Then science fiction great Theodore Sturgeon came to town to give a workshop. I had grown up reading his work; his influence on me as a young reader had been enormous. I paid my fee, mailed in the manuscript he agreed to read as a part of the workshop curriculum, and sat down to bite my nails and wait for his judgment.

During this time of waiting, it occurred to me that over the two-week course of this workshop, he and I could run into each other at the coffee machine or something, and actually speak to each other, one-on-one. The thought left me star-struck. What on earth could I possibly say to the great Theodore Sturgeon?

I could ask him a question. I knew the prospect was not likely; surely there would be thousands of people at the workshop. Nevertheless, I set out to prepare myself so I wouldn't be caught with my pants down, so to speak, if the opportunity came to speak with my hero privately. I wracked my brain and spent sleepless nights, torturing myself over this idea. What would be The Definitive Question to ask Theodore Sturgeon? In retrospect, I think this was my way of not dwelling on the fact that he was reading my first attempt at novel writing.

My musings came down to one question that seemed to synthesize all that had been troubling me. The question was: "What do you do when you want to preach?" I had the urge to write, I had a message to disseminate, I had the time, the space, the knowledge and a teensie bit of talent for the task. But everything I wrote sounded preachy. Every time I reread what I had written, it felt as if I ought to be writing op-ed pieces, or essays or how-to books. At one point, I even talked with my minister about actually preaching. His response? "My collar closes the door to 90 percent of the people in the world. You, as a writer, have no such boundaries." Wow. A fiction writer has such opportunity.

Such responsibility.

So what do you do when you want to preach?

Satisfied that I would not only find out the answer to that question, but that I would have something intelligent to talk over with Ted Sturgeon, I set about to wait with a calmer heart.

The first night of the seminar, I was astonished that there were only about ten students. This was going to be an intimate setting. I would probably get to know him over the course of the two weeks.

And I did. He and I became friends in the limited time he had left on this planet, but I never had the opportunity to ask him that question because the first words out of his mouth on that first night of class were these: "It doesn't matter what you write, what you believe will show through."

I was stunned.

I'm not sure I heard anything else Ted said that night, because this was so clearly the answer to all my questions, and it was so simple, and tasted so strongly of the truth that I was awash with the possibilities for my future career.

Did he mean that I could write a vampire book and my message would come through? I could write a romance novel? A western, science fiction, horror, a comedy about dogs? And still, that which had been shown to me, that which had been given to me, the life-saving philosophy that I had developed (and that surely would save the world) could still be served?

Of course. I have only one story to tell, and that's my story. I can't tell yours. But mine is large and encompasses much, and it can be sliced into myriad tales of truth and fantasy.

I realized that it was the message showing through in the writing of my favorite authors that attracted me to their work. Singly, a book may not contain impressive spiritual insights; but over the entire body of work of a certain author, a reader cannot help but get to know the writer's heart.

When I realized the truth of what Ted Sturgeon said that night, not only did my career spread before me like a vast playground, but I was filled with confidence and questions. Before he died, Ted Sturgeon and I spent a lot of time together, and in fact he wrote the introduction to my first book, *When Darkness Loves Us,* which went on to be published, the first of a half dozen books. But more importantly, I could relax. My job as a novelist needn't be unnecessarily complicated. It is difficult enough to tell the truth within the fiction; I don't have to consciously worry about what message the reader is receiving. That isn't my job. I don't have to save the world. I only have to ensure that the reader enjoys reading what I've written.

It has been my fortune to have a challenging career as a writer, teacher, editor and publisher. Through my relatively brief association with Theodore Sturgeon, I have learned that the surest way to make my own dreams come true is to help others achieve theirs. The fate of empires does not hinge upon my work or upon any one piece of work. But those of us to whom this gift has been given have a responsibility to be persistent about writing and publishing our work until a sufficient body of work has been assembled. Our message is important. The world needs it. That's our job.

Never forget: It doesn't matter what you write. What you believe will show through.

Elizabeth Engstrom

Legacy

I was fortunate to grow up in a household where books were treasured. My parents were voracious readers and, early on, they taught my sister, Ann, and me the pleasure of the printed page. My father C. W. "Chip" Grafton, was a municipal bond attorney in Louisville, Kentucky, and spent forty years of his professional life dedicated to his passion for the law. In his spare time, he nurtured a passion of a different sort—writing. Many evenings he returned to the office after hours to devote his energies to the crafting of fiction. In his lifetime, he published two novels of a projected eight-book mystery series, a mainstream novel, and a "stand-alone" crime novel, entitled *Beyond a Reasonable Doubt.* His first mystery, *The Rat Began to Gnaw the Rope,* won the Mary Roberts Rinehart Award in 1943.

During my childhood, he often talked about writing. He was a teacher at heart, having taught both college English and law school classes in the course of his career. Listening to him, I had no notion in the world of being a writer myself, "when I grew up." In those days, women were generally encouraged in one of three vocations: you could be a nurse, a teacher, or a ballerina. Since I was ill coordinated and was not only squeamish at the sight of blood, but also phobic of needles, I had naturally fixed my sights on teaching. As to subject matter or grade level, I had no clear concept.

My father's lessons about writing, while peripherally entertaining, seemed to have no relevance to my goals. Still, I absorbed his advice, which he might well have offered as a way of reaffirming his own self-generated code of writing conduct. He used to say, "You have to keep your writing simple. It's not up to you to revise the English language. You should always spell correctly and use proper punctuation." He thought it was a miracle that a writer could conjure up an image in his own head, translate that image into marks on a page, and then, through the catalytic action of reading, have the same image appear in another person's head. How could an idea leap like that from one mind to another? I'm not sure my father ever figured out how such alchemy transpired, but he believed that a writer's first responsibility was to foster and promote that magic. In his mind, good grammar was essential to keeping the communication pathway clear.

He believed in plain old hard work. He believed that in a novel the transitions were important. He'd tell me, "Every writer has the big scenes in mind, but if you don't take particular care with the scenes in between the moments leading up to the crowning moment in your book, the reader may not be with you. The reader may, in fact, become bored or impatient and toss the book aside before reaching the critical passage that inspired you to begin work." He also felt minor characters were important and took special delight in making them come alive in his own books, even if their appearance was confined to a paragraph.

Probably the most important advice he ever gave me was how to handle rejection. He'd say, "Bend with the wind. When disappointments come along, as surely they will, don't stiffen with bitterness. Be graceful. Submit. Think of yourself as a sapling, yielding to circumstance without cracking or breaking. Bending with the wind allows you to right yourself again when adversity has passed." At the ages of eight and ten and thirteen, none of this seemed pertinent, but I recognized the sincerity with which he spoke and unconsciously took note.

Not surprisingly, in time, I too began a lengthy love affair with the written word. In college, I wrote poetry and short stories, graduating with a BA in English, still convinced that I'd teach. By the time I moved from Kentucky to California in the early sixties, I was married, raising a family and working full-time as a medical receptionist. Like my father, I, too, returned to my desk at the end of the day and devoted myself to writing.

At the age of twenty-two, after an adult education creative writing class, I started work on my first full-length novel, *Maggie*. This book was never published. I suffered my rejections (not always gracefully, I confess) and set to work on my second full-length novel, *The Monkey Room*, which went nowhere. The third completed novel, *Sparrow Field*, was summarily dismissed, garnering as many form rejection letters as the first two. Sometimes, a kind soul would pen a single sentence of encouragement at the bottom of the page. I didn't even know enough to take heart from this anonymous support. All three early novels ended up in my "bottom drawer" where they remain to this day.

Looking back, I can see that the writing in these manuscripts, while earnest, was nonetheless amateurish. The characters were either flat or manufactured. The story lines were poorly realized, clumsily executed, or sometimes absent altogether. Without knowing it, I was now teaching myself three vital lessons about writing: persist, persist, and persist. The fourth full-length novel I wrote was completed under the unwieldy title, *The Seventh Day of Keziah Dane.* I entered this manuscript in what was then called the Anglo-American Book Award Contest, probably long-since defunct. If memory serves, no award was given that year. . . . At least, I didn't win one . . . but I did receive an offer from a British publisher, a sum that in those days translated into perhaps as much as three hundred and fifty dollars. I was thrilled, ecstatic. I thought I'd died and gone to heaven. With the counsel of an experienced writer of my acquaintance, I used that publishing offer to net myself an American agent, who then secured me an American publisher. *Keziah Dane* was published in 1967 and a fifth novel, *The Lolly-Madonna,* came out in England two years later.

Soon afterwards, a British producer bought the film rights to this novel and together we wrote the screenplay, a form he taught me in ten days flat. Eventually, we made a deal with MGM and the movie, *Lolly Madonna XXX,* was released in 1973, starring Rod Steiger, Robert Ryan, Season Hubley, Jeff Bridges, and Randy Quaid, among luminous others. While the film itself was not financially (or aesthetically) successful, I earned sufficient money to begin to write full-time. I suppose at that juncture, having sacrificed my R.N. and my appearance in *Swan Lake,* I must have realized I wasn't going to be teaching elementary school, either.

I spent the next fifteen years working in Hollywood where I supported myself and my children writing numerous movies for television. At the same time, I completed yet another full-length novel, my sixth . . . never published . . . and followed that one with a seventh, which has never seen the light of day. By then, I was restless writing teleplays, and even more restless with the necessity for writing by committee. Film is, by its very nature, a collaborative medium, and I was not suited to the impact of all those egos. By 1977, I was keenly aware of how destructive *group* writing was to someone of my stubborn and recalcitrant disposition. It occurred to me I'd best get back to solo writing if I hoped to reclaim whatever talent I had left. I began work on my eighth full-length novel, a mystery, which I knew from the outset would be entitled *'A' Is for Alibi.*

I relate this progression in some detail because at every step of the way, I was utilizing the precepts I'd literally learned at my father's knee. Meanwhile, he—pragmatic, hard-headed, practical soul that he was—had one day added up the total of all the monies he'd earned from his books and realized he couldn't support his family on the proceeds. At that point, he set aside his publishing ambitions, moved his literary projects to the back burner, and renewed his commitment to municipal bonds. He still wrote when he could, but he'd relinquished all hope of trading in his career as an attorney for one as a novelist. He intended, on retirement, to write full-time. To that end, he'd completed a portion of *The Butcher Began to Kill the Ox,* the third in his mystery series. He'd also written a hefty six-hundred pages of a novel about his experiences growing up in China, the son of Presbyterian missionaries in Shanghai.

At the age of seventy-one, still actively engaged in the practice of law, he began teaching bond law to young attorneys coming up behind him in the firm. He had, by contract, only three years to serve until his long-awaited freedom. One Sunday morning in church, he was stricken with a heart attack and died within hours. This was January 1982, four months before the publication of *'A' Is for Alibi.* The dedication to my first published mystery reads:

For my Father, Chip Grafton, who set me on this path.

In dying, my father taught me yet another lesson, one I wish I'd had the power to teach *him.* Follow your heart.

Summon the courage to live out your dreams. None of us really know how much time we have left. Writing is our task. It's what we were put on this earth to do. If you're passionate about writing, don't postpone the process. Write every day, filling your life with fearless imagination. Your writing may prove to be a struggle, but the discipline will give form and shape and substance to your life. Work hard. Persist. And remember—please—to spell correctly. Use proper grammar and punctuation. Keep your writing simple and mind your transitions. Tend to your minor characters and above all else, dear hearts, learn to bend with the wind.

Sue Grafton

B.C. *Reprinted by permission of Johnny Hart and Creators Syndicate, Inc.*

A Writer's Real Worth Is Inside

How did I become a writer? That can be answered in one line—the back of my seat to the seat of the chair. Why did I become a writer? That's a little more complex. I became a writer because I was a writer, because wherever I looked there was a story I had to tell. Sometimes, I think it started in the womb, but that's a bit too far back for me to remember. I began to tell stories by the time I was three, and I suppose it drove my poor mother crazy. Her recourse was to teach me to read, and by the time I was five, I was reading quite fluently.

I had two brothers and a sister. My sister was the oldest, and she informed me that my stories were lies. I responded that they were stories. It didn't matter that things had not happened; the point was that they could have happened.

When I started school at age six, I encountered my first and most daunting difficulty: I was and am left-handed. My teacher, as with all teachers then, insisted that I write with my right hand, and since I was not at an age where protest by a six-year-old mattered, I attempted to do as she said. The result was my handwriting, which, at best, would be marked deplorable. To this day, almost eighty years later, I still write with my right hand—if I use my left, it does mirror writing—and reading back what I have written is very difficult.

I must say at this point that one day, many years later, I encountered Norman Corwin, who gave form and meaning to radio drama, sitting on a bench in Central Park, with a large pad on his lap and a pencil in his hand. *He was writing.*

"Norman," I said, "you are doing what I always dreamed of."

"Which is what?" he asked me.

"Sitting in the shade on a spring day and writing with a pencil on a yellow pad."

Ah well, such were my dreams.

At that time, not when I met Corwin in the park, but when I was a six-year-old, engaged in the very difficult business of growing up, we were poor. My father, with six mouths to feed, when he was working and not laid off, brought home between thirty and forty dollars a week. Then my mother passed away when I was eight years old, and my sister took over. And then the Great Depression came. It was very difficult, and it is almost impossible today to comprehend what "poor" meant in the thirties.

At eleven, I got my first after-school job, delivering the *Bronx Home News;* and between then and the time I was married, in 1937, I always managed to find some kind of job: delivery boy, library page, road work, cement work, factory worker. Perhaps because of these jobs, I came to the conclusion that I had only one way out—I had to be a writer who was paid for his work.

I began the process at age twelve. I read magazines in the New York Public Library, and I wrote stories and sent them to various magazines. I wrote in pencil on notebook pages, but of course, even the most charitable of editors could not read them. I wrote about everything; all was grist for my mill, and at long last, I received a note from an editor: "Listen, kid, get a typewriter."

I was fifteen by then and earning five dollars a week. Good money, considering the times, but never enough. We had too many hungry mouths. Nevertheless, the future called, and I went to the typewriter shop and asked what a used Underwood Upright cost.

"Twelve dollars, kid."

Out of the question—way beyond my horizon. Twelve dollars—we could live on that for a week, and often enough we lived on less.

I knew about my handwriting. I knew that I would never sit in the park and write on a yellow pad—still a dream today.

"Do you rent them?" I asked.

"Fifty cents a month."

I had exactly fifty-five cents in my pocket, and I plunged, signed all the papers, and lugged that big Underwood home. I couldn't wait to sit down in front of it and try that beautiful, wonderful machine that translated my dreams into proper words that anyone could read; and here I must say something about the Underwood Upright. Not only was it the most wonderful endurable machine on earth, but like the Deacon's One Horse Shay, it ran nearly forever. When I married in 1937, I bought a new Underwood out of our wedding money. In 1981, I retired it—because typewriter shops could no longer cannibalize parts. Meanwhile, I had turned out at least eighty books, at least one hundred short stories and newspaper columns beyond numbering.

But, to get back to my story. How did I find time for school, after-school jobs, and the Underwood? The answer is that I have no idea, but I did, and the stories poured out. For the next two years, I sold nothing, but I kept on writing, and then, at age seventeen, I sold my first story to *Amazing Story Magazine,* for thirty-seven dollars. By God, I was a writer!

No, it's not as simple as that. I had to learn how to write, to punctuate, to understand the shape of a story. I had to learn an art—one of the most difficult arts known to man; and I had to learn it well enough to consider it a profession—and not have to haul bricks and cement to stay alive.

I came to understand that art and creation is not simply another profession, but a reason for being alive on this earth. I had to listen to people and learn all the subtleties of language, the cadence and rhythm that distinguishes one from another. This is a process I am still engaged with, and that will be for the rest of my life.

Today, I am eighty-five years old, and I still write. A day without writing, for me, is a day lost, tossed away.

So if I were asked the question, "What must I do to be a successful writer?" I would answer that you must want it more than you want anything else. Whether you write for a magazine or a newspaper or as a novelist or playwright.

Most writers do not make much money, and in this world where money is the measure of everything, or I should say almost anything, you must find another measure. There are writers who make millions, and there are other writers who earn a mere pittance, but that is no measure of worth. The real worth is inside of you and can only be measured by your understanding of the human condition. Learn to think clearly, understand your medium and understand people.

I might add one thing to this. Read the writers you admire most, unravel the net of words that they spin, and let them be your teachers. You can learn a great deal about the mechanism of writing in school, but the real picture lies in your understanding of the human heart. No school can teach you that. Only your own ears and eyes.

Howard Fast

Writer, Teacher, Peaceful Warrior

I wanted to tell the world just one word.
Unable to do that, I became a writer.

Stanislaw Lec

In my high school and college years, I was better known as an aspiring athlete than as a literary lion. My eventual success as an author surprised me almost as much as it would have surprised my English teachers who believed me better suited to bricklaying than wordplaying. Still, I had ideas percolating inside me—stories I wanted to express—and a surging desire to share, to communicate, to somehow make a positive difference.

What I lacked in quality, I made up for in quantity—words that echoed my own deepest yearnings, which, like seedlings, waited to sprout. But during my literary latency period, these seeds lay buried under piles of dry essays, required thesis statements—papers bearing little relevance to the world I knew or cared about. So I put my imagination on hold until the day I completed my last college essay. Then, to my surprise, I discovered that I *liked* writing. There was something about sculpting with

words—mining gems from the creative unconscious—
that made time fly. Armed with little more than the belief
that I had something worth saying, and the hope that I
could say it well, I set out, with more love than talent, on
the road to literary success.

I might have dreamt of reaching the heights of Hesse or
the depths of Dostoyevski, but I would be content if I
could stretch towards the likes of Washington Irving, Jack
London, or Robert Louis Stevenson. So I set my sights on
simple storytelling. The only problem was, I didn't know
much about writing stories. So I signed up for a correspondence course where I learned enough of the basics to
get started. The rest would depend on my willingness to
rewrite and rewrite again until I got it just . . . write.

Training in gymnastics had taught me that elbow
grease mattered far more than genetic gifts; that talent
was made, not just born. As a coach, I learned to break
large tasks into manageable steps—and applied the
lessons of sport to the field of writing.

I knew I needed writing skill, but also something to
write about, so I began writing articles for a gymnastics
magazine. Over time, what I already knew got old—like
exploring in my own backyard, when I yearned for the
Amazon, the outback, the road less traveled. Over time,
my writing topics expanded beyond the athletic arena—
from the basics of sport to the fundamentals of living.

Through the lean years, I held to five rules for writing
and living: Show up; pay attention; tell your truth; do
your best; don't be attached to the outcomes. "Show up"
means sitting down in the chair in front of your computer
or writing pad. "Pay attention" means to look, listen,
touch, smell, taste of life and write for the senses; then
read your writing, notice the weaknesses, and improve
your work. "Tell your truth" means to write as only you
can, for no one else can write exactly as you do. "Do your

best" means constant rewriting until you are certain you cannot improve another sentence or word—then setting it aside for awhile before doing an even better draft. "Don't be attached to outcomes" means that you cannot control the outcomes, only the effort—that the effort itself is success. Not even Michael Jordan could control whether he made a basket—only whether he took the shot. That's all any writer can do—and by taking the shot, we vastly increase our odds of making literary baskets.

For ten years I felt like The Invisible Writer. No one, save my beloved wife and a few relatives, knew or cared that I was fighting the good fight; no one appreciated the hours of solitude striking the keyboard with little to show but crumpled pages. Getting noticed is only one facet of success, but when it happens, it has the taste of pink lemonade on a summer day. And when it happens, it seems to occur overnight—but, for me, overnight success took more than ten years. What began as a series of gymnastics articles became a treatise on training and life, which when nurtured and nudged into shape as "the natural laws of learning" evolved into a ream of paper. When the stack got heavy enough, I began to fancy it as a "non-fiction book manuscript."

I had ascended to the rarified heights, rising (mostly on hot air) above the crowd of would-be authors. Now I was a would-be author *with a heavy ream of paper filled with words. My words. And they were typed in nearly the right order.*

That's when I began reorganizing, rewriting, and reshaping—cutting and pasting on the living room floor with scissors and scotch tape. Back then, I lacked both the skill to structure and the will to outline. So, five drafts and nine years later—during which time I got married, had a child, became a college professor, moved across country, traveled around the world, was divorced, meditated, contemplated, climbed and fell and climbed again—I completed what I believed to be a finished book.

I sent the manuscript to a few publishers in New York, all of whom were unanimous in their lack of interest—it was returned unopened. Then I married Joy, we started a new family, and my luck changed. Joy suggested I call a literary agent. I looked in the phone directory, found one, cast my bread upon the waters, and waited.

Actually, I cast two bits of bread on the water, since my original manuscript turned into two—and within several months, I had sold *Way of the Peaceful Warrior* and (a book now titled) *Body Mind Mastery.*

My career took off like a rocket—then blew up just off the launching pad. Within a year, both books were out of print. My agent couldn't resell either one. He told me to go out and write another book. So I did. But no one was interested. (Not a good way to get an auction going.)

A successful book needs to be sold not once, but eight times: First, you must sell the book to yourself (if you aren't excited about it, who else will be?); then you sell it to an agent, who must sell it to an editor, who has to sell it to an editorial board and publisher, who sells it to the sales force so they will enthusiastically sell it to the bookstores (or it never sees the light of day). Next, the bookstore sells to the public. Finally, and most important, readers sell it to the other readers by word-of-mouth.

I learned that getting an agent to take a book, or even selling that book to a publisher, does not often translate into fame and fortune. As I've noted, the demise of my athletic book was soon followed by the death of *Way of the Peaceful Warrior.* But some books have a way of rising, Phoenix-like, from their ashes.

Three years passed. I occupied myself with helping raise our daughters and finding work where I could—as a typist, house painter, office administrator and personal trainer. My career as an author seemed a fleeting dream.

Then, as fate would have it, a woman acquaintance to whom I'd given an out-of-print copy of *Way of the Peaceful Warrior* passed it on to a friend of hers named Hal Kramer. Hal, then in his seventies, had started his own publishing company, Celestial Arts, made it successful, and had finally sold it and retired. When he read my out-of-print book, he decided to start a new publishing company, H. J. Kramer Inc.—featuring my book.

He offered me a one-hundred-dollar advance for *Peaceful Warrior*—the best offer I'd had in years, so I accepted. With a staff of one—himself—and almost no marketing budget, Hal wrote letters to bookstores telling them he was back in business with a new book he believed they would like. It took him two years to convince the major bookstore chains to carry a single copy in each store.

Then word of mouth took over and the rest is history: Sales began to pick up, and the snowball that started rolling steadily has continued for two decades, with nearly two million copies in print in twenty languages worldwide, and a film project. My advances have ranged from one hundred dollars to more than a million.

As *Peaceful Warrior* sales took off, another small publisher republished my athletic book under a new title. Over the years, two books turned into three, then four, and as of this writing, I look back on two novels, two children's books, and seven nonfiction works each revealing a different facet of "a peaceful warrior's approach to living well."

Hard work makes luck, and I've been lucky. It all started with showing up—writing through the good times and bad. I've learned that I could write for self-expression, but to become an author, I had to develop not only the craft of writing, but empathy for my readers. Many writers can spread beautiful words upon the canvas of the page, but professional authors appreciate that they are creating a product that readers must like enough to select out of thousands of other volumes.

Francis Bacon wrote, "We rise to great heights by a winding staircase." And Issac Bashevis Singer wrote, "Life is God's novel; let God write it." Truly, who can guess what twists and turns the path our lives may take? All we can do as writers is to take the shot, put in the effort, sow the seeds, and reap with pleasure and gratitude whatever harvest is given.

Dan Millman

Counsel from a Veteran of the Writing Wars

I once overheard a professor say to a beginning writer: "Everything has been written about already, and written better than you can do it. If you intend to write about love, tragedy, adventure . . . forget it, because it has all been done by Shakespeare, Dickens, Tolstoy, Flaubert, and the rest. Unless you have something absolutely new to say, don't try to be a writer. Take up accounting."

That was silly—really stupid. Everything has not been said, and will never be said. Human emotions may have always been the same, but there was never anyone on earth before you who was exactly like you and who saw love and hate exactly as you see them through your eyes.

And you need not have lived something to see it, to write about it. You were provided with imagination. Use it. Da Vinci did not have to attend the *Last Supper* to paint it.

Use your imagination daily. Writing is not only an art but also a profession. While inspiration is an enormous factor, the writing of a book is a profession. You have to prepare for this profession by practicing it—write diaries, journals, letters, fragments—and by studying the works of authors you admire, to learn how they create characters, insert conflict, move a story.

And then you have to write not just when the spirit moves you, but every day. If there are bad days, you can discard what you've done, but write every day, pretending you're on a salary, pretending you must deliver something or be fired, yet working on and on for yourself and by yourself.

When I was doing short magazine pieces and screenplays, I feared undertaking anything as formidable as a book. One day, while I was collaborating with novelist Jerome Weidman on a screenplay for a studio, Weidman advised me how to overcome my fear. "Think about writing one page, merely one page, every day. At the end of 365 days, the end of a year, you have 365 pages. And you know what you have? You have a full-length book."

Finally, you must want to write rather than to be known as a writer. That's why you must treat your actual writing as a career. You must not talk about it. You must do it—want to do it, love to do it despite the loneliness, feel there is nothing more important on earth while you are doing it.

Because there is nothing more important. Despite what that professor contended, there are things left to be said. The world around you is different from the world Shakespeare wrote about—your world today has trod on the moon, by God. For every new writer, every new year remains unexplored until he or she explores it.

Irving Wallace

Coded Messages and Kindred Spirits

Many years ago I sent a letter to Mary Carter, the author of *Tell Me My Name,* saying I loved her novel and confessed that I was a neophyte writer. She wrote back a wonderful letter which adorned the bulletin board over my desk for years. Her reply is lost now, but I can still see her words—even the typeface—in my mind.

First, she thanked me, as if my letter was the best thing that had happened all day. Then she wished me good fortune with my own work. "Writing," she said, "is like sending coded messages into space. You never know if someone is out there receiving." She was glad to know that, this time, a connection had been made.

A few years later, I attended a writers' workshop where the keynote speaker equated compelling writing with storytelling. He quoted a king commanding his minstrel: "Speak to me a tale of love and death."

Love and death, the speaker explained, are the two great universal emotional experiences that connect people no matter who they are or where. Joy and grief, delight and sorrow, passion and abandonment.

I went home from the conference and devised a story about love and death for a confession magazine. A young woman is torn by love for her bereaved mother-in-law and resentment that the mother-in-law won't "get over it." Finally, one day she realizes she's grieving, too.

> *"I've been so busy trying to comfort Mama, it just now hit me," I said (to my husband). "I'll never see Papa again, either. I'll never open the kitchen door and see him there with a big bag of zucchini because he planted too many." Joe opened his arms and held me as I began to sob. "He always planted too many."*

I wept when I wrote those words twelve years ago; if I read the story today, I weep again. Those tears are my signal that I've made the connection Mary Carter wrote about. If I cry when I write, I touch something in others.

Back then I wrote a couple dozen stories for confession magazines and sold them all eventually. I found that if I cried as I wrote, the story invariably sold the first time out.

Of course, everything can't have that connection to something deep within. But now and then, a magical moment happens. My own words trigger my own tears, and I know this message will reach someone.

I remember my awe and incredulity at my first fan letter. I'd made contact! I always think of Mary Carter when I receive a letter and I always reply.

My best example of a story that clearly touched people has to be an essay that was first printed in my local paper, and later published in *Reader's Digest.*

My husband, Glenn, was in the Air Force, so we moved a lot. The essay was about the used Plymouth Valiant we bought when we returned from an overseas base and the dog Nelly we got at a local pound about a year later.

As we moved from Ohio to New York to Alabama to Virginia to California, the Valiant (christened Blueberry), went from the "new" car, cozy in the garage, to the "old" car shivering at the curb. Nelly grew from puppy to a deaf old soul. Our boys changed from toddlers on booster cushions in Blueberry's backseat to teenagers arguing about whose turn it was to drive her.

Finally, it was time to sell her, although Glenn asked for so much money in the newspaper ad, I could tell he didn't really want to. Too bad we couldn't put her out to pasture like a well-loved old horse. But a man who doted on old Valiants showed up and without dickering, peeled five $100 bills from his wallet.

> *Glenn swallows, takes the money and hands over the keys* [the essay concluded]. *It isn't easy, seeing his old sweetheart go away. Even if it wasn't love at first sight, it's been an enduring romance for nearly two decades.*
>
> *Nelly studies the stranger in the Blueberry, then looks at us, puzzled.* "It's okay," *I say.* "She's going to a good home."
>
> *I take Glenn's hand.* "It's just a car," *I say. But she's more than that, more than steel and fabric and a little fiberglass fender patch. She's double cushions in the backseat for our little boys. She's part of the continuity we clung to as we traveled from state to state. She's almost twenty years of our lives. On thousands of mornings, I stood and waved as Glenn drove her down the street to work. Now she goes down the street one last time.*
>
> *And I burst into tears.*

I've never had so much response—even long distance calls from people who found me through directory assistance. Now here's the funny thing. No one mentioned the Blueberry. Or my family. Or my writing. They all wanted me to know about their own cars. Old Henry. Goldenrod. Sweet Sue.

"Logically it's ridiculous to become attached to a collection of inanimate parts," admitted a woman who then spent two paragraphs extolling her VW Bug named Daisy, "but your article touched a nerve with me."

"The article touched home with me," wrote a woman from San Jose who described, in detail, the car she'd had for more than twenty years.

"It really struck a chord with me," wrote a woman from Michigan who had an identical blue Valiant, and put in parentheses after her signature "a kindred spirit."

And there's the connection—the "with me" that each of them felt. Touching the kindred spirit. When we write about things that people everywhere share—hard times, tender times, despair, delight—the code goes out, a kindred spirit intercepts it and that essential connection is made.

And that's why we write.

Marilyn Pribus

"My sales have shot through the roof since I made
the switch from rambling, hare-brained manifestos to
fashion and fitness tips for the lucrative women's market."

5

MENTORS

We are all apprentices in a craft where no one ever becomes a master.

Ernest Hemingway

A Gift to Myself

Have compassion for yourself when you write. There is no failure—just a big field to wander in.

Natalie Goldberg

I believe in miracles.

I was on a beach in Thailand when my life changed forever. Though a typhoon brewed a thousand miles to the south and the waves on this tranquil beach would be pounding thirty feet and higher in a couple of days, that day the Thai Sea was flat as a pond. Strolling beside me was a Buddhist monk, his saffron robes fluttering along the sand.

"And what about your Angels?" he asked me.

"My Angels?" I shrugged. "The problem is, you can never be sure who's going to show up, can you? The good Angels or the bad."

"Yes," he laughed. "I know what you mean." He walked a little farther mulling over the season to come.

"Well, how about the Dodgers then?"

"Fourth place. And lucky to be there," I said with a shrug of my shoulders.

My uncle had always loved baseball but especially the Los Angeles Dodgers. But he hadn't always been a Buddhist monk. That had come ten years before. Not long after he gave up on a writing career I had admired for years and moved 10,000 miles away to a small monastery outside Bangkok.

After I graduated from UCLA I had been his assistant—a lot of research, proofreading, retyping. My pay was minimum wage but what I learned was priceless—hours of mentoring about the craft of writing and the business. "Understanding the beast you must slay" is how Frank put it.

One day as I sat next to him in his apartment in San Clemente, we talked about writing. He was drinking wine from a large tumbler. It was just noon and he had downed three of them already. By the evening he would switch to straight vodka. I had learned to be somewhere else by seven or eight o'clock. If it was true that Frank was a damned good writer, it was also true that he was an out-of-control drinker.

"See these ads," he said, as he thumbed through a magazine. "They put your story in here in order that the reader will turn the page and see the next ad."

After twenty years as a writer he was hard-headed about the business. A professional writer who had written for all the major magazines. he was a regular contributor to *The New Yorker*. In the past year he had written a novel that had been optioned by Columbia Studios. The money he had received for the screenplay had finally freed him financially. But it was Hollywood that would eventually destroy him, that played to all his darkest weaknesses, that set him on the course that would land him on a beach in Southeast Asia beside another writer who was falling apart.

"But I didn't bring you all this way to talk baseball," he

said as we stopped beside a jetty that speared a hundred yards into the sea. "You're in trouble."

Frank was direct as always. That had been the wonderful and terrible dimension to our relationship. He had a laser for a mind, and it cut right to the heart of things with only a question or two. I knew it was no use to resist. So I told him everything.

The life of a writer is a lonely day-to-day battle waged largely against oneself. If it's not a sluggish imagination that stalls you, it's too much imagination—wondering where the next mortgage payment is coming from. It's a labyrinth that the fortunate find their way through with one book, one blessed attempt that shoots to the top of the bestseller lists. That, of course, is a million to one, the *People* magazine profile of the ad exec or lawyer who hits a grand slam on his first try. There's always a picture of him sitting in his new Ferrari, or standing on the porch of his new house on a body of water somewhere, the foreign rights rolling in, the film premiering next week, a seven-figure advance for book two already in his bank account.

That never happened to me and I have no regrets. I took the road thousands of other successful writers take. I was a journeyman. I wrote for dozens of magazines, some small, some big, until I was thirty. Then I wrote my first book. A how-to. That was followed by a history, a biography, and a book about Halley's Comet when that phenomenon was in the sky, and my agent thought I could make a few bucks writing about it. I moved up the writing and publishing ladder with every effort both in the quality of what I wrote and in the paydays. By the time I had written my tenth book, I was getting six-figure advances and decent sales. I owned a home, and my wife and daughter were reasonably well cared for.

And then my luck just ran out. For three years I couldn't sell anything to anyone. I lost everything—the car, the home, my self-respect. What's more my talent had dried up fast and utterly. I couldn't seem to write anymore. I remember just staring at myself in the mirror, looking at the lines on my face. I wasn't young anymore, either. My youth had dried up with my talent. If I couldn't write anymore, I'd had to start over. But doing what? I had never worked for anyone. I had been a writer my whole adult life. The lines in my face seemed to deepen everyday as I searched that mirror for an answer. I would take my shower in the morning, a long, slow one to kill time. Then I would end up just staring at that mirror because the next step would be to open the bathroom door and face another day. Another day in which I had no idea what I was going to do.

Then one morning I heard my wife knocking on the door. "There's a letter for you," she said.

I took a deep breath and opened the door. I wasn't ready to face another rejection letter. I looked at the envelope and saw it was from Thailand. I had not heard from Frank in almost ten years, since the blustery day I had dropped him off at the San Francisco airport to fly off on some hair-brained, desperate journey to become a monk. I remember shaking my head as he disappeared through the gateway. *What the hell was he thinking?*

The letter said simply, "Why don't you come see me? We can talk, Frank." In the envelope was a round-trip ticket to Bangkok. I had nothing better to do.

Now as we strolled the beach together, I poured it all out. "It's all over for me," I said.

"What is?"

"The writing. I'm off it for good," I said. "And I'm afraid I don't have what it takes to be a monk."

He had a smile that sort of peeled its way across his face and usually wrung out in a huge laugh. But this time the laughter never came.

"No, you don't," he said. The statement seemed to hang in the air like an accusation. From that black place where I now lived, everything I did or thought seemed to be an accusation.

"You're a writer," he said finally. "You can't turn your back on this the way you think I did."

"I never thought that . . ."

He held up his hand before I could finish. "Of course, you did. That's why you came. To see if I could offer you an escape like the one I found."

He started walking quickly down the beach again and without looking back he said, "Come on. I want to show you something."

He started climbing the bluff that led to the monastery. It was a good lung-searing march but Frank took it effortlessly. When I got to the top, he was a hundred feet in front of me. I ran to catch him.

"Where are we off to?" I puffed.

He didn't answer. We were almost running now as if we had an appointment we couldn't miss. We entered a small temple with a golden Buddha sitting watch, walked through to another room and out the back door and into a garden. A young monk was ringing a bell, slowly swinging a mallet that sent a deep gonging through the countryside.

We wound our way through a terrace of sprouting rice, the golden shimmer of the water in the sunlight blinding me as I followed this mad monk. It was hard to believe that this strange, shaven-headed creature scurrying through this strange and beautiful land was of my blood.

He stopped finally at a wooden rail that looked down into another courtyard. Below a couple of dozen children played. He beckoned me with a wave, and pointed down at the children.

"That is why I came," he whispered as if we were going

to disturb these children who were running around, chasing each other, screaming. "They are my students. I came to teach them."

I looked at him doubtfully. "I thought you came to be a monk," I whispered back for no reason I could think of.

"So did I," he laughed quietly. "They let me sit around for a month before they introduced me to my students. I guess they were checking me out. See how I ticked, I guess you'd say."

"Yeah, what'd they find out?"

"What just about everyone who comes here finds out. That we're too wound up with ourselves, tied up in knots worrying about what's going to happen to ourselves, to ever be able to help ourselves."

He pulled me away from the rail so we wouldn't disturb the kids in their important business. "I want you to go home and give to other people."

"Give what? I'm broke."

"Give whatever you can to whoever you can." He started walking again. "The bus leaves in the morning."

"You want me to leave? I've only been here a few hours."

"Then there's no time to waste, is there?"

The next day I was on a plane wondering the whole way back what it was I was meant to give. I got my answer very quickly. The first week back I got calls from three different people to come and speak to their groups about writing. I readily accepted as it worked into my new plan, or rather Frank's new plan for me. I was supposed to give what I could. At these talks my eyes were opened, and I knew I had found what Frank had sent me on my way to find. I saw how hungry people were to learn not just about writing but how to get their words into print. I was suddenly inspired. It was right up my alley. I knew the writing business inside and out. The ups and downs. This was something I could give.

That week with the help of a few friends I planned to hold a writers' conference in Maui and six weeks later the first Maui Writers Conference was held. One hundred people attended. The next year 500 people attended. In two more years the Maui Writers Conference and Retreat became the largest event of its kind in the world, now attracting nearly 2,000 writers to the retreat and conference. It has become a phenomenon, a gathering place for writers. Nearly a hundred of the top editors and agents and film executives in the business come every year to help writers learn their business and the craft of writing. Thousands of writers have found agents; countless books have been sold. Bestselling authors not only line up to speak at the Conference but many donate large sums of money as well to the nonprofit Maui Writers Foundation so the work of helping other writers can continue.

Soon after the first Conference ended, I began to write again and quickly sold two novels that became bestsellers. And the greatest miracle of all—the love of writing was reborn in my heart. Now I wake up everyday thinking, planning what else I can do to help other writers find their dream because I am convinced the more I help other writers, the more I am helping myself.

Yes, I believe in miracles because I saw one with my own eyes.

John Tullius

My Dad Story

My dad may have been a carpenter, but in his own way he taught more about the discipline of writing than anyone else.

I was the tenth of eleven children. When I was a kid, I didn't understand why my dad was always away at work. He got up at nine, worked at the lumberyard until about 2:00 P.M., came home, ate lunch, napped, showered, went to his second job (for the Postal Service), came home at around 1:00 A.M., talked to my mom till about 2:00 A.M. went to bed. He did that every day for thirty years, so we could go to school, and so our mom would have food to feed us.

Once, when I was sixteen, I asked him why he worked so hard. He looked at me for a long while, as though he didn't quite know how to answer. Finally, he said, "It's what I have to do."

My dad usually spoke better with his hands than with words, especially when it came to emotional stuff. When I went away to college, he made me a redwood-stained clothes tree which I still have.

When I was twenty-one, we got into a big fight over a car. I needed one, but he wouldn't help me finance it.

Looking back, I now think he really knew I needed the damned thing but was afraid I couldn't handle all the other costs indigenous to owning a car. He was right in the sense that it was more costly than I'd originally anticipated, but somehow I made it work. And he saw that, too; he just didn't want to admit he was wrong.

Or maybe he just didn't know how to say it. One night, six months after I had bought the car, I was at my parents' for dinner. "Before you leave, I got something for you," he said. He went into the basement, came back with a case of Castrol oil. "I heard you tell your mother the other day your car was low on oil," he said. "You never want to risk burning out your engine, so I thought you could use this."

I didn't know what to say, nor what to think. We looked at each other for a long while. I finally said, "Thank you."

My dad was a serious reader. He liked westerns and spy novels, but he also read a lot of nonfiction. He was a quirky old dude. He'd go through the pulpy stuff cover to cover, yet he'd also drop a book, no matter how far along he was, if he came across something which he knew was factually incorrect. He once stopped a Len Deighton novel with about thirty pages to go for that very reason.

"Don't you want to know how it ends?" I asked.

"Doesn't matter," he'd said. "You write about a period of history, you get your facts right. Facts aren't right on one thing, it ruins the entire book."

I made the argument for creative license, but my dad wouldn't budge. "Dammit," he said, "it's the principle."

My dad liked that I was a writer, even if he didn't quite understand what my first book was about. Every time I saw him, we'd have the same conversation. "Now, what kind of book you writing again?"

"It's about the TV show *The Fugitive.*"

"So, you're writing a script."

"No, not writing a script. It's a book about *The Fugitive.* The

TV show. You know David Janssen, the one-armed man. . . ."

"Never saw it." My dad read westerns; my dad watched westerns. Now, if I told him I was writing a book on Bret Maverick . . .

"Well, it was a big hit in the sixties, and it's still popular today."

"So you're writing a book about a TV show."

"Yes."

"See, I'm trying to explain this to your Uncle Galen, and . . . "

"Well, you tell Uncle Galen that your son likes television, likes David Janssen, and thinks *The Fugitive* was one of the best shows ever made."

"So, it's sort of a history book."

"That's it, Dad. It's a history of *The Fugitive* on television."

"Well, if you're gonna write about history, son, just get your facts straight. I can't stand it when I read something I know to be wrong. I ever tell you about this Len Deighton book I read?"

I finished the book proposal for *The Fugitive Recaptured* in August 1992. I sent it out to several publishers but also made extra copies for my family and friends to read.

On Labor Day Monday, I got a call from my dad around 9:00 P.M. My dad just wasn't the type to pick up the phone and call you. You always had to call him. That's just the way he was.

"You know, I just finished reading this thing you left with your mother."

"You mean the book proposal?"

"Yeah, the book proposal."

"So what do you think?"

"Well, I got a problem."

Great, I thought. *I must've missed something.* No, I mentioned the parallels with the Sam Sheppard case. No, I specifically said William Conrad was the *radio* Matt Dillon.

My dad continued. "See, I think it's very good. Very well written, very interesting. I enjoyed reading it."

"So what's the problem?"

He paused, like he wanted to make sure this came out right. "Well, I don't know if it's good, because it's good, or if it's good . . . because my son wrote it."

My voice cracked. "Hey, that's okay, Dad," I said. "You can say it's good because I wrote it."

About a month later, I found a publisher and finished the manuscript the following April. The book would be published in August, to coincide with the release of *The Fugitive* motion picture.

I showed my dad the finished manuscript. His eyes glistened. "Very impressive, son."

"You wanna read it?"

"Nope," he said. "I want to wait till it's an actual book, with your name on the cover, and all that."

"Fair enough," I said.

My dad never did see the actual book. Less than a month later, he died suddenly of a heart attack.

I never did tell him, at least in words, how much that phone conversation meant to me. But somehow, I think he already knew.

This is for you, Dad. Thanks.

Ed Robertson

Writing from the Heart

When you write from the heart, you not only light the dark path of your readers, you light your own way as well.

Marjorie Holmes

I was pulling together materials for the first night of my Advanced Writing for Publication class when I was interrupted by a confident, demanding voice.

"Are you Bud Gardner?"

The man standing in the doorway to my office stood about 5 feet 8, weighed about 125 pounds, and was all business.

"Yes, I'm Bud. Have a seat. How may I help you?"

"I'm Joe Howard. I came by to meet you, to decide if I want to take your class beginning tonight. You see, I'm over sixty, and I don't have enough time left to waste even a minute of it."

Joe Howard, I learned, was a retired, veteran reporter for the *Los Angeles Times,* now living in my home town.

"I still do a little stringing for the *Times* now and then. I covered Ross Perot when he came to town a while back."

"With your background as a seasoned journalist, why on earth would you want to take this class?" I asked.

"Because I'm looking for a change. I've spent most of my life writing hard news stuff. I want to look at other types of writing. I know I have a couple of books in me. Maybe some fiction, too." His eyes narrowed. "The question is, what have you got to offer me?"

"In this advanced class, we begin by reviewing how to sell articles to magazines."

"Been there, done that," he snapped. "What else?"

"We'll study how to get a nonfiction book published— either by sending out a book proposal to a trade publication or by self-publishing."

"What?" he scolded. "Self-publishing? Isn't that for amateurs who can't interest major publishers?"

"Not really. Self-publishing allows a writer to get a great idea to the marketplace first, to control the book project from start to finish, to become a publisher. Three of my former students have become millionaires because they chose to self-publish. One author, Jane Nelsen, has self-published fourteen books, which nets her one million dollars a year from her writing and speaking engagements."

"Phfffftt! Not for me," he said, irritated. "What else?"

"We'll take a look at the short story structure, and many students will want to begin working on a novel."

"Oh really," he said cynically. "Just how many novels have your students turned out anyway?"

"I'm not sure. Nancy Elliott, Bettina Flores, Naida West, Jim Dearing, Ethel Bangert, and many other fine authors have turned out novels since taking classes in our writing program."

"Anything else?" he said, unimpressed.

"The whole purpose of this advanced class is to step up production, to turn out more articles, make multiple sales from one idea, to sell to the global market, and to get books published."

"You can do all of that in one semester?" he growled.

"Oh yes, we'll get some articles in print this semester, but the class will be long over before any books appear. That's okay. Knowing how the publishing industry works and having step-by-step processes to follow—that's what this class is all about."

"Is that it?" he said, beginning to tune out.

"We'll also talk about how to run an efficient home office, how to use the five energy levels we experience each day to turn out our best writing, and how to handle rejection, procrastination and writer's block."

"Writer's block? Give me a break. No serious writer ever gets blocked."

Wow! What an irascible, old curmudgeon, I thought. If he took the class, I knew I was in for it. He'd constantly challenge me on every concept I presented and would make life miserable for me. I'd had enough and decided to get rid of him.

"Then I guess the class isn't for you," I said firmly.

"I'll decide that," he snapped. "What kind of writing do you see me doing?"

As I looked deep into his eyes, for the first time I saw the pain he was feeling. I had nothing to lose.

"Why don't you try your hand at poetry?" I said softly.

"What? Poetry? Me? For God's sake, why?" his voice rising.

"It just might help you get in touch with your true feelings."

That stopped him cold. He sat there staring at me. It was a long time before he spoke.

"I've never thought about writing poetry. I'm not sure I want to reveal my feelings in print," he said, no longer fighting.

"I understand." It was time to bring this to an end. "Look, why don't you come to the first session tonight, then make up your mind about taking the class. Okay?"

As he walked down the hall, he stopped and stared back at me for a full minute. Then he was gone. I thought I'd seen the last of him. *Good riddance,* I thought. But I was wrong. He not only showed up but sat through the full three-hour class, then asked to see me after class.

"Okay, you're on. I'll write you three poems a week. Deal?"

"Deal," I said, trying to act confident, my stomach churning.

Joe Howard was true to his word. The next week, the week following, and every week after that he turned in three poems for me to critique. At first they were rather stiff and formal but carried great energy and power. Then as the weeks wore on, I began to see a softness appear in his poems.

I wish I hadn't agreed so quickly to Joe's deal of turning in three poems each week. Why? Because he turned in three poems to me each week—for five years. I couldn't get rid of the guy. He joined a poetry group in town and read his poems in public readings. He even read some of them on radio. Eventually, he produced a play of his best poems that was presented one weekend in our campus theater, featuring some professional actors and readers.

As students read their work aloud during the class, Joe pulled no punches in critiquing them. He always gave good, solid advice—even if it was harsh at times. Students respected and admired him, but didn't dare challenge his authority.

Then one night during the second year, he asked to read a poem to the class. I was taken aback. He'd never asked to read aloud before. The poem he read was about a conflict he'd had with his daughter. As he began reading it, he was confident, self-assured. About a third of the way into the poem, he burst into tears. The students and I were shocked. This old curmudgeon was actually crying.

I didn't know what to say. In thirty years of teaching, I'd never faced a situation like this. I decided to wait.

Joe got under control and began to read again. He broke into tears a second time. Again I waited, not knowing what to do.

Embarrassed, fighting for control, he read again . . . cried . . . stopped . . . read again . . . then finished the poem, weeping.

The room was deadly quiet. I waited what seemed like an eternity. Then I finally spoke.

"Thanks for sharing, Joe," I said quietly.

Emotionally moved, the class exploded into applause. Everyone was cheering, smiling, and wiping tears away.

"Hold it!" shouted Joe, now back in control. "I've got something to say." Then he told how he had interviewed me before the first class a year and a half ago and how much he had enjoyed the class and writing poetry.

"When Bud first asked me to write poetry, I couldn't believe it. It was difficult at first because I couldn't get in touch with myself. Then as the months passed by, I began to go below the layers of the crusty reporter I'd been to the core me. What you heard and saw tonight with this poem came from the real Joe Howard. I finally got in touch with my true feelings." His eyes filled with tears again. "Thank you for sharing this moment with me."

Triggered by this experience with Joe, I created and have delivered a speech all over the western United States and Alaska titled "Writing from the Heart," which opens with Joe's story. And to show the brilliance of his great talent, during that speech I read the following poem:

"The Black Stallion"
by Joe Howard

He was wild and free.
Small, muscular, hoofed.
Ranged far and wide.
Knew no boundaries.
Except those of hunger,
fatigue, disease.

Wild he was.
Strong he was.
Free he was.
Fearless he was.

Till they trapped him.
Threw him off his feet.
Tied his legs.
Dropped a tarp over him.
Beat the fight out of him.

Then they pulled the tarp off.
Burned him with their brand.
Took the bindings from his legs.
Jerked him back upright.
Saddled him, rode him,
fed him, drove him.
Until the memory
of what he'd been
was lost in the pain.

Time passed.
And he grew old.
Grey. Spindly.
No longer usable.
Worthless to them.

Feed cost.
So they took him back.
To where they'd found him.
Cast him out.
On old ground.
To face what was now strange.

Alone, he stood . . . For a while.
Alone, he did not move . . . For a while.
Then, deep within, memory stirred.
And his head lifted.

His eye caught sight of sky.
Of peak. Of wild others.
And he bent to feed,
not yet dead.
Rose to see, not yet down.
Moved to explore, not yet lame.

Life returned . . . Slowly . . . Slowly.
Healing began . . . Gently . . . Gently.
And the old black stallion
heard his heart beat . . . once more.

The old black stallion found his
soul . . . once more.
Knew he was alive . . . once more.
Knew he was free . . . once more.
Knew he was home . . . once more.

Like the black stallion, all writers at times despair, but if they will dig deeper within themselves, they, too, will find the resilience to push on, to reach their goals.

I learned from Joe Howard, my dear friend and

seasoned writer, that we must always write from the heart, and not just from the head. When we write stories from the heart, we connect with readers on a deeper level as we guide them to new levels of thinking, feeling, seeing, perceiving, and being. In short, we allow them to change. As writers we must see ourselves as change agents, but not manipulators, who—through heartfelt stories—offer readers changes of thought patterns that can inform, entertain, or persuade them with new ideas.

Thank you Joe Howard, my good friend. I'm a better person, writer, teacher and speaker because you passed my way.

Bud Gardner

"I'm sorry, Mr. Mentel. Now that you've been published, I'm afraid you'll have to leave the writers' group."

ByLine
June 1998

Tom Prisk's cartoon reprinted by permission of ByLine *magazine, June 1998.*

Accused of Plagiarism—
My Highest Compliment

It seems to me that all writers, including those who deserve to be classified as geniuses, need encouragement, particularly in their early years. I always knew I could write, but that just meant I wrote a little better than the other kids in my classes. That I might one day write well enough to derive income from my efforts, oddly enough, never occurred to me during my grade school and high school years.

There was a particular teacher at Hyde Park High School in Chicago, Illinois, who, simply by concentrating her attention on me, made me believe that I might be able to master the knack of writing well enough to consider the craft as a profession. Her name was Marguerite Byrne, and she taught English, which, of course, involved writing skills. Whatever instruction she shared with me was exactly the same as all her other students enjoyed, but the difference was she encouraged me to begin the process of submitting things I was writing, in that day, chiefly poems.

To my surprise the *Chicago Tribune* not only thought enough of several of my verses to publish them, but also

paid me—inadvertently—the highest compliment a
fledgling author can receive. The editor wrote a confiden-
tial letter to Miss Byrne, asking her to see, if by chance,
one of her students—a certain Stephen Allen—might be
guilty of plagiarism. The editor's suspicions had been
aroused because, he was kind enough to say, he found it
hard to believe that a seventeen-year-old could create
material on such a professional level.

When Miss Byrne shared the letter with me, I was
ecstatic! It was wonderfully encouraging. *Maybe I really
was a writer,* I thought.

Miss Byrne also encouraged me to enter a contest
sponsored by the CIVITAN organization. The assignment
was to write an essay titled "Rediscovering America." I
was literally astonished when I received a letter saying
that I was the winner of the contest. The prize was a
check for one-hundred dollars and an invitation to an all-
the-trimmings banquet at a hotel in downtown Chicago.

My mother, at the time, was not even aware that I was
interested in writing, or if she had somehow found out
about it, she took little notice. When I arrived back home
that evening, she didn't ask how the evening had gone. I
placed the one-hundred-dollar check on the breakfast
table where she would see it when she awoke in the
morning—and went immediately to bed.

This scenario demonstrates the tremendous importance of giving young people caring attention and
encouraging them to develop and practice such gifts as
they might have. Years later, I was able to repay my debt
to Marguerite Byrne by dedicating one of my books, *Wry
on the Rocks—A Collection of Poems,* to her.

On the other hand, without encouragement talented
students may never be motivated to learn, develop skills,
or reach their full potential. For example, at the same high
school, there was a teacher whose Spanish language

classes I attended but from whom I, unfortunately, learned very little simply because of the woman's cold, sarcastically critical attitude. She seemed to know nothing about encouraging students, and she was gifted at speaking contemptuously of those of us who were not learning fast enough. Her negativism drove me away. Partly because of *this* teacher's negative influence, I am not fluent in Spanish today.

You see, I had already learned that one can derive instructive benefit from bad examples—by avoiding that behavior. Alcoholism was a serious problem in my mother's family. As a result of having seen enough examples of alcoholic excess in my childhood, I have never had any interest in drinking. The same applies to smoking. My poor mother was a two-pack-a-day victim of nicotine addiction, and because of the endless clouds of smoke, the coughing, the overfilled ashtrays, and the ugly smell of cigarette smoke in the house and in my clothing, I have never smoked a cigarette in my life.

Again, young writers need to be encouraged. Because of Miss Byrne's influence, I have enjoyed a lifetime of writing books, songs, and TV scripts. And guess what? I haven't plagiarized a single word of any of it.

Steve Allen

Sometimes the Biggest
Are the Nicest

Frustration began to overtake me as I filed away yet another "nice" rejection letter. With two mainstream novels and one mystery completed, another mystery in the works, I was not inexperienced at writing. But I was having no luck whatsoever in breaking into the world of the *Published Author.* And the worst part was, I didn't understand why.

I truly believed I'd done everything right. I'd studied writing and attended writers' conferences for years, absorbing nuggets of wisdom from the best of them. I'd even concentrated on the marketing aspect of writing, realizing that merely writing a book was the first step— selling and promoting it were also high on the list.

My two mainstream novels made the rounds of every big publishing house, starting with those whose editors I'd met at conferences. Naturally, I hoped that having a personal contact within the company would get me a bit higher up on the list of wannabees. Still, it just wasn't happening. What was I doing wrong?

By the time I began writing my second mystery novel,

my discouragement level ran high. The rejection letters were always "nice." Each editor complimented me on some aspect of the book, or several aspects. "I really love the setting," one would say. "Your characters are great," another would add. "But . . ." There was always a "but."

Most times the "buts" were vague and innocuous. "It doesn't really fit our list." "It isn't quite right for me." Why wouldn't they tell me what was really wrong with my work? Why wasn't it grabbing them?

At writers' conferences and workshops, I heard all the standard advice. "Avoid the passive voice." "Write what you know." "Edit, edit, edit. Find the perfect word for every sentence."

Without benefit of a critique group (since I live in a very rural area), I felt increasingly lost. Finally, after yet another "nice" rejection letter arrived in the mail, I gathered my courage. The biggest-name mystery writer I'd ever met in person was Sue Grafton. She'd been the keynote speaker at a local conference, and although I seriously doubted she'd remember me, I decided to ask her advice.

Having no idea how to contact her, I pulled one of her books off my shelf, got the publisher's address, and wrote a letter to her in care of them. I explained briefly my dilemma and asked—begged, really—for her help and advice. The worst that could happen were either that she would say no, or that I'd never hear anything. Expecting the latter, I mailed my letter, then promptly put it out of my mind and got back to my writing.

Several weeks later, my phone rang one afternoon and the voice said, "Connie, hello, this is Sue Grafton."

I had to sit down. I was nearly speechless, but realized that this was my one and only shot to talk to this great writer. She was most gracious and didn't mention that I probably stuttered my way through the conversation. She offered to review the first chapters of each of my three books—the two mainstream and one mystery—and to give her opinion. She warned me that she would be honest in her thoughts and that this was a one-time offer. Knowing what a busy lady she is, I was thankful for anything she was willing to do. I photocopied my chapters that day and mailed them the next.

Expecting a page or two critique at best, I was surprised when she called me again within a few days. She had received the material and read it. As any good and sensitive critic will do, she started with the good stuff, pointing out the strong points in each story. One, in particular, she felt had a good first chapter.

So, why did she think I was receiving those nice rejections, I asked.

"I think you need to get back to the basics," she said. She told me she got the feeling that I'd written and rewritten, and tried so hard with them that I'd sapped the originality and muddled them more than I'd helped them.

Back to the basics. The basics.

We chatted a bit longer about writing and the publishing business in general. I thanked her repeatedly for her kindness in looking at my work and in calling me with her words of wisdom.

I hung up the phone, wondering exactly what "getting back to the basics" meant. After all, I'd attended all those conferences, and there were all those writing books on my shelves. Although I was still elated by the call from Sue Grafton, I wasn't quite sure where to turn next. I took a deep breath.

Among the how-to books on my shelves were two on the topic of writing mysteries. I pulled them out, unsure whether I'd read them when I first bought them or if they'd become shelved with good intentions but no action. I read them again—they covered the basics of mystery writing—topics such as plotting, planting clues and creating believable heroes and villains. My own stories pretty well filled these requirements, so I still wasn't sure what I was doing wrong.

A few days later I was in the city and stopped in at a large bookstore. Browsing the writing reference shelves, my eye caught a bright yellow cover. *Techniques of the Selling Writer.* The basics, I thought. Suddenly I remembered a writing workshop I'd taken several years earlier. The instructor, a much-published romance author, had recommended this book. In fact, she'd told us how she would go back and reread her own copy before starting each new book. She'd told us that it was a constant inspiration to her.

The copy of *Techniques* in this store was shrink-wrapped, but that didn't matter to me. I bought it without even needing to browse through the pages. I began reading before I even got it home.

The basics. Here they were, completely outlined and illustrated with plenty of examples. Where other books instructed writers not to use the passive voice, this one gave examples of what that meant, and ways to rewrite sentences to avoid those deadly pitfalls. I devoured the information like a hungry wolf. Then I went back and reread chapters that pertained to my current work. I began to understand the meaning behind the carefully phrased rejection letters.

My improvement was immediate. Two of my short stories won writing awards. My mysteries were soon published with minimal editing needed. Editors have commented that each successive book gets better. I, too, go back to that book before starting each new novel. I wrote to thank Sue Grafton and have met her again at mystery events, where she has been as gracious as always.

Getting back to the basics. I doubt that she will ever know just what impact those five simple words had for me, but I will never forget how she took the time from her busy life to help me—a struggling writer—get back on the right path.

Connie Shelton

PEANUTS. *Reprinted by permission of United Feature Syndicate, Inc.*

So Long Lives This

My mother was a writer. Maybe it's genetic. I had already been bitten by the writing bug. Once bitten, the itch continues. Only fellow writers can identify the itch, its course, and its cure. Never mind doctors—we need an acceptance to that act of penned love we labored over.

I was sixteen years old when my mother began writing her murder mystery/romance novel. I knew when she got that glazed-over look that she was lost in one of the chapters. Intrigued, I asked to read the chapters as she churned them out. I sat, mesmerized, begging for completion of the novel until finally, two years later, the mystery saw its way to a spellbinding conclusion.

Tragically, my mother got sick and died before being able to submit her manuscript. It was willed to me. I placed it in my closet where it remained, as the years wore on and circumstances changed. After eight years, it was as if an alarm had sounded in the closet: The birth of my son, Graig, pushed me to my mother's manuscript. The moment my son was placed in my arms, I felt a continuum, a link to my past, present and future that I had never before felt in quite the same way. And at that moment, I ached for my mother—I ached at *her* losses, for *my* loss, for her to see my son. With those thoughts, the seed was planted: It was time to reread the book. I knew I'd be facing the pain of reading my mother's words and emotions, of witnessing lost dreams. It would bring me back, but it was a way I could be close to her again. I took out the manuscript and read all 325 pages in one sitting. I couldn't put it down. It was as good as I had remembered—no, it was better! I knew I couldn't leave it in my closet any longer. It was ready for a new home. But time has a way of running away. Another move, the baby, work . . . so, the manuscript was placed in yet another closet.

But I didn't forget. From time to time, the pages would call out to me. Reminded of the circle of life by having my own child now, I went back to the closet, pulled out the manuscript, had it photocopied and decided to submit it. *Everyone* I knew in the field discouraged my submitting it. Reason: there could be no second novel, and no editor would buy a murder mystery without the chance for follow-up books. I wasn't daunted. With a recommendation from my aunt, Bobbie Polin Bayuk, I stuck it in an envelope, said a prayer, and sent it off to Dick Whittemore at Doubleday & Company with a cover letter *not* mentioning that the author was deceased. I wanted to give it its best shot. Six months passed, and I had forgotten about the submission. After all, everyone had said it didn't have a chance.

It was in the middle of a hectic day when the doorbell rang. A messenger delivered a letter to me: Doubleday wanted the book! Just like that! Stunned, I ran to my grandparents' house to let them know a piece of their daughter, my mother, would live on. It was the first time their eyes had lit up (save for the birth of my son), since my mother had died.

Then came the nerve-wracking ordeal of having to tell

the editor who accepted the book, Sharon Jarvis, that the author of the book was no longer living. I was afraid my mother would lose her dream once again. Terrified, I called the editor to thank her. "Who are you?" she queried. "An agent?" I didn't answer, asking only if we could meet and talk in person. Puzzled, she acquiesced, agreeing to a meeting the following day.

My legs were jelly as I entered her office. Before I even sat down, I explained the situation. "I love the book," she said. "I still want it."

Living Image by Gladys Selverne Gallant, was published by Doubleday & Company in 1978. I notified everyone possible that my mother had ever known. Fortunately, my grandparents lived to see the work published. It was printed in America, Canada, France, New Zealand and Australia. It also ran as a condensed novel in *Cosmopolitan* magazine.

My eleventh grade English teacher, Ross Newman, taught us Shakespeare. He made us read, understand and memorize many of Shakespeare's sonnets. One, Sonnet XVIII, stood out that had driven me to defy all the odds:

> *So long as men can breathe, or eyes can see*
> *So long lives this, and this gives life to thee.*

My mother had given both love and life to me and, at last, I was able to give her something in return, something that, perhaps, gave her a touch of immortality.

Pat Gallant

From Noah's Ark Writer to Bestseller

It was a warm September day in San Diego, California, where I was enrolled in a freshman English class at California State Normal College. It was my first hesitant step towards becoming an English professor at some distant, unknown university, and my teacher was reading from my maiden effort at creating literature.

I lay still in the dim, dark recess of the ancient, smelling boxcar. Through the black, threatening shadows, I could make out the burly, muscular shape of a fellow hobo coming towards me . . .

Miss Florence Smith paused to look over the class in my direction. I fearfully awaited her criticism.

"Mr. Linkletter," she said admiringly, "you are a born Noah's Ark writer. I've never seen a better example. Did anyone ever tell you that before?"

"No," I replied, "and I don't even know what a Noah's Ark writer is."

"Your adjectives come in two by two!"

And thus began my painful climb towards being a writer.

Under her tutelage, with many a crumpled paper ball of discarded efforts filling my wastebasket, I entered the California Phi Beta Kappa Essay Contest for State

Colleges two years later and was astounded when my entry won third prize.

And a year after that, I was tentatively (and temporarily) nominated for a Rhodes Scholarship at Oxford.

Fortunately (or, unfortunately) this honor was withdrawn when it was discovered that I was not a U.S. citizen because my adopted parents had not completed their citizenship application.

However, in the meanwhile, encouraged by this wonderful teacher, I had written a weekly humor column in the *Aztec* college newspaper, and then at the urging of my classmates, wrote the Annual Musical Comedy produced by the junior class.

I had never *seen* a musical comedy, or even read about one, when I confidently accepted the challenge. I immediately went to the library, looked up a recent Broadway hit, *Of Thee I Sing, Baby,* and after a quick read, optimistically assumed I could do as well.

The play did not win a Pulitzer Prize, much to my disappointment, but it did attract the attention of a young man in the audience who was the manager of the local KGB radio station.

Several weeks later, while making Waldorf salads in the kitchen of the college cafeteria (one of a half dozen jobs that got me through college during the depression), I answered the telephone and had a life-changing conversation with Mr. Lincoln Dellar who offered me a job as a part-time radio announcer at KGB.

How many times in the next sixty years have I recalled this unexpected phone call. And how often have I reflected that life is what happens to you while you're making other plans.

Two years later, after my graduation in 1934, I had moved ahead to executive positions as radio program director at KGB, and then radio director of the San Diego

Centennial World's Fair, and the Broadcast Director of the
Texas Centennial World's Fair in Dallas in 1936.

Two months before the Texas fair opened, the main
attraction at the centennial was floundering with a bad
script and production problems. The show was a huge
outdoor presentation called "The Cavalcade of Texas." It
had been crafted by a university history professor who
had little knowledge or experience with show business.

To my astonishment, the officials of the fair came to me
and asked if I could rewrite and restage this gigantic production involving a 300-foot stage, 180 actors, a herd of 200
cows and a real turn-of-the-century train. Recalling my
college "leap of faith," I sprang to my typewriter and
turned out a new play and suggested new kinds of staging
never tried before. It was a success beyond my dreams.

The following year, I wrote a second cavalcade, "Texas
Under Six Flags," and then moved on to the 1939 World's
Fair in San Francisco to write and co-produce the
"Cavalcade of the Golden West."

Hollywood beckoned and I was invited by the famed
MGM producer-director, Mervyn LeRoy, to an interview
where he promised to get in touch with me soon with a
long-term writing contract to make movies.

After this thrilling interview, I waited, and waited, . . .
and waited . . . for the promised call. It never came.

Undaunted, I went on to write and co-produce (with
my lifelong partner, John Guedel) two triumphant, long-
lived radio and TV shows, *People Are Funny*, which ran on
NBC weekly for nineteen years, and *House Party*, shown
five times a week for twenty-six years on CBS.

In 1947, with all of our network shows in the top TV
brackets, with two Emmy Awards, four nominations, and
a Grammy Award for a talk record, I was finally ready to
climb the Matterhorn of the writing world—a *book!* This
was a long-time dream of mine, but no publisher was

pushing me to try. All of my other leaps into writing had been inspired by the faith and persuasion of my teacher, my classmates, and my show business jobs. This time it was to be up to me!

So without a contract or an agent, I wrote a humorous, non-fiction, backstage book about my misadventures on *People Are Funny*. I mailed the manuscript to ten publishers. To my surprise and delight, Doubleday & Company sent me a contract which specified, among other things, that I personally would actively promote the book on the radio network. (Later I learned that was the *only* reason I got the contract.) After nine months of writing and rewriting my first book, it went on sale and did a glorious dive into the tank. I think we sold 4,500 books, most of them to my fans and family. So much for book writing.

Then several years later, I had a call from an agent in New York, named Berney Geis. He explained that his wife kept telling him about an afternoon show where a guy named Art Linkletter interviewed children. She thought it would make a good book. So did he. And finally after some serious arm-twisting, so did I.

Six million copies later and number one on the national nonfiction list for almost two years, I began to take this book-writing business seriously.

Fast forward to 2000, and my list of books is now twenty-four, all published by nationally known companies.

Somewhere, I hope, Miss Florence Smith is looking down on me, and saying, "Mr. Linkletter, you have begun to show some real talent."

Art Linkletter

Angels over My Keyboard

Be not forgetful to entertain strangers, for thereby some have entertained angels—unawares.

Hebrews 13:2
(English—King James version of the Holy Bible)

When my father left us, I was just beginning high school. His words of hate still burn in my heart as he answered my mother's question, "What about this girl going to college?"

"Who cares?" he snarled. "She's not worth it!"

However, something inside gave me another answer. It is the knowledge of the great gifts our Heavenly Father has given to each of us. Rudyard Kipling called it a muse, others believe it is an angel or God speaking within our hearts. My inner voice said, *Dottie, you were the youngest child to have your poem published in* Wee Wisdom *magazine, when you were six. You wrote out in longhand your little news-letter for the neighbors on your block. Your teachers say you have a gift. You can write! It does not matter what your father or any-one else says. You know you have a precious gift within, and you have a library card. Use them both.*

Talent is a secret you share with God, and those who have the eyes to see and ears to hear.

My high school English teacher was an angel who insisted I take journalism. I wrote stories and articles for the *Alhambra High Moor* at the midnight bakery I worked in every afternoon and evening. After I scrubbed the floors and cleaned the cases, business was slow. I wrote articles, editorials, poems, ad copy and stories for my "shopper's column" on paper bakery bags for my beloved teacher.

When my sweetheart came home from the war, we married and had two beautiful babies. We bought a small tract home and, with the help of relatives, a small dry cleaning business. Then recession hit. No one was having any dry cleaning done. We were about to lose the business and the home. Because I had lost my home several times as a child, I determined not to let that happen to our children.

I remembered my English/journalism teacher and wrote a sample Shopper's Ad column using the display ads in the small country weekly, the *Baldwin Park Bulletin.* I borrowed my neighbor's typewriter and some paper, cut cardboard for my shoes, used clothesline rope to tie pillows on the back of my rickety old baby stroller meant for one child, put my two children on board and headed for the rural newspaper office. I took off my shoe and hammered the wheel back on with my heel every time it fell off.

The publisher stopped setting type on the linotype machine and spoke to me. I showed him a copy of my high school paper. He had no jobs to offer. But he did allow me to buy ad space at wholesale and resell it at retail to the local merchants as a shopping column, like the one I had written in high school. The profit paid the house payment. He gave me a chance, another angel in my life.

The people in the town liked my column. Then several merchants, a bevy of angels, called on me at my home and asked me to start my own advertising business. They

would be my first customers. I was able to buy an old
Model T Ford, a used typewriter, and enough reams of
paper to pay back my angel neighbor. My little business
was off and running. What a thrill it was to order my own
first business cards!

I eagerly read business, sales and inspirational books
from the local library. My favorite was Dr. Norman
Vincent Peale's *The Power of Positive Thinking.*

One night at the library, the thought grabbed my mind
that there were no books about sales, for women. They
were all by, for and about men. I think I was inspired by a
line from one book suggesting that I should "hand out cig-
ars." I suddenly knew I was the one. I must write a book
for women in sales. I would call it *Never Underestimate the
Selling Power of a Woman.*

Then one day my neighbor bought two tickets for the
Dr. Norman Vincent Peale program at the Pasadena Civic
Auditorium. She invited me to go. What a thrill! Dr. Peale
told the audience about his dream of creating *Guideposts
Magazine,* only to experience a terrible fire that burned all
the equipment and even the subscriber names. Radio
shows across the country put out the word. All the subscribers wrote to Dr. Peale and gave him his subscription
list again. A miracle!

After the program, I waited in a long line to speak to Dr.
Peale. He had such a kind face. I told him that his story of
recovering *Guideposts* despite disaster had given me great
courage. Then I hesitatingly gave him one of my new business cards. I told him about how I had started my business
on foot, pushing my two babies in the rickety stroller, and
then how I had run out of cardboard for my shoes.

To my amazement he took it in his hand, read it carefully and placed it in his inner coat pocket! The lump in
my throat and tears in my eyes were hard to hide. Dr.
Peale had not thrown me away. He kept my card.

Two days later I received a note, handwritten, from Dr. Peale. Just six words. "I am so proud of you."

I wonder how many thousands upon thousands of notes that wonderful angel man sent to people. I am so grateful I was one of them.

Later that year, Dr. Peale sent a writer to interview me. My story, how I expanded my tiny advertising business to all of Southern California, opened four offices, hired and trained 285 people and sold 4,000 annual advertising contracts, appeared in *Guideposts*. Under my picture was the dream I had told the writer, "I am working on the first book for saleswomen!"

Several months later, Dr. Peale called me. He said he was telling my story in many of his talks. I was astounded. He asked me which publisher was publishing my book, as so many people in his audiences wanted to buy it. I gulped and confessed that eighteen publishers had turned it down because they believed that there were no women in sales and there was no market for such a book.

"Well, that is not right!" he told me. "I will speak to my publisher, Prentice Hall. I will call you in a few days."

I was stunned. Dr. Peale spent his entire life helping and loving people. He was truly an angel.

He called me back later that week and said, "The man who refused your book at Prentice Hall has just retired. There is a new, younger man who is waiting for your manuscript!"

Prentice Hall sold out the entire first edition to Tupperware, which was giving opportunities in sales to American women.

Dr. Peale wrote the foreword for several of the books my daughter Lilly and I have written. What an encourager he was, as are all angels.

When Mark Victor Hansen and Jack Canfield, two more angels, asked me to write the story for *A 2nd Helping of*

Chicken Soup for the Soul about our daughter Lilly Walters losing her hand in a terrible forklift accident, I wrote "Angels Never Say Hello." (The angel message is "Arise and Go Forth!")

I wrote that I found by the most amazing coincidence a one-hand touch typing book for Lilly. When I called IBM from the hospital, the manager said, "I have it in my hand!" That angel man arranged for a rebuilt electric type-writer for Lilly as a gift, as well as the wonderful book.

Since she was only eleven years old and too young for the typing class, the typing teacher told her to come at lunchtime, and he would teach her one-hand touch typing then. Still another angel.

When the book was published, letters, faxes and E-mail began. Teachers, rehab professionals, grandparents, parents, aunts, brothers, priests, nuns, ministers and rabbis from all over the world wrote to ask us where they could find the one-hand touch typing book. It was then that I learned that Lilly had given it away to her English teacher the year of the accident (after she taught him how to touch type with one hand). So we did not have the book.

When we called IBM, they said they had never published such a book! Evidently when I called their manager that day, he was holding in his hand a sample someone had given him!

The angels at the Glendora Library did a massive search for us. They found the book publisher! We have purchased many cases of the one-hand touch typing books and have arranged to supply them at cost to all who inquire. Lilly, who is the computer whiz in our office and author of many successful books, sends with it a personal letter of encouragement addressed to the person with the disability.

Because of the story I wrote for the *Chicken Soup for the Soul* book, still more were helped. Jack Canfield and Mark

Victor Hansen arranged for my story about Lilly to be picked up by magazines all over the U.S. and Canada.

The most recent was especially precious. The first edition of *Positive Living,* a former publication of The Norman Vincent Peale Foundation, featured my *2nd Helping of Chicken Soup for the Soul* story about Lilly and the angels.

In my heart, I know. It must have been Dr. Peale sending out another angel message, "I am proud of you."

Dottie Walters

PEANUTS. *Reprinted by permission of United Feature Syndicate.*

6

MAKING A DIFFERENCE

A book should serve as the axe for the frozen sea within us.

Franz Kafka

Painting Portraits on Our Souls

The thieves who burglarized our home almost stole my heritage. My husband and I were attending a Maui Writers Conference where he was a keynote speaker, and I was debuting my first book, *The Angels Speak: Secrets from the Other Side*, coauthored with Rosemary Dean. I was excited about meeting all the prominent authors, agents and publishers gathered at the Grand Wailea Resort hotel. Then a call jolted me awake at midnight.

Thieves had broken into our house, twenty-five hundred miles away, kicking in our front door. Rick, our vigilant next-door neighbor, sprang into action. He grabbed a 204-10 shotgun and ran up to our front porch, shouting, "I'm coming in!" The robbers dropped the duffel bag they'd stuffed and escaped out the back door, never to be seen again.

Little did they know what precious cargo they had left behind. Nestled in the bottom of the bag, amid credit cards, check books and other valuables, lay an old cigar box in which my mother had stored my father's love letters. Written when they had just fallen in love until a year after they married in 1928, these letters, jotted in pencil and tied together with a faded pink ribbon, were not only a legacy of a lifetime, but also were the key to my understanding my parents, especially my mother, who had piqued me most of my life.

Born prematurely and kept in an incubator until I gained enough weight to leave the hospital, I had been adopted at four weeks of age by Mary and Tony Martin. While I loved them both and appreciated the stable home life they had given me and my adopted brother, Ron, I often chaffed under the strong thumb of my mother who was bent on controlling my hairstyle, clothes and every other aspect of my life.

During my elementary school years, for example, she insisted on fixing my hair "the Spanish way." Every night I'd howl in pain as she'd yank a lock of my hair around her finger, plaster it with Stay-Back gel, and bobby-pin the curls in place. The next day at school, these curls, minus the bobby pins, would bounce like stiff springs poking out of my sore head. She thought I looked beautiful, and I felt hideously set apart from everyone else.

While she took great pride in sewing my dresses, using patterns that she liked even though they were woefully out of date, I longed for store-bought clothes, cashmere sweaters and tight wool skirts. She wanted me to look unique, but I just wanted to look like everyone else.

Of course, it didn't help that I looked nothing like her. I was tall, olive-skinned, gangly and flat-chested as a teenager; she was short, stout and buxom, with white porcelain skin. I was self-conscious not only of our physical disparity, but later of our educational one. By the time I got to college and eventually earned a master's degree, her limited third-grade education created a chasm between us that, I'm ashamed to say, grew wider with each passing year.

Like my father, she'd been born in Spain and migrated to California as a young girl. While my dad eventually mastered English, my mother never really tried. She spoke a version of "Spanglish," mixing metaphors and mangling words. A stingray became a "stingwing"; a Mitsubishi was a "Mr. Mishi." When I was in the third grade and cloak room monitor for the day, the teacher asked me to describe the contents I'd found in a lunch box. I replied, "An apple, some cookies and a peanut butter and jelly sangwich." Everyone laughed as my cheeks stung from embarrassment. I was so angry at my mother for mispronouncing words for me that I vowed that day to become an English teacher so that no one would ever make fun of my English again.

After my father and brother died, my mother's care came to rest entirely on my shoulders. She was eighty years old then, suffering from a host of diseases including Alzheimer's, diabetes and colon cancer. For more than two years, she lived with me as I tried to juggle my everyday life as a wife, mother, English teacher and writer, with the added tasks of being her chauffeur, psychologist and caregiver. The illnesses taxed my patience, and coupled with the resentment I felt that my favorite parent, my father, had left me the sole survivor in an increasingly nightmarish existence, the burden was too much. My anger deepened.

There were times when I'd be cleaning up her colostomy bag or tucking her into bed after finding her wandering about my bedroom in the middle of the night, that I'd moan, "What did he ever see in her?"

I learned the answer to that plaguing question when cleaning out her old house to ready it for sale. I found my dad's love letters. Without them, I never would have been introduced to the hazel-eyed, raven-haired beauty he fell in love with long before I entered their lives. She no longer was the bewildered, weak and helpless child in my life. Through his words, she was transformed once again into a shy, giggly coquette, sitting out on her lawn, petting her white Angora cat and hoping he'd stop by. When she went away to work in an asparagus cannery, he began writing of his love:

> *Mary, it has been only a short time since we have become acquainted, but it seems to me as if I knew you all my life. Well, love is blind and it comes all of a sudden and it came to me for you, little girl. And I must let you know this, that I am wishing to see you again and be by your side and see you smile and talk to you once more. For now my love for you is getting greater every minute.*

He closed his love note with "an ocean of love and a kiss on top of each wave" and wrote S.W.A.S.K. on the envelope: "Sealed With a Sweet Kiss." Less than a month later, he was hinting of marriage:

> *Honey, my love for you is very great for when I love, I love the Spanish way on right 'till the end, and my heart craves for you to its fullest extent.*

Then he drew an arrow with their initials on it with hearts falling from his initials. Later when it became clear that she could marry him only after her older sister, Julia, married first, a Spanish tradition, he lamented:

> *For you I live and for you I die, just for you, Mary, and now you surely have my heart burning with love for you and honey, my poor heart is calling, just calling for its mate which I am sure is you, for since I met you, it seems to me as if this world is different and better than before, and you are the one that has made this happiness come to me. . . .*

Tony and Mary eloped and, although they lived in San Leandro, California, she continued to go away to Isleton, about a fifty-mile trip, with her siblings during asparagus season, and he resumed his love letters. He wrote about his struggles through the Great Depression, working during the week at a factory and painting cars on the weekend for a dollar an hour. He chronicled family spats and gossip, his garden laden with tulips, pansies and flowering peach trees and his reluctance to buy a much-needed battery for his car at a whopping $8.50. But, mostly, he revealed his strong feelings for her and how much he missed her. Because I had loved him so much, I couldn't help but start to appreciate the woman who clearly was the love of his life.

In the middle of the night, when caring for my mother's ailments had left me wide awake and frustrated, I'd reach for those letters and read them line by line until peace would at last descend upon me, and I could fall asleep again. I have since thought of the lyrics of "Amazing Grace," about being blind then seeing—how true that was for me. As each page lifted another filter I had placed through years of resentment and misunderstanding, a clearer, brighter picture of my mother shone forth.

Through my father's eyes, I finally began to understand just what it was he saw in her. His words painted a new picture for me. I began to recognize what he had always seen: her basic goodness, hard-won wisdom and practicality—those qualities which he admired so much about her and which in my childishness I had refused to see. He looked forward to the faithful, though ungrammatical, letters she wrote to him. He was proud of her "Spanish way," because it was strong and true. She loomed before me now like a wise genie released from a bottle, imbued with wisdom and deep understanding . . . taking shape as a lover of life with its shifting colors and hues . . . then reforming to reveal an innocent soul with an unwavering faith in a God that would see us through all things . . . and ultimately emerging as a simple, contented woman, intent on being the best wife and mother she knew how to be. My father's words were like teardrops on snow, melting my heart and releasing old disappointments and stubborn hurts. I realized that I loved her—and always had. It just took his words of love to help me discern the truth about myself.

I shudder to think of Dad's love letters almost being stolen by thieves. Without them, I would never have been given the gift of insight which bolstered me through a most difficult passage in life. During my mother's final years, she was in a nursing home in a wing specializing in Alzheimer's patients. I went to see her nearly every weekend, often taking her to a nearby park where we'd feed the ducks, play the game Aggravation, or watch the canoes glide across the lake. I enjoyed those times immensely, savoring those moments when she'd connect with the present and her surroundings. I noticed her sense of wonder, her appreciation of nature and her reverence for all of life. We'd talk for hours about the old days, this time laughing about my Spanish ringlets and skirts with petticoats. At times I felt my father's smiling presence, like a soft glow in the periphery, whispering, "See, Jennifer? Now you know why I love her." At her funeral, I sang her praises in a loving tribute to a life well-lived.

Although I became a published author long after my father died, I'd like to think that somehow he knows what a significant impact his words had upon me and how much I have come to value the written word for its illumination in our lives. His love letters were a holy legacy, as all heartfelt writings are. How sacred is the written word that paints portraits on our souls.

Jennifer Martin

The Boy Who Saved Thousands of Lives

The shot heard "round the world."

Ralph Waldo Emerson

It was a day like any other in a busy hospital. Among dozens of incidents of joy and fear, a small boy was brought in, dying from a road accident. When the end came, one of the nurses took a deep breath and did what her job required her to do: She asked the boy's parents if they would donate his organs. Their reply was sharp and clear, an emphatic refusal, pain mixed with anger at having been asked such a crass question at the worst moment of their lives.

"I understood how they felt," the nurse told me later. "The bottom had fallen out of their world." But all she could think of was that on the third floor of that same hospital another little boy, of much the same age and with a mother and father very much like these, was also dying that night—because the heart that could have saved him didn't arrive.

I often think of that little boy and how close he came to making it. I also know how his parents felt: my own

seven-year-old son, Nicholas, was shot by highway robbers six years ago while we were on vacation in southern
Italy and, when the doctors told us there was no hope, I
still remember vividly wondering how I would ever get
through all the years ahead without him. Maggie, my
wife, and I, however, did donate his organs to seven very
sick Italians, some of whom would certainly be dead by
now, and we have never for a moment regretted the decision. After living in the shadow of death, some of them for
years, all seven are back in the mainstream.

What we thought was a purely private act took Italy by
storm: the president and prime minister both asked to
meet us privately, letters poured in by the hundreds.
We've been given honors in Nicholas' name that previously went to some of the world's greatest humanitarians
and scholars.

Today's front-page story, however, is often almost forgotten tomorrow as some new tragedy comes along to
take its place. Unless we do something to etch this story
in the people's minds, I thought at the time, it will have no
permanent effect on their actions, and thousands will
continue to die every year because organ donation rates
fall short of need in virtually every country in the world.

And so, having been a daily newspaper writer much of
my life, I did what comes naturally: I wrote. And wrote.
And wrote. At first for the obvious places: medical journals, parents' magazines, newspaper features, then for the
less obvious: the scouting magazine, Italian newspapers,
newsletters, then further afield still: a Dutch magazine, a
travel magazine, the weekly paper of the town where I
was born in England. I faxed and e-mailed and telephoned editors, feature writers and syndicated colum-
nists. I got up at 2:00 A.M. to talk to European editors or
stayed up until midnight to call Australia. Maggie and I
crisscrossed this country talking to audiences of every

imaginable kind, and everywhere I went I called on the local newspaper and television stations.

There were many rebuffs, but there were many achievements, too. Better yet, writers all over the world picked up the story from our words and wrote memorable pieces of their own. To think of just one: virtually every overseas edition of *Reader's Digest* led off with Nicholas' story, and we have a collection of clippings in Chinese, Portuguese, Swedish and twenty other languages. A television movie, *Nicholas' Gift*, starring Jamie Lee Curtis, picked up many of the sentences I had written. And recently I wrote a book *The Nicholas Effect*, which, though much of it was written through a veil of tears, shows how his example has saved literally thousands of lives.

Nicholas was a remarkable little boy—gentle, imaginative and, yes, wise—and we all expected him to do great things. When he died, all those expectations seemed to have died with him. But in the end, as the words written and spoken about him found their way to the four corners of the world, he did more than we could possibly have foreseen. More even than saving lives, his brief innocent life sent an electric charge through the human spirit, reminding us all of the preciousness of life and hence the importance of living up, rather than down, to it.

In his last few days we played a game with Nicholas in which he was a Roman soldier about to return home. "When you get there," we told him, "they'll write poems to you, your name will be cheered by people you've never met." It was only a game, but it all came true with this difference, however: that Nicholas conquered not by the force of arms but by the power of love. And that, of course, is much stronger.

Reg Green

The Christmas Box

And the trouble is, if you don't risk anything, you risk even more.

Erica Jong

In 1992, I wrote a story called *The Christmas Box* as a Christmas gift for my two little girls, Jenna and Allison. I was not a writer by profession, I just wanted to give them something that would express my love for them. But as I started to write, it became an almost mystical experience. The story began to write itself, pouring into my mind in torrents of inspiration. The whole story took only five weeks. As I completed the story, I had the strong impression that I had been inspired by my sister Sue, who had died when I was only two years old. *The Christmas Box* was, perhaps, also a gift for my mother, to help her heal after thirty years.

I knew I needed to share this story with more than just my two daughters. I photocopied twenty copies and gave them out as Christmas presents to family and friends. Within weeks, something happened that I had not expected. I began receiving calls from strangers telling me how healing my book had been for them. At the encouragement of a bookstore manager, who had received multiple orders for my unpublished book, I sent the manuscript to local publishers. Every one of them turned it down. Still receiving many requests for the book, my wife Keri and I decided to publish it ourselves.

That next Christmas, we sold 20,000 copies of the book in my home state. As letters and phone calls poured in, I began to believe that God had given me a mission with this book. Since those meager beginnings, *The Christmas Box* has now sold more than seven million copies and been published in eighteen languages. The movie based on the book has been viewed, so far, by an estimated sixty million people around the world. It is the only book in history to simultaneously hit #1 on *The New York Times* hardcover and paperback bestseller lists. But the greatest moment of *The Christmas Box* was not a public event. It was something very personal. Something the world would never see.

As Christmas of 1994 approached, Keri and I decided to publish *The Christmas Box* nationally. Still without a publisher, I quit my job, used our savings and convinced one of my former clients to invest nearly a quarter of a million dollars. Simply stated, we put everything on the line.

I knew the book had tremendous potential, because it had become the number one book in nearly every bookstore that carried it. However, we soon discovered that few of the booksellers on the East Coast or in the South were fronting my book. If you've seen the back storerooms of a Barnes & Noble or Waldenbooks at Christmas time, you know that the boxes of books climb to the ceiling. In most of those stores that I was fortunate enough to even get into, my little book was buried somewhere beneath those other titles. I knew the danger this posed. After Christmas, the books would all be shipped back to me. Not only would we lose all our money, they would never order my book again.

I needed publicity to get the stores to notice my book. I needed something big. I had two aces up my sleeve. A reporter from *People* magazine had already interviewed me; then I got an invitation to be on the national cable network. The program producer wanted to do a fifteen-minute segment on my book with live call-ins. As I counted the calendar down to Christmas, this was my only chance.

We were also near the end of our money. I spent our last promotion dollars on a plane ticket to New Jersey for a cable show. I planned to do a booksigning in Atlanta, Georgia, on my way back.

I arrived at the Newark airport at one in the morning. All I could afford was a cheap hotel. I remember standing out front of the airport trying to catch a shuttle to my hotel.

The next morning, I called a cab. I learned that it was nearly $100 to drive me to the studio. I arrived with my suitcases and a woman met me. "What's with the luggage?" she asked.

"I brought some extra things, just in case you wanted to change my wardrobe."

A wry grin crossed her face. "Don't worry about it. You won't be on long enough for anyone to notice."

I was wondering what she had meant by that when I was taken to the green room. Waiting to go on the show with me was a large man, talking loudly about his great product. It was guaranteed to stop snoring, he said.

When it was my time to go on, the director met me at the door. "Sorry, we had to cut your segment."

"Cut my segment? I just flew all the way from Utah. No one told me about this."

"Yeah, we got this great segment on snoring. Maybe we

can squeeze you in during the cooking segment for a few seconds. You can hold up your book."

I talked him into 45 seconds. As I took off my microphone at the end of the segment, I asked the producer if I could stay and watch the rest of the program.

"Why?" she asked.

I took off my microphone, handed it to her, and walked out.

Out front I asked the receptionist if I could use the phone to call a cab.

"Is it long distance?" she asked.

Back at the hotel, I called my book's distributor. They had not received a single phone call from the program.

That afternoon I flew to Atlanta, rented a car, and drove to the bookstore in a mall. I walked up to the front counter. "I'm here for my booksigning."

The woman glared at me. "We don't have a booksigning today."

"I came three thousand miles for this. Where's your manager?"

"He just left," she said. "What book did you write?"

The Christmas Box."

"Never heard of it," she said dryly. "I don't think we have it."

I thought of what I should do. "May I use your phone?"

"Yeah, I guess. There's one in the back."

I went to the backroom. Surrounded by hundreds of unopened boxes, I wondered if my book was somewhere in there. I called the salesman who had set up the event.

"They aren't expecting me here," I said. "In fact, they haven't even heard of my book."

"I'll check into it," he said. "I'll call right back." A few minutes later, the phone rang. "Is the manager there?" he asked.

"No."

"It's because he's hiding. He forgot about your signing, and he didn't want to face you."

I sighed.

"How did your cable show go?"

"Bad. They pretty much canceled my segment."

"That's too bad," he said sadly. "Especially in light of *People* magazine."

My heart froze. "What happened to *People*?"

"You didn't hear? They canceled."

"Canceled. Why?"

"No one in New York has heard of you."

The announcement took my breath away. He'd just told me I'd lost everything. I felt numb. As I walked out of the bookstore, the clerk stopped me. "I found your book," she said. "It was still in a box. But there's only eleven copies."

"Do you want me to sign them?" I asked.

"No," she replied. "Why don't you just leave?"

It was almost poetic: it was raining. Humiliated and discouraged, I sat in the rental car with the rain pounding on the hood as my world crashed around me. "God," I said aloud, "you have given me just enough rope to hang myself."

Instantly, the inspiration came. A powerful voice that I couldn't wipe from my thoughts. *"Why are you doing this?"* it asked.

I did not respond.

"Are you doing this for money?"

"Money? No," I said aloud. "I've put every dime back into this. It's never been about money. But now I've lost everything."

The inspiration came again. *"Are you doing it for your pride?"*

I had to think harder about that. "No," I finally said. "I wrote this book for my daughters. I pursued it because it mattered. But I don't like looking like a fool, pursuing a dream that everybody told me was impossible."

Then the voice said: *"Do you believe that I inspired you to write this book?"*

"Yes!" I replied.

Then came the final inspiration. *"Then what does it matter? I will do with my book as I will."*

Those words took my breath away. I knew that all was lost. Or at least I thought I did. And I wondered how I would tell Keri. Keri and I had been trying to have a baby for four years. Now, finally pregnant, Keri had had serious complications and ordered to bed by her doctor. It was a stressful time when she had been warned to avoid stress. How would I tell her that we're going to lose everything?

Still, something in the back of my heart cried out, *"Thy will be done."*

I flew back late that night. As I drove home on a snow-shrouded roads, I decided that I would not tell Keri the bad news until morning.

As I walked into our darkened bedroom at three in the morning, Keri said, "Hi, honey. Welcome home. How did it go?"

I couldn't hide the truth. "Not very well. *People* magazine canceled." Keri knew what that meant. "Honey, we're going to lose a lot of money," I said.

The dark night hung heavy with grief and loss. Then from the darkness came Keri's sweet voice. "But, Rick, think of all the good you've done."

In that moment of total bleakness, I thought, *"I am a lucky man. My life is going to get very hard for the next few years. I've lost my business; I've lost our savings. But I'm a very lucky man!"*

The next Monday morning, unwilling to give up without a fight, I decided to rewrite the marketing plan. Around 10:00 A.M. the phone rang. It was the reporter from

People. "How many books have you sold?" she asked.

"What does it matter?" I answered indignantly. "You canceled my story."

"We did," she said. "But I got a call last night from the editor. He wants to run with it."

The next Monday morning, the article was on the newsstands. A full page proclaiming the book "A Christmas Treasure." By noon, I had received a call from NBC, *The Today Show,* asking me to come onto the show with my daughters. I flew back to New York with Jenna and Allison. We got off the plane to find a chauffeur with a sign that read, *"Mr. Evans."*

"Yes, I am!" I said. The respect was like water to a man dying of thirst. They took us in a stretch limo to a suite that was as large as my home. It had three bathrooms!

Katie Couric did a wonderful interview. The book soared. Within three weeks *The Christmas Box* had hit #2 on the *New York Times* bestseller list. Publishers and movie makers were calling from all around the world. The book was put up for auction. The reality of what had happened didn't occur to me until the morning my agent called. "The auction is down to the last two houses."

"Where are we?" I asked.

"Are you sitting down? We're up to 4.25 million."

Later that afternoon, my mind reeling with the revelations of the day, I drove to *The Christmas Box* Angel statue in Salt Lake City—a spot where I often go to meditate. As I looked out over the Salt Lake valley, I finally understood. God knew what was going to happen. He knew that in the coming years my life, my family, my marriage would all be faced with tremendous challenges and temptations. To prepare me, He gave me an incredible gift. He gave me the chance to know that both Keri and I were doing this, not for money or acclaim, but because it was the right thing to do—even if it cost us everything we owned. He gave both Keri and me one of the greatest gifts we can hope to receive in this life. He gave us the chance to see our own souls.

Richard Paul Evans
Submitted by Sharon Linnéa

Writers in Prison

A moment's success pays for the failure of the years.

Robert Browning

I was doing a guest writing workshop at Susanville State Prison near the Sierra Nevada foothills in northern California. Most of the men doing time there are sentenced to prison because of drugs. They are housed in huge dormitories in bunk beds. They have no privacy, no place to be alone, no place to think quietly. I had great apprehensions when I walked onto the prison grounds. I had taught writing workshops at many California prisons, but those prisons had cells. In cells, even if they are shared with another inmate, one can find at least a little writing time. Surely the men here at Susanville were not going to be interested in what I had to offer.

I had decided to spend my two days giving a monologue workshop. I wanted the men to have a chance to write and then perform before a camera. I wanted them to see themselves on video before I left the prison at the end of the second day. I felt that life in this prison had probably stripped

them of most of their identity and that writing and performance art might restore some sense of who they were
or who they could be.

I was pleased that twenty men had signed up for the
class. This was the maximum number I had said I could
take. I spent the first hour with them, talking about what
it was like to be a writer. Telling them that there is a joy
and a freedom in the words. That no matter how much
they were all forced to be alike, dress alike, eat the same
food, keep the same hours, that in their writing they could
finally be different. As different as they wanted to be.
Writing, I told them, can be the most liberating of all the
arts. You can be free with the word. There are no limits. I
told them that every time I picked up a pencil or sat down
at a computer or a typewriter that it was as if I was coming home, coming home to my art, my words, that this
was a world that no one else could take away. This art
would sustain me throughout all my days.

The men listened well and when I finally had them start
their writing projects, they worked hard. There was only
one, a young, very handsome blond man, who I worried
about. He was reluctant to share during that first day
when I had them writing their monologues. Every other
student read and rewrote and read again, but this man sat
quietly, erasing, writing, tearing up drafts, starting again.
Whenever I would approach his desk, he quietly covered
his paper with his arms.

"Can I see?" I would ask.

"It would be easier for me if you didn't," he would
answer and then a shy smile would appear.

I figured, what the heck. Even if he doesn't share his
writing with the class, he's writing. He is choosing to
spend his whole day in this hot, stuffy classroom working
on something called a monologue. That morning he probably didn't even know the meaning of the word. This

should make me happy. But it didn't. I was concerned about his need for privacy, about his inability to share, knowing that he didn't think his writing was good enough. I had worked in prisons for too many years to be fooled by his shyness. I knew that many of the inmates had learned at a very young age that they could do nothing right. They had been abused and tormented as children and lacked any self-confidence. But no matter how much I praised the other prisoners he wouldn't relent. He went back to his dormitory that evening with his writing tucked into his jeans pocket. Many of the other men just left their work on the desks. Not him. He was taking no chance that I would read it after he was locked away behind the bars. He was right, of course. I would have made a beeline right for his desk the minute he got out the door. He had judged me right.

The second day all the men returned to the classroom. This was particularly pleasing to me. Even the young blond man. This was the day for reading and taping. I wondered how the silent, shy student would handle this. I was actually surprised to see him there. He had combed his long, blond hair and his shirt was neatly pressed. He had obviously thought about the fact that he was going to be filmed and wanted to look his best. At last I was going to hear what he wrote.

He didn't say much during the performances. I had given the men fairly loose instructions about who should be speaking in their monologues. I had, though, told them that I wanted to hear their characters tell me what it is they really wanted, what it was that no one understood about them, and why they needed to talk. He sat there quietly, watching the work of his fellow inmates. One of the men had written a monologue for God, and another had been Abraham Lincoln, another Martin Luther King, Jr. Some of the monologues were funny, others serious. Even though they hadn't had time to memorize their lines, once they began reading, the scripts in their hands were hardly noticeable, and I was extremely moved by their work.

Finally, he was the only one who hadn't read his monologue. When all the others were finished I asked him, "Are you ready now?"

"I don't think so," he answered in such a gentle voice.

Then the men were on him.

"Man, if I can do it, you can do it. Try it. You'll like it. Come on man, don't be shy. Nobody's going to judge you here."

So he got up, took his script to the performance area and stood before the camera. He looked so young. The papers in his hands were shaking like frightened birds, but he looked with determination into the eye of the camera and opened up his monologue.

"My name is Bruce. I am twenty-one years old and I am dead. I am dead because I spent time in prison for drugs and I didn't care. I didn't care about me. I went to bed every night just counting the days 'till I could get out and get that next fix. I would kill for my next fix. I would die for my next fix."

He went on about his life, how he was raised in poverty by alcoholic parents, beaten, hungry, no life at all, shuffled back and forth through foster homes. While he read, he showed scars on his body, the burn marks on his arms where a drunken father had extinguished cigarettes, the cuts on his wrists where he had tried to take his own life. I couldn't help it. The tears began forming in my eyes, hot and painful. My God, why had I asked him to share this horrible pain? Then he got to the end of his story.

"Even though I died right there in prison, I want to tell you something. The reason I need to talk to you today. I have risen again, just like in the Bible. I am reborn. One day a woman came in and told me to write. And I had never written before, but I did it anyway. I sat for eight hours in a chair and focused the way I have never focused before. I could never even sit still before! I wrote out my ugly life, and then I was able to finally feel something. To feel pity. For myself. When no one else was ever able to feel it. And I felt something else. I felt joy. I was writing, and what I was writing was good. I was a writer! And I was going to get up in front of all those men in that class, and I would say that this . . ." At these words he held up his little manuscript. "This is more important to me than any drug. What I wanted to tell you was that I died a drug addict, and I was reborn as a writer."

We all sat there stunned. The camera kept running. He took a self-conscious little bow. Then he said, "Thank you," once again in his quiet voice. And then the men broke out in spontaneous applause. He walked over to me and took my hands. Inmates are not allowed to touch their teachers, but I let him anyway. "You have given me something," he said, "that no drug has ever given me. My self-respect."

I think of him often. I pray that he has continued to find respect for himself through the written word. I know, though, that that day in that room with those men, a writer was born. After a long and terrible journey, a lost soul had come home, home to the words.

Claire Braz-Valentine

A Season with
the Great Sinclair Lewis

There is nothing to writing; all you do is sit down at a typewriter and open a vein.

Red Smith

Although largely unread today, Sinclair Lewis was the most famous novelist of his time and, in 1930, the first American to receive the Nobel Prize for Literature.

Books like *Main Street, Arrowsmith,* and *Elmer Gantry* made him a vast fortune, and thanks to his novel *Babbitt,* that word is in most dictionaries meaning "a middle class businessman epitomizing narrow-mindedness and self satisfaction."

In 1947, when I was twenty-five, I returned from adventuring in Spain and Peru to visit my parents in Santa Barbara. I read in the newspaper that the renowned novelist was spending a few weeks in Santa Barbara while writing a screenplay. With the brashness of youth, I wrote him a letter saying I was a would-be writer and asked to meet him. To my surprise, he invited me to his rented house for tea the next afternoon.

I was let into the house by a servant and waited in the living room. Suddenly I heard a Midwestern voice say, "How d' ye do!"

I turned and rose to see Mr. Lewis coming into the room, his head back, his skeletal hand extended and held high. He was a startling sight. At sixty-two, he was tall and fiercely ugly, quite the ugliest person I had even seen. I recoiled from the haunted eyes sunk in his scarlet face which was ravaged and scarred, pocked and cratered from countless operations for skin cancer. His once blazing red hair was now thin and orangy-white.

Yet I swear that ten minutes after I met him—when he started to talk and ramble—I no longer thought him ugly. He was kind and rapacious and charming and witty and factual and fanciful and reverent and irreverent and gossipy and profound, and I was no longer aware of a face but only a powerful personality and a towering imagination and great boyish enthusiasm. We talked about all manner of things; I learned later that this was a talking period for him. A lonely period. Subsequently, I would know his long, silent times; both were equally compulsive.

He fumbled a cigarette from a crumbled package and put it in his mouth. The words spilled from him: "So you're a writer, eh? I remember way back when I was at Yale— dreadful place—and I said to a Professor Tinker—y 'know, the great Tink—that I wanted to be a writer and nothing but a writer and he said, 'But you'll starve,' and I said, 'Don't care if I do,' and he said, 'Then you'll succeed!' "

He was a great mimic, a remarkable imitator of infinite accents and dialects, and he reproduced Professor Tinker's refined intonations to perfection.

"You write every day? Work on a schedule? That's what you have to do. None of this bunk about waiting around for the muse to strike. I always say the art of writing is the art of applying the seat of your pants to the seat of your chair. Can't just sit around talking about writing. Gave a lecture once at Columbia and started out by saying to the students, 'How many of you here are *really* serious about becoming a writer?' They all raised their hands and I said, 'Well why the hell aren't you home writing?'—and sat down. Only two ways you can learn to write, by reading and writing, and lately I'm not even so sure about the former."

I had the feeling I was in a Creative Writing Workshop for one, but he was so enthusiastic and enjoying himself so much that I felt very privileged to be the audience.

"Keep notes? You have to keep notes; every writer has to keep notes. I wouldn't be without old Ebenezer here."

He picked up the notebook and handed it to me. I leafed through it as he talked. Terribly neat and orderly, it had such headings as Dutch-American Names, French-American Names, Mannerisms, Peculiarities of Dress and so forth. Under "Titles", I got a little thrill when I saw such literary landmarks as *Main Street, Elmer Gantry, Dodsworth, Arrowsmith, It Can't Happen Here, Babbitt,* with a line drawn through them and the word used next to them.

When I told him I was writing a novel, he sent me home to get the first seventy-five pages.

The next day I screwed up my courage to call him. "Mr. Lewis, excuse me for bothering you, but have you by any chance had time to read those seventy-five pages?"

"Well, Barney," he said, "yes, I've read them."

There was a silence. Finally I said, "And?"

"I would be inclined," he said, and he said it not unkindly, "my inclination, that is, my first reaction . . . would be to throw away the first seventy-three or four."

"Words?"

"Pages."

I couldn't find my voice for awhile. "Throw . . . away . . ."

"Sure, just toss 'em out."

"Not rewrite—rework—revise—?"

"Hell," he said, conspiratorially, "let's just get rid of them!"

"But—" I croaked, "why?"

"Barney," he said, "do you know what every story has in common, from *Little Miss Muffet* to *Moby Dick*?"

I hesitated and he boomed back over the phone, "Conflict! Supposing the spider had been a nice little spider and hadn't frightened her? No story. Supposing instead of always trying to elude Ahab, Moby had spouted and said, 'Hey Cap'n, flensing-time, I'm over here—come get me!' No cross-purposes, no conflict, no story. Ennui."

"But I had to set the scene," I protested.

"For seventy-five goddamn pages? Look, when I want to read about the Azores, I'll buy the *National Geographic!*

"But there was some good stuff on the last pages, get me seventy-five more."

Reluctantly, I did.

At two in the morning the phone rang. I stumbled out of bed and answered it. There was no salutation. Just an enthusiastic voice.

"Now she's moving!" exulted Mr. Lewis. "Yessirree, at last it is going! That girl is a honey, and I care what's going to happen to her and to him, and you don't need to save anything in those first seventy-five pages at all!"

My heart leapt.

"Well, I'll let you get back to bed. Say, I have a good idea today: Do you know how to play chess?"

I said I didn't.

"Well," he said, "you take some lessons and then come East as my secretary. Forty-five dollars a week and expenses. I'll send you the ticket tomorrow before I leave."

And that is how the most stimulating and productive five months of my life began.

Barnaby Conrad

Dean Has AIDS—A Father's Story

It was one of those lazy Sunday afternoons, and I was watching professional football. My wife decided to call our third son, now living two thousand miles away, to clarify a comment he made in his last letter.

I became aware of my wife's silence as she sat motionless on the floor holding the phone. "Honey, what's wrong?" I asked. Slowly she looked up. Finally she said, "AIDS—Dean has AIDS."

The ordeal lasted twenty-one months with our son moving in with us for the final fifteen. Caregiving our son, we experienced nine life-and-death situations. Two of our three remaining sons abandoned us; we were rejected by our church and shunned by many friends. AIDS will do that.

Help started coming after the local newspaper began running a series on AIDS featuring Dean, my wife and me, and our trials for community education and awareness.

Dean died May 23, 1993. In the aftermath, my wife developed a frozen shoulder and was an emotional wreck. She knew immediately the price paid both physically and mentally.

Six months later, I lay on a hospital bed with doctors

advising me to retire immediately; my immune system had crashed and psoriatic arthritis had immobilized my joints. All as a result of the stress just experienced.

How does a man grieve and release pent-up emotions? Women seem to be able to ventilate to friends and talk out feelings. But us men? We spend our time talking about athletics, hunting or fishing, our jobs, hobbies, politics or "the old days."

I began to write, first remembering certain episodes, then listing all that had happened to us. I expanded on areas that represented our greatest hurts. I needed answers to questions relating to why people acted the way they did. I knew I would remain emotionally sick unless I could begin forgiving. But I had to identify what had to be forgiven. On paper I identified all options and reasoned why certain options were chosen: more organizing, more outlining, more fleshing out the outline entries.

Soon I had a handwritten manuscript. A former secretary typed the manuscript on her computer, and the editor of the newspaper that ran our story did the editing.

Fifty publishers were contacted, seventeen read the manuscript and one requested a ninety-day exclusive option. I talked to several editors. All agreed the quality of the writing was good, the story neatly developed and that its message should be made available to the public, but ". . . we're a business. Unless you are a known individual like O.J. Simpson, the public won't buy a biographical story—even when the subject is AIDS. My list of books for publication will be approved only if I can convince my review committee that the projected profit on your book is higher than another candidate."

On the recommendation of a friend, I contracted with a printer to self-publish my book.

My book arrived two years ago. To contact my antici-pated audience, I wrote to every hospice, infectious disease physician and community-based AIDS support service in the country and offered the book through direct mail. Then, through two distributors and the Internet, I offered the book to the general public.

Having published my book gave me instant acceptance as an expert on the social impact of AIDS. Newspaper articles resulted in opportunities to give talks in churches. The distributors opened doors for talks and signings at bookstores.

I now realize that publishing my book gave me an opportunity to first write out my feelings and then talk them out while providing emotional support to those affected by AIDS or any other disease that takes life prematurely. I began to feel my head emptied of that which could have destroyed me emotionally. I have now grieved my loss, and my life is back together again.

Even though Dean is gone and can never be replaced, writing has allowed us to move on with life. Having a newfound skill in writing is helping me to feel like a "Grandpa Moses"—but writing, not painting. Funny, I barely passed English in college and never considered myself a writer. Now a second manuscript is almost done, and a third book is in the thinking stage. My lemons have become lemonade.

Edmund Hansen

7

OVERCOMING OBSTACLES

When I face the desolate impossibility of writing 500 pages, a sick sense of failure falls on me, and I know I can never do it. Then gradually, I write one page and then another. One day's work is all I can permit myself to contemplate.

John Steinbeck

In Spite of It All

All my life I had three dreams. I wanted to have a big family, get a college degree and become a published writer. The first turned out to be the easiest! I married at nineteen and by the age of twenty-six, I had five children. Back then, I had no time or money for college, and the only thing I wrote was the grocery list! I didn't mind because I knew I would have time for my other dreams when the kids grew up.

When my youngest daughter was nine months old, I began having serious health problems. For six weeks I went blind. I was sent to a Columbus hospital, and after two weeks of tests, I was diagnosed with multiple sclerosis. A short time later, I experienced additional complications and was told by my doctor that I would probably die. I prayed that I would live long enough for my children to remember me and know how much I loved them. I was so frightened. Encouraged by a former teacher, I wrote a book. In my own words I told my kids how very much I love them, just in case I died before they had a chance to learn for themselves. My book was the beginning of my second dream.

About ten years ago, when I was hospitalized for my

MS, my neurologist discovered something that he called *funny* in one of my blood tests. *Funny* turned out to be lupus. I knew little about the disease, but I figured it was rather serious because my doctor, who is also a friend, cried as he said he hated to "hit me with another rotten illness." Looking back, I guess maybe my ignorance helped me to accept it.

As my kids were growing up, I was hospitalized about seventy times for ten days of IV's. Somehow my husband, friends, God and I held the family together. I had some terribly rough times, and yet some very special times where, because of my illness, our family became stronger.

The kids grew up and eventually left home. All five married in two years. Suddenly, in spite of my illness, my dreams of going to college and writing rekindled. I was determined that nothing would stand in the way of finally fulfilling my dreams. I enrolled at Terra Community College in Fremont, Ohio, and set my goals to get an individualized Associate of Arts degree in writing, psychology and computers. Because my hands had become extremely numb, my teachers worked with me to do things that were difficult. Again, for a brief time, my world seemed so perfect! I had waited all my life for the opportunity.

In my first college writing class, my teacher would return my papers with little notes, saying, "This is great!" or "Beautiful, keep writing!" Just for fun, I submitted one of my papers that I had written about being blind to two different magazines, and both wanted to publish it. During that class, I had nine of my homework assignments published.

Then at the end of 1993, all hell broke loose. In one week's time both my parents were diagnosed with Alzheimer's, my grandmother died, my sister had a major heart attack, my aunt died and a cousin burned to death in a fire. Looking back I don't know how I made it through all this.

Perhaps agitated by the other problems, by the end of the next quarter, my own health once again started to cause trouble. I tried to ignore it, but finally my doctor insisted I begin a series of thirty daily shots. I knew from experience that the shots would cause me to be very sick, and toward the end of the thirty days, I would have to miss college. I was devastated. I confided in my instructor, who told me it was "okay" to miss class, that he would help me in any way. He stressed that my health was the most important thing. My emotions were mixed. I was deeply touched by his understanding and kindness, yet I was upset he could possibly think that anything was more important than going to college after waiting a lifetime.

A few months later, I started having different symptoms. I tried with little luck to push it out of my mind, hoping the pain would disappear. When it didn't, I finally went to my doctor who confirmed my lupus was out of remission. X-rays showed my spine was disintegrating, and although my doctor didn't say directly, "You are dying," on some days that seemed like a good idea! The forty-four steps to the third-floor classrooms, where most of my classes were, had become a challenge. They always left me short of breath and often caused much pain. I knew there was an elevator, but as long as I was able, I would climb slowly and thank God at the top that I had made it!

With the help of my college teachers, the support of my beautiful family and friends, I finished taking my classes one-on-one with an instructor. In 1996, I graduated *summa cum laude,* and got my long-waited-for degree in creative writing. I was so excited.

Shortly after graduation, the college opened up a

writing lab where students needing help on any writing assignment could get help with their papers. When I was asked to be one of the tutors, I was ecstatic. I could be where I loved to be, with people I love and do what I love to do most: write.

As my lupus progressed, I once again felt my heart bursting with emotions that wanted out. I loved life and so many people so deeply, and I wanted to find a way to let a part of this love live on even after I am gone. I started writing a romance novel, based somewhat on my reality of living with lupus. (My lupus specialist edited the medical material for me.) After eight months of hard work, editing and changing, learning about agents and publishers, my novel *Stolen Moments* was published in March 1999.

Life has been very good to me. I know, when I wake up each morning, the pain will be there. I have been so blessed in life that it seems selfish to ask for more, but yet each night before I retire, I ask God to let me see just one more sunrise. I so want to take just one more class, write one more book, get just one more kiss from each of my little grandchildren. My body is aching to take just one more walk in the woods in the spring, to witness the entire world as it wakes up from the winter. In spite of my illness, or perhaps even because of it, I have fulfilled ever so many dreams, and I am always hoping for just one more. . . .

Barbara Jeanne Fisher

The Professor and Me

Let me glimpse the face of truth. Tell me what the face of truth looks like.

Jack London

I was born a writer. I understand that some writers are made, but I was quick on the uptake. I knew what I wanted to be.

My mother was quite ill during my childhood. Having two brothers and a sister all younger than myself, I entertained them by telling stories since my father refused to buy an "idiot box," i.e., television. I didn't write my stories down since this was pre-kindergarten and early learning-to-read-years, but by the time I was six, I used to grab the Sunday *Chicago Tribune* and shoot to the comics. Brenda Starr was the most intelligent woman I could imagine. Her journalism took her to foreign countries, paid her enough to afford a fabulous hairstylist and equally incredible lingerie, and her boyfriend, Basil St. John, was always stuck in some jungle leaving her free to pursue her career. How good was that?

By the time I reached college I'd had a lifetime of parents, family and teachers supporting my dream of becoming a journalist. I was bright-eyed, swallowing my education without chewing and naïve as any seventeen-year-old could be. I should have seen it coming, but I didn't.

On the recommendation of the head of the English department, I was chosen to participate in a creative-writing seminar intended for second-semester seniors headed by a travelling Harvard professor who would be on campus for six months. I was the only freshman in the group.

After a month of lectures and small assignments, we were instructed to write our first short story. The stories would be read aloud and then critiqued by the rest of the class. I had no clue I was the Christian. They were the lions.

The night before I was to read, the professor telephoned me to come to his office "for a chat."

This quintessential professor, well over six foot six, tweed jacket with leather patches on the elbows, horn-rimmed glasses and booming voice, commanded me to enter and sit down. My behind hadn't hit the chair before he slammed my folder containing my short story down on the desk with such force that it skidded across and landed in my lap.

"Frankly, Miss Lanigan, your writing stinks."

Shock kept me from bursting into tears. I saved that for later. "What's wrong with it?" I asked, my dry lips sticking to my teeth.

"You have absolutely no idea about plot structure or characterization. How you were ever recommended for this class is beyond me. You have no business being here. One thing's for sure, you'll never earn a dime as a writer."

"There's not anything redemptive?"

"I'll give you that your description is nice," he said dismissively.

Nice? I felt like Catherine in *Washington Square* at the part where her father has just paid off her lover, and she hears the carriage wheels on the cobblestones and her father says, "Don't worry, Catherine, at least your embroidery is nice."

Visions of Brenda Starr's overly stamped passport faded fast. I'd never considered other options in my life. I'd only had one dream. It was a mission. It was my life. Wringing my hands, I fought tears (badly) and asked, "What will I do?"

"I don't know. But," he said raising his forefinger triumphantly in the air, "you are a fortunate young woman, because I have caught you at the crossroads of your life. Your parents are spending a lot of money on your education. You wouldn't want to waste that money and your time on something to which you're not suited?"

"No."

"I suggest you change your major. Get out of journalism."

"And do what?" I was aghast at the thought.

"You could be a nurse."

Comebacks have always eluded me. I didn't even know I was doing it at the time, but I looked him in the eye and said, "Jeez, I could be a teacher."

It went over his head.

"Miss Lanigan, I'm mindful of the fact that you have declared your bid for *summa cum laude*. To do that you can't take anything less than a B in this class. [And I'd have had to have straight A's throughout the rest of my courses.] You can't even do that without a great deal of assistance . . . from me. So, I'll make a bargain with you. I'll be your crutches. I will get you through my class and give you a B if you promise never to write anything ever again."

In my mind's eye, Brenda Starr was gone. All I saw was a gaping black tunnel as my future. I felt dead inside. Being a devoted Catholic, I was taught to revere authority under any and all circumstances. Including logic.

I didn't know I was looking into the face of the devil, but I was. I knew he was asking for my soul, but I was very inexperienced in devil-deals. I wanted my writing. I wanted that *summa cum laude.*

"Okay," I said weakly.

I took my short story with me and went back to my dorm, grabbed a metal trash can, matches and went to the roof. It was night. I burned my story and as the ashes spiraled up, I promised God that I would never believe in childish dreams again. I would be smart. I would use logic. If I couldn't see it, taste it, chew it and spit it out, I wouldn't believe in anything again.

For fourteen years I didn't write. Instead, I read everything I could get my hands on. If I couldn't write it myself, I'd read what others had the talent and courage to do.

The summer of 1979, I was in San Antonio with my family the weekend after Judge Woods had been assassinated by the Hell's Angels. Every journalist, television producer and film crew was in town. Sitting under an umbrella table around the pool was a group of writers, and I did something I'd never had the assertiveness to do. I went up to them and said, "I just want you to know that I think what you do is the most important work in the world. Searching for truth. I always wanted to be a writer," I gushed.

One of the writers, cigar in his mouth, looked at me and said, "If you wanted to be a writer, you'd be writing."

"Oh, that's okay. I have it on good authority that I have no talent as a writer."

"Who told you that?" he asked.

I related my tale about the professor. Finally, he said, "Why, I'm ashamed of you. You haven't even tried. Here's my card. If you ever write anything, give me a call."

I'm ashamed of you.

Of all my mother's key guilt-layering phrases, that was the one that spurred me into action. When I went home, I bought a stack of looseleaf lined paper, a pack of pens and started writing a novel about World War I. Since I didn't own a typewriter, I borrowed one from a friend, typed up the four hundred pages I had and sent them to the writer. He called me a month later and said, "I read your manuscript and it was good. I sent it to my agent, and she's going to call you in half an hour."

Thirty minutes later, Kathy Robbins called me from New York and said, "Catherine, you are startlingly talented."

Shock prevailed for the second time in my life. She asked me questions of whether I saw the book as a "softcover" or "hard-cover." Maybe we should go "trade." Industry terms came rattling at me like gunfire. Finally, I stopped her and asked, "Does this mean you liked it?"

"Yes! I want to sign you with my agency today. I'll send the contracts out. I think I can sell this by Christmas."

She did. In fact, she had two publishing companies bidding for that book. September 1999, marked twenty years and twenty novels I've published, including *Romancing the Stone, Jewel of the Nile* and *Wings of Destiny.*

I met a psychologist one time at the place where I worked days while getting my writing career to more financially stable ground, who explained to me about the professor. "Don't you see what happened? His response was violent and angry. To coerce you into a bargain like that means that he was jealous. He saw something he didn't have. He saw talent."

I don't know about that, but I learned that writers make something out of nothing. We make dreams into reality. That's our nature, our mission. We were born to it.

I will never give up my dream again. Never.

Catherine Lanigan

You're a Loser, Cunningham

And it does no harm to repeat, as often as you can, "Without me the literary industry would not exist; the publishers, the agents, the sub-agents, the sub-sub-agents, the accountants, the libel lawyers, the department of literature, the professors, the theses, the book of criticism, the reviewers, the book pages—all this vast and proliferating edifice is because of this small, patronized, put down, and underpaid person."

Doris Lessing

I hadn't thought much about writing until my senior year in high school. Then a teacher gave us an essay test about a certain historical incident. She said to write two pages about it. I wasn't too sure what had happened or why, but I started writing. I put down everything I could remember about it, and everything the teacher had told us.

I had three pages when done, but I was still not sure I had the facts right. When the papers came back, I received an A grade. I decided writing was fun and that I was good at it.

The next year, I went to college at a small school, Pacific University in Forest Grove, Oregon, and signed up as a journalism major. There were only twenty of us in the whole department. The journalism professor, Professor Rowe, called me in after class one day and said he wasn't sure that I'd be able to make the grade in journalism. I had failed the entrance exam on English and was put in the "bonehead" English class. That made me a loser.

I told him I really wanted to be a writer and that I'd study hard on English grammar and sentence structure and spelling. He said I was a "provisional" major until I proved I could do the work.

I was devastated. Big guys don't cry. Hey, I was nineteen. Instead, I promised myself I'd work three times as hard as anyone else and prove to Professor Rowe that I could be a journalist. A few months before, I'd read a writer's magazine and decided doing feature articles for newspapers and magazines would be a good place to start selling what I wrote.

It was only two weeks after my talk with Professor Rowe that my article came out in the magazine section of the *Portland Oregon Journal,* "Willow Witt, Willow Weaver." It was about a local man who wove willow branches into clothes baskets. He'd learned to do it in Russia. I showed the article to Professor Rowe who nodded and said that one article didn't make a journalist. By the end of the school year, I'd had three more articles published—one in a national trade journal—and Professor Rowe grudgingly accepted me as a journalism major.

When I graduated with my journalism degree, I went to work on a small paper in central Oregon. My first real newspaper job. The editor hired me before he realized that I didn't have a car. In a small town, a car was a must for a reporter. I did the best I could on a second-hand bicycle.

Then I was drafted into the army. I tried to get into the Public Information Office, where I could use my journalism skills, but they never let me transfer. So I wrote a series of twenty-five feature stories about my life in the army, then about army time in Japan and finally about the days of war and combat in Korea. My hometown paper in Forest Grove, Oregon, published the series once a week with my picture and byline. Yes! Another small step to becoming a journalist.

After my army stint, I went back to newspapering, then into writing audio-visual training and motivational slide shows and motion pictures in Detroit. But I wanted to write novels. I had my Korean war novel almost done. It was episodic, a little like *South Pacific,* but not that good. Twelve times I sent the manuscript out, and twelve times it came home to roost.

By that time there were four mouths to feed at the Cunningham ranch, and I had to keep my day job. No such thing as the luxury of taking off a year to write my great American novel. Fiction, short stories and novels were my dream. I wrote another novel I couldn't sell and more short stories. We formed a fiction writing group in Detroit, where I worked, but that didn't help me sell my novel.

At last I decided I had to specialize. I'd try Western novels. They weren't as long, and somebody told me they paid the least of the novel genres so there shouldn't be so much competition.

Something kept driving me on. "You can do it, you can do it," I kept telling myself. I remembered Professor Rowe who had groaned when he looked at my English exam score and labeled me as a loser and only a "provisional" major. I had to become a selling novelist.

I went to used bookstores and bought twenty-five different Western novels. I sat down and read them all.

During reading I wrote down on 3 x 5 cards words and phrases common to the era and the cowboy business. I put down all I could find out about old Western guns and gunplay. By the time I finished reading the twenty-five books, I had a hundred 3 x 5 cards with Western words and phrases on them. Most gave explanations and details.

After I read each Western, I wrote out a one-page summary of the plot line, the characters and any theme.

Gradually, I learned what a plot was, how characters interacted and how a story could be plot-driven or character-driven. Slowly I learned, but I did learn.

I forgot about *Combat Boots and Japanese Slippers* and the other novels I'd tried to write. I locked them in a drawer and started fresh.

I drew heavily from the novels I'd read for plot ideas and characters. I came up with a plot for my first Western novel and wrote it. The first place I sent it bought it for the amazing sum of three hundred dollars. That was in 1968. It sold to Thomas Bouergy & Co. of New York. They published books for rental libraries.

I'll never forget that day when the finished book came in the mail. I opened the envelope with nervous fingers and then turned over the brown plastic-covered book. *Bushwhacker on the Circle K.* There it was, my first published novel. I could hardly put it down. My first novel! All the years of yearning and wishing and studying and training and then working at writing had finally paid off. I read the first paragraph of *my book!* The editor had not changed a single word. I was euphoric.

The editor had told me sometime before to send her another idea, which I did, and I was off on writing my *second* novel, which was a sure sale.

I saw all sorts of Western-series novels on the stands. In this type of novel, there is a main character who is the hero in each book. I wanted to do a series like that, so I spent weeks creating my character, fleshing him out, making him real. He'd be a Secret Service agent, working for the government and taking on assignments all over the West. I wrote the book and sent it out.

I'll never forget the letter I got back from the Pinnacle Books editor. "While this is not the best Western I've ever read, we have decided to publish it." That was in 1972, and I received half the advance on signing the contract, and the other half when the book was published.

So I was over one more hurdle. I'd made it into the paperback field, where volume and speed of writing were important. I wrote five more Westerns about Jim Steel in his gold series, and all were published by Pinnacle.

Somewhere along the line I was tagged as a "fast" writer. An editor called me one day and said he had a "hole." A writer was supposed to deliver a long-overdue book. He didn't. The editor needed the manuscript to go into production in seven days. I wrote the Western novel in five and overnighted it to New York. It was 160 type-written pages. Glories of the computer!

Looking back, I'm not sure if I ever would have become a writer if it hadn't been for that professor who said I probably couldn't make the grade, and he doubted if I'd ever get out of the "provisional" category. I made it out.

By now I've written and had published 286 books, mostly fiction, but twelve non-fiction books as well. Motivation? Yes, that "provisional" tag still bugs me. But I realize that I had used that tag to help me make my dream of being a novelist come to pass.

I'm going to keep on writing novels until I learn how.

Chet Cunningham

The Obsession

Nothing splendid has been achieved except by those who dared to believe that something inside them was superior to circumstance.

Bruce Barton

An obsession can lead to tragedy or triumph. In my case, it led to a career as the author of two books, credits in regional and national magazines, contributor to a number of Writer's Guides, a weekly column in the *Los Angeles Times*, and an invitation to host a radio show about the publishing business at a National Public Radio station.

I had just launched my freelance writing career after working as a political reporter at a small suburban newspaper. And naturally, my mission was to write and submit publishable articles. I thought of myself as an archer, aiming the arrow with manuscripts which would find their way (without wounding) into the hearts of magazine editors.

And then the obsession took hold. I was determined to be published in *Los Angeles Magazine*, figuring such a credit would really jump-start my career. In addition, I fantasized about becoming their television columnist, which would catapult me into a very glamorous world.

So, beginner that I was, I marched into the office of *Los Angeles Magazine* (without an appointment) and asked most graciously to see the editor! The receptionist said, "Nothing doing!" Well, she smiled.

Obsession, obsession. I returned a week later. "May I see the editor or can I make an appointment?" Same response: "We simply can't have the editor meet with every writer who walks in off the street. How would he get any work done?"

Now the obsession really takes hold. I must get in to see that editor. He will melt when he hears my pitch. But how, how? The wonderful, kooky idea takes form. I'll make my friends buy subscriptions to the magazine.

I choose the supermarket as the locale (sooner or later, everyone goes to the market) and as each pal or acquaintance stops to study her grocery list, I approach. "Would you be interested in subscribing to *Los Angeles Magazine* and investing in my career as a freelance writer?" Two consecutive days at the market results in my gathering twenty-five checks made out to the magazine.

I am now armed. I have my newspaper clips in a folder and once again march into the magazine offices. "You again," sighs the receptionist. Ah, but I have a calling card. I explain that I am delivering twenty-five new subscribers and trust that the editor might be willing to see me under the circumstances. The receptionist walks back into the hallowed inner sanctum where the man who can buy words sits and I hear a booming laugh. He'll see me! He's curious enough to want to meet this obsessed writer who goes to such lengths to get an interview. Here's where persistence, preparation and luck intersect.

As I dump the twenty-five checks and a typed list of subscriber addresses on his desk, the amazed and amused editor says, "Just what do you want to do for us?" He waves away my television column suggestion, looks at my newspaper bylines (which are about political campaigns) and says, "We assigned a political story to a writer who can't deliver. We need the article in ten days. If you can get an outline to us by Monday [it's now Friday], you have yourself an assignment."

There's a presidential primary in progress and political headquarters are open all weekend. I know who to contact. Armed with camera and notepad, I'm off and running. I gather information all day and write Saturday and Sunday night. By Monday morning, I'm numb, nervous, worried. Everything is riding on whether I've done a good job. My husband offers to deliver the outline. And I pace at home all day. Finally, at 5 P.M. the editor calls. It's a go!

So the obsession paid off. I had cracked the pages of *Los Angeles Magazine* with a photo feature, and realized very early in my career, that creative marketing and persistence are as important as writing talent.

Frances Halpern

Sometimes Secret Writers

When I write stories I am like someone who is in her own country, walking along streets that she has known since she was a child, between walls and trees that are hers.

Natalia Ginsburg

In grade school, they tried to teach me to diagram sentences. I tried to figure out why you'd want to break up words that way. I never did learn to do it. I heard language flowing in my head, loved the way words made images, how they stirred up thoughts and feelings. Writing was magic. Reading was magic. Diagramming wasn't.

Mrs. Hauk flunked me in English and said I'd never be a good student. She told me that in front of the whole class. Meanwhile I was writing my first novel. I wrote at night, under the covers with a flashlight. Everyone knew I was bad at English, so I had to write in secret. Sounds silly, but that was how my young mind put things together back then.

I read Jack London. I read John Steinbeck. I read William Faulkner. And I continued writing, secretly.

They passed me through high school, mostly to please my mother. She was a teacher. Everyone said I was a *bad* student.

After high school, I got a job in the construction trades. I liked working outside, away from stuffy classrooms. Six years after high school, I took a creative writing class at a community college. People liked my poetry, and I got some of it published. My writing teacher, Mr. Hill, urged me to go to college full-time and get a degree.

After considerable badgering from Mr. Hill, I agreed to take the college entrance exams. I flunked the grammar test and got put in bone-head English. Mr. Lautner's first assignment was a big challenge. He told us to write on our favorite subject and turn it in the following week.

I asked how long it should be.

"As long as it takes to exhaust the subject," he answered.

I wandered back to the coffee shop, dejected. Here was yet more proof that I was not college material. The assignment was way over my head. My favorite subject was the writer William Faulkner. I read all his novels. How would I ever exhaust this subject by the following week?

I had to try. I called in sick at my job and got out my books. The next week, I handed in my paper, neatly typed. Thirty-five pages, not including footnotes and bibliography. Title: "The Theme of Nature's Power in Three Novels by William Faulkner."

The following week Mr. Lautner returned our papers. Mine had a word I didn't know scrawled at the top: "Plagiarism!" It also had a big F made by a marking pen. My classmates all had two- or three-page papers with A's and B's at the top. This college stuff was going to be even tougher than I thought!

I went to Mr. Lautner and asked him what plagiarism meant. He told me it meant I had copied the whole thing. I swore I hadn't. After considerable begging, he told me to come to his office in two days and write a similar essay. On the appointed date, I wrote while he corrected papers and talked to his friends on the phone.

After awhile he asked to see what I'd written. He started reading. He tipped back his chair and swung his feet up on his desk. He nodded.

"This is good," he said. "Damn good! How long have you been writing like this?"

"Since the sixth or seventh grade, I guess."

"Let's go have a beer," he said. "I'll buy."

We went down to the local pub and shared a pitcher of brew. He wanted to know why I'd been assigned to bone-head English.

"I flunked the grammar test," I said.

"You know, except for some comma splices and mis-spellings, your writing is excellent." He fell silent. I waited expectantly.

"What bothers me," he continued, "is that I wrote my master's thesis on Faulkner's novels. Only, your bone-head English paper was better than my thesis." He laughed and shook his head.

That's the day I thought maybe I was a writer, in spite of what Mrs. Hauk told me back in the sixth grade. Why I believed her all those years, I will never understand, but I think a lot of kids' minds work that way. We get hurt and embarrassed by our early failures and forget to go back and take a second look at what we're feeling. We get disconnected from who we really are and what we can do.

John Lautner and I kept in touch for several years, but I finally lost track of him. I'd like him to know what he did for me that day. He'd be happy to know I became a writer. Sometimes it's nice to imagine that he read one or two of the twenty-plus books I've had published over the years. And maybe he even likes what I've had to say!

Hal Zina Bennett

How to Write Your Way
Through College

Twenty-five years ago, at the midpoint of my thirties, I decided I would like to go to college. The idea was startling to a number of people who assumed that I had already been there. I was a professional writer, wasn't I? Didn't that mean that I was educated?

It was startling to my husband, who had accepted the financial challenge of educating five children but had never considered the possibility of having to add a wife to the list. Where was the money going to come from, especially since my own contribution to the family income would be reduced by time spent in classes and studying?

The answer to the first question was easy. A writer isn't necessarily a college graduate any more than a college graduate is necessarily a writer. A tremendous number of writers, myself included, are too excited about being out of high school and free at last to spend their golden hours putting words on paper to want to devote another four years to formal education. It's part of the eagerness of youth, I guess, but after a couple more decades of living, it begins to become evident that there is a lot of interesting activity going on behind those ivy-covered (or, in my case, "adobe-covered") walls. At a certain point in life, philosophy, psychology, history and literature can sound pretty exciting. But "Where is the money coming from?" was a more difficult question. I pondered a long time over that one before I came up with an answer. When I found one at last, it was deceptively simple: "I'll sell the things I learn."

"I'll believe that when I see it," my husband said.

So we made a deal—I would enroll part-time at the University of New Mexico, but if I could not put myself through college by marketing the knowledge gained from my classes, I would drop out.

Happily, that didn't happen.

Luck was with me when I minored in psychology. I chose it because I thought it would be interesting, but the way it turned out, I had tumbled into a gold mine. Take a look at the women's magazines and what do you see there? A million *how-to* articles on such subjects as how to make marriage work, be a good friend, raise your children, handle aging parents, deal with emotional crises, break bad habits and get along with the in-laws. Few of these are written by specialists. Most are turned out by ordinary people who have read some textbooks and presented the subject matter in terms the average reader can relate to.

I made my first major sale during Psychology 101, where we were training rats to run through mazes. The rats did what we wanted more willingly and were happier, better-natured animals when given rewards for running than when punished for not running. During the course, we learned to transfer this principle to dealing with human beings, and I wrote an article called, "Our Son Was Uncontrollable," to show how these techniques could be applied to one's own children. The article sold to the "My Problem and How I Solved It" column at *Good Housekeeping* for enough money to cover a full semester's tuition.

With this success to bolster me, I signed up for a class on psychology of education, which provided me with material for "Those IQ Scores—What Do They Really Mean?" for *The Woman*. Other articles followed: For example, "What Ever Happened to Childhood?" (the psychological problems that confront adults who have not spent the necessary time in various phases of childhood); "Second Marriage—Ready or Not?" (the importance of an adjustment period after an emotional crisis); and "The Togetherness Myth" (the need for people to have freedom to develop their own identities). All those articles were based upon things learned through lectures, and in them I quoted our speakers, all authorities in their fields. Although I, myself, could not tack Ph.D. onto my own name, the articles were liberally sprinkled with the opinions of those who could.

The second most lucrative classes were journalism courses, especially those in news photography. Starting as a novice with a borrowed camera, I was soon able to illustrate my own articles and hugely increase their sales potential. My first photo series was taken for *Black Belt Magazine* to illustrate an article about a class of blind karate students. One of these students was a pretty teenage girl, so I wrote an article about her, slanted toward a youthful audience. That story and accompanying photographs sold to *American Girl* and, subsequently, to two textbook publishers. During the course of my college career, using a university dark room, I sold more than 150 photographs to periodicals and a book of children's poems, illustrated by photographs, to a religious publishing house.

English classes also proved fruitful. A poetry-writing class at sophomore level brought sales to numerous magazines, including *Guideposts* and *Woman's Day*. A literature class on American writers introduced me to the works of Poe and inspired me to try my hand at a Gothic novel.

With Poe's *The Fall of the House of Usher,* for inspiration, I wrote a book—*Down a Dark Hall*—which, amazingly, is still in print today. A class in Greek mythology led me into an attempt to rewrite some of the beautiful myths at an easy-read level and resulted in sales to the Encyclopedia Britannica Educational Corporation.

For a Shakespeare class, I utilized information from a psychology class to write a term paper modeled after the "Can This Marriage Be Saved?" articles in *Ladies' Home Journal.* I wrote the three sections from the conflicting viewpoints of Othello, Desdemona and their (fictional) marriage counselor, who sent a protesting Othello off to a neurologist to be tested for epilepsy. Although I was chagrined to receive a C minus grade, I submitted the article to *Ladies' Home Journal* with the suggestion that they might want to consider it for April Fools Day. They declined, but the editors were so impressed by the fact that I'd captured the style of those pieces that they began to give me assignments to conduct real life interviews for that popular series.

Of course, there have been many courses that have not been directly profitable in the financial sense. None of those was time-wasted as far as my career went. A study of literature exposed me to the work of writers whose abilities so surpass mine that I set new goals of excellence to strive for in my own work. Classes in philosophy have deepened my thinking and helped me to enrich my characterization. History courses provided me with background for future novels.

On the day of my graduation, I sat down at the typewriter (no computers back then) and triumphantly pecked out an essay called "A Graduate in the Family." Six months later, that personal experience piece appeared in *Good Housekeeping,* illustrated by a picture of my middle-aged self, in cap and gown, exuberantly waving a diploma.

My husband snapped that photo.

We both got paid.

All in all, attending college proved quite profitable for me. My writing income, instead of decreasing as my husband originally feared, actually tripled immediately, and, in the years since then, has gone far beyond that.

Lois Duncan

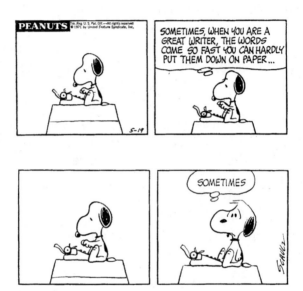

A New Yardstick

*T*alent is long patience.

Gustave Flaubert

I was riding high before the accident. I had two books in print—one with editions on four continents. I'd just signed a contract with a major publisher for my third book and received the first half of a good advance. I gave speeches all over the U.S., and I had a booming practice as a psychotherapist.

Then, on December 30, 1994, it all changed. While walking down a corridor in a small airport in upstate New York, I rounded a blind corner and was knocked unconscious by a metal flight information monitor hanging from the ceiling. The impact of the blow threw me backwards, and my head hit the concrete floor.

After a paramedic examined me at the airport, the doctor in the nearby urgent care facility diagnosed me with a concussion. That night I felt awful—dazed, confused, exhausted—my head throbbing.

I awoke the next day with a severe headache, still feeling dazed. But I had work to do, so I returned to the airport for a flight back to California. I still felt terrible when I got home, but my doctor, and later a neurologist, said that the symptoms would probably pass. So I forced myself to keep going, though all I wanted to do was sleep.

I gave a few speeches, finding myself strangely lethargic as I spoke. I didn't want to talk with people before and after the speech. I began seeing fewer counseling clients. Even worse, I couldn't get organized on the book I was under contract to write. I'd already done most of the research, and had traveled to China to conduct interviews, but now I couldn't bring the information together and make sense of it all. Finally, I asked a colleague to co-author the book with me. Our collaboration failed when my editor rejected the book.

My problems continued—daily headaches, exhaustion, poor concentration, minimal motivation and mediocre memory. What was going on? I'd gotten knocked on the head, but certainly there wasn't anything wrong with my brain. I had a picture in my mind of what someone with a brain injury was like—poor speech, strange physical mannerisms and a very slow mind. That wasn't me!

Yet when doctors finally gave me a neuropsychological test and an imaging test, both showed brain damage. They called it Mild Traumatic Brain Injury. And they said that a head injury I'd had many years before had made my brain more vulnerable to the second assault, even though I hadn't noticed problems after the first accident.

Even then I thought the problems would clear up. But three and a half years after the airport accident, my counseling practice was down to five or six clients a week. I hadn't given a speech in years, and I couldn't write anything longer than a letter. I began thinking seriously of suicide.

Finally, I enrolled in an outpatient rehabilitation program for brain injury. The program was intensive, fast-paced, and fortunately, covered by a grant from the state. I went to groups with other brain injury survivors, had individual sessions with various therapists and counseled with a neuropsychologist.

Though I felt overwhelmed by the pressure of the program, I began making progress. When the other patients talked about their problems—unexplainable rages, confusion, lethargy, and disorganization—I recognized myself. And most of them had also been "achievers" before their accidents.

The therapists helped me begin retraining my brain. Using a special planner we called a "Brain Book," I learned to meticulously plan each day. We created index cards with tasks written on them to keep me on track and set a timer to monitor the minutes. I even used a tiny tape recorder so I could remind myself of important things. Unfortunately, I kept losing the recorder.

After a lot of hard work and more than a little despair, the new strategies began to help. I could actually get places on time, something I hadn't done since the accident. But could I still write?

Two months into the rehab program, I saw a flier about an upcoming speech by Dr. Claudia Osborne, a physician who had suffered a severe brain injury. I had read Dr. Osborne's fine book, *Over My Head,* and wondered if she had written it herself. What an inspiration that would be.

When the day of the speech arrived, I got to the hall early and took a seat in the second row. Dr. Osborne looked normal and spoke more eloquently than many people without brain injuries. But I knew that she had spent two years in rehabilitation after her accident.

As I listened, tears began running down my face. Dr. Osborne gave me hope. She talked about "compensatory strategies"—the kinds of things that I was already using—planners, timers, scheduling, detailed planning and memory aids. And she stressed that these aids required dedication. "Practice, practice, practice," she said.

Dr. Osborne also talked about "using a different yard-stick." In her busy life as a practicing physician and professor before the head injury, she often accomplished more in one morning than she did in a typical week after the brain injury. Rather than using that as an excuse to feel bad about herself, she now applied a different yardstick and realized that smaller accomplishments were now cause for bigger celebrations.

After the speech I was the first in line to have Dr. Osborne sign my copy of her book. I had only one question for her. "Did you write it yourself?" I asked.

"Yes," she replied, looking up at me. "I had a lot of help with editing, and it took me seven years, but I wrote it myself."

Inspired, I began brainstorming about a writing project. Considering the reduced power of my brain, it was less a brainstorm and more of a "light drizzle," but I knew that I wanted to write again.

As I thought about the task ahead, the voice of the neuropsychologist at the rehab echoed in my head. "Break down the steps you must take to get to your goal. Write down each small step, and how long you think it will take. If the step will take longer than thirty minutes, make it a separate goal, with its own steps."

I realized that the small steps should apply to the size of the project too. I'd been struggling to get going on a book project. A story might be a better way to start. I'd recently been invited to submit a story for *Chicken Soup for the Writer's Soul*. That thought scared me. But I remembered the comment of a former client when she learned of my head injury. "Now you'll have to write with your heart, rather than your head." My head was foggy, but I knew that my heart was getting stronger. I decided to write a story about learning to write again. That night, after my kids went to bed, I planned the following day in my Brain Book. I'd have half an hour alone before my son's basketball game, so I wrote a reminder to pack a pen and paper.

The next morning, I stayed in the car while the rest of the family went into the gym early. Grabbing my pad, I outlined the story, using a "mind-map"—a circle with the topics I'd cover branching off it. Later that morning, I began planning my timeline for completing the story. I used the guidelines the neuropsychologist had suggested—and they worked. By afternoon I had a detailed timeline and a sense of accomplishment I hadn't felt in years.

Next came the outline. I thought it would take half an hour, but after thirty minutes, I was exhausted and had to rest. Later that day, I worked on it for another half-hour, rested, then finished the outline the next day.

Because of the detailed outline and timeline, the actual writing went well. Still, I had to rest more often than I had planned. And when I stopped scheduling the writing time in my Brain Book, two weeks went by with no progress.

I want to write, I told myself. *Yet I've been putting everything else first.* I wrote "Write *first*," and put it on a Post-it note in my Brain Book. Back on track, I completed the rough draft. It had taken me a lot longer and wasn't as polished as before my accident, but I learned I could still write. At that moment, joy, excitement and hope washed over me. I knew I was going to make it.

Finally, two and a half months after the speech that had inspired me, I finished editing and polishing my story, *this* story. Rereading the manuscript, I remembered Dr. Osborne's words about using a new yardstick, the importance of practice and honoring what we *can* do.

This is only one small story. Yet my new yardstick tells me it's time to celebrate. In spite of the long, bumpy road, I am riding high again.

Erik Olesen

Writing Is My Destiny

When you speak, your words echo only across the room or down the hall. But when you write, your words echo down the ages.

Bud Gardner

I didn't start out to be a professional writer. Somehow the gratifying concept of words echoing down the ages had previously escaped me. Besides, everybody knows that for a novice to break into the hallowed field of publishing is—of course—impossible.

So attempting to transform myself into a published author wasn't the lure that drew me back to college like an invisible silken thread. Delving into psychology was my desire, and with three children in their middle-to-late teenage years, I could finally afford the luxury of quality time for myself.

I wandered into my writing class without the foggiest notion of the miracle about to take place in my life, or how desperately I would need that miracle fifteen years later. My only concern at the time was the free hour, sandwiched in between important psychology classes, sixty precious minutes five times a week that I didn't plan to waste. I enjoyed writing. Putting words on paper was an easy way to pick up three credits. This course would be a snap.

Then Bud Gardner's first pronouncement to the class caught me by surprise: "If you pursue writing as a career, you'll discover that it's the hardest, most demanding job you'll ever tackle." I almost laughed out loud. Hard? Obviously I would never publish (didn't plan to try), but the act of writing, itself, was as easy as falling off a log.

But before long I found—to my horror—that to pass the course and earn those three dangling credits, we were expected to contact real, fire-breathing editors with actual proposals for articles, which was another matter entirely. Scary. We armed ourselves by privately repeating, "I am a published author." We wrote 3 x 5 cards to that effect and attached them to all surfaces our glances might fall on. Did it help? I'm not sure. The first time I called the entertainment editor of a local newspaper and mumbled, "My name is Kris Mackay. I'm a writer," I held my breath and awaited the hysterical laughter my bald-faced lie would surely elicit. Strangely enough, he didn't laugh. He agreed to look at (and later published) my article.

Now with great gusto and unbelievable bravado, I queried *Parade* magazine about a new method of identifying fingerprints by computer. Two weeks later their letter reached me: "You may have a winner here. Send us the piece. On speculation, of course."

I turned hot and then cold. The possibility of thousands, maybe millions of people reading my words made it suddenly difficult to breathe. Smoke poured from my computer as I added to and laboriously fine-tuned the basic article I'd read aloud in the safety of the class. *Parade*'s next letter held a check so hefty I suspected I must be dreaming. Hey, this was getting fun!

Buoyed by success, I attempted a book based on true incidents of great courage, commitment or love in the lives of ordinary people acting in extraordinary fashions. Two publishers were interested. More feverish work—and yes, it is work—and finally my first book graced the shelves of bookstores, winking, I swear, at potential buyers strolling by.

Reader's Digest reprinted one chapter from my book. I remember editor Phil Osborne's letter as if it were etched permanently on my brain. "We have read your suicide prevention story and find it absolutely riveting!" The highlight of my career as an author, bar none, was the day I approached the cash register at a local grocery store, saw stacks of the current *Digest* at each counter and realized that "A Life on the Line," by Kris Mackay, was nestled between its covers. Using every ounce of self-discipline I possessed, I refrained from wrestling the public address phone from the hand of the checker and screaming, "Attention shoppers. My story is in the *Digest!*"

Fifteen years flew by, magical years. Four more books. More interaction with the *Digest.* My "Drama in Real Life" reenacted on TV's *Rescue 911.* Travel with and co-authorship of a book with Barbara Barrington Jones, trainer of beauty queens, including the winners of the Miss USA pageant five years in a row, from 1985 through 1989. Speaking engagements. Hearing almost daily that the courage and heroics of people featured in my books had affected a satisfying number of lives.

Another favorite quote, source unknown, goes like this:

"Deep in your coded instructions, your Creator has placed a very special job that only you can do . . . You are patented and copyrighted in Heaven."

More enthralled with writing every day and loving the idea that my words might be of some benefit to others, I came to feel that I had truly found my niche.

Then my life changed. The events of the past four years are almost too painful to describe: My beloved father died after a lengthy, exhausting illness. Our daughter was diagnosed with breast cancer and endured six months of treatment so aggressive we wondered if the treatment might not be worse than the disease. Then my mother followed my father. As I reeled from blow after blow without time to properly heal, my psyche suffered the cruelest blow of all.

Ed, the handsome, healthy husband I idolized and leaned on, died with no warning at all, with a brain hemorrhage so massive that had he been lying in bed in the operating room at the hospital, nothing could have saved him.

My whole world fell apart. I floundered. Nothing prepared me for such emptiness. Ninety percent of my own person seemed irrevocably gone. Activity of any kind was pointless, but I grudgingly forced myself to follow up on speaking engagements already in the works, fighting my inclination to slam the doors, turn out the lights and sit alone in the dark. Friends and family were amazingly supportive. People reminded me I am lucky to have writing to sustain me, but secretly I doubted I'd ever again pull myself together for that kind of effort.

Three weeks ago, I suddenly began to hear my type of stories. Wonderful stories that stir my sleeping imagination. Every day now some phrase in casual conversation piques my curiosity. Without conscious volition I find myself asking, "How did that happen, exactly?" I feel the first faint stirrings of hope that the miracle wrought by stumbling into Bud's class fifteen years ago will be the instrument to bring me back to life. That writing will allow me to return to what I was "patented and copyrighted" to accomplish.

I'm going to make it, after all.

Kris Mackay

Writing for My Health

Opportunity . . . often it comes in the form of misfortune, or temporary defeat.

Napoleon Hill

When I was growing up as a kid in the Bronx, I was allergic to everything. I didn't have seasonal allergies like most people do who take a pill and get relief. I was allergic to more than two-hundred foods and pollens that plagued me all year long. Sometimes I thought if I had to reach for one more tissue, I'd die from frustration. And, in fact, when I was growing up, I thought I might really die. When I was eight years old, I overheard a doctor telling my parents that if we didn't move to Arizona for my health, I could die. Each week after that I'd mutter, "Anybody packing my suitcases today? Anybody going on a trip?" Nothing. We never moved, and I've been suspicious of my allergies and my parents ever since.

I spent most of my childhood in bed because of my relentless allergies. From my bedroom window, I could look out across the main street called the Grand Concourse and watch other children playing basketball, football and baseball in the park. One of my favorite things to do was play sports, but, unfortunately, because of my allergies, I couldn't play sports that often. I was not altogether that good at sports, but I still loved to play. And even when I did get the chance to play, I often wound up injured from a ball to the head or a bat to the knee. One time I was lying in the street bleeding and my grandmother nervously said, "If I give you a dollar, will you stop bleeding?" That's how routine my ailments had become to my family. They offered me bribes to stop the pain as *if* I wielded that much power over my own body.

When I was sitting in my bedroom watching the other kids play outside (this was before TV), I did the only thing a kid really can do in bed during the day besides read—I wrote. I started writing jokes at first to amuse myself. I would read through my stack of comic books so quickly that I was always in need of new material to make myself laugh. Then I started sharing my jokes with my younger sisters, Ronny and Penny. My mother would often make them sit at my bedside, and I thought the least I could do was repay them for their attendance with a giggle or two.

When I wasn't holding court from my bed, I would dream of some day leaving the Bronx. I knew that in order to leave I would not only need a ticket, but also a profession to carry me on my way. My father once advised me, "Son, find a job you can do with a toothache." I was also known for having bad gums, so this comment was meant philosophically and realistically. When it came time to apply to college, I signed up for the only thing that seemed up my alley—journalism. If I was not meant to play ball, maybe I could become a sportswriter and follow the careers of other athletes with fewer allergies than me.

Some say going to college is meant to be a journey of discovery. If that's true, then I uncovered a very interesting thing about myself: I was on the totally wrong journey. I went to Northwestern University to study journalism and discovered that I was a terrible journalist. I had no patience for facts and details and often wiggled my way out of tight spots by writing jokes. One of my first assignments was to write an obituary. Each student was given a living person and then told he had just died. (I got Danny Kaye.) Then we were instructed to go to the library, do the research and return with an obituary suitable for newspaper publication. Unfortunately, I met a red-haired girl at the library. We started talking, and soon my deadline arrived before I had done any research at all (except on the percentage of red-haired girls with freckles making it into politics). While other students in my class turned in lengthy, well-written obits, mine was merely three sentences long: "It was reported today that actor Danny Kaye died. The rumor was false. He's fine." The teacher was not amused by my humor.

Journalism was all about the accuracy of information, and truthfully I was only interested in the accuracy of comedy. I left Northwestern and, after a short stint in the army in Korea (where I discovered I was also rather allergic to bullets), I moved to New York City and started writing for several nightclub comics. My new career choice was anything but successful at first. One comic hated a joke I had written so much that he lit it on fire with his cigarette lighter and let it float into a trash can. It was my first flaming rejection. But I liked writing for the comics, and I continued to do it despite the high-frustration level and low pay. Eventually, comedian Joey Bishop took me to Hollywood with him to write for his new sitcom. I was finally leaving the Bronx for good, but I had no idea what lay ahead for me out west. My parents gave me hugs, kisses and the names of two good doctors in California before sending me on my way.

I think because I was such a sickly child, I was never thrown by disappointment. That which did not kill me or make me wheeze, inspired me and encouraged me. Whether I had a good day at work or a bad one, at least I was alive and I was a working writer. I put in long hours and advanced to writing for television shows like *I Love Lucy* and *The Dick Van Dyke Show*. I learned from some of the best writers and producers in the business such as Harry Crane, Carl Reiner, Sheldon Leonard and Danny Thomas. Nobody cared whether I was healthy or sick. If I wrote a funny joke, they would laugh just like my sisters had in the Bronx. Only—unlike my sisters—people in Hollywood finally paid me money when I wrote jokes.

And they kept paying me enough money to make a living. I went on to create fourteen television sitcoms, write three produced plays, direct eleven feature movies and publish an autobiography about my career while spending four years playing Murphy Brown's boss as an actor. Whether I was writing, producing or directing, it all boiled down to being able to write and create material that amused people and hopefully brought them joy, too. Two years after moving to Hollywood, I married a nurse, which was a very wise move on my part. Along with being sick, I often developed hypochondria when I *wasn't* sick. So the union between a nurse and a hypochondriac is a match made in heaven. My wife and I have been married for thirty-six years, and we have three grown children and twin granddaughters who, I am proud to say, did not inherit any of my allergies or ailments.

Since moving to Hollywood four decades ago, I have been back to visit the Bronx many times over the years. However, my trips always conjured up painful memories for me as I recalled how ill I had been and how many things I was never able to do from my bed. If Hollywood represented the best I could be as a writer and a person, then the Bronx still symbolized my weaknesses and my vulnerabilities. That was, until 1998, when I went back for a very special occasion.

Each year the Bronx honors several celebrities and public figures who grew up in the borough and went on to have successful careers in different fields. In 1998, I got a letter that I was to be honored along with comedian Red Buttons and actress Rita Moreno, also Bronx natives. My wife and I flew out for the ceremony, and I traveled with the same trepidation that I always had when I returned to my hometown. My head was never filled with images of nostalgia, but rather flashbacks of tissue boxes, medicine bottles and doctors with horse needles longer than my arms.

But this trip back to the Bronx would be different for me. At the event, we were ushered onto a parade float that traveled down the Grand Concourse. Local residents and merchants lined the streets eager to wave and send their good wishes into the air. At one point in the parade, we stopped in front of the Bronx County Courthouse, and I noticed a street sign that carried my name. The city was presenting Red, Rita and me with permanent street signs along the Grand Concourse.

As I looked up at my sign called Garry Marshall Street high above my familiar Grand Concourse, I remembered it was near the same spot where I once lay bleeding in the gutter when my grandmother had offered to give me a dollar to stop. It made me realize how far I had come from the Bronx and for the first time made me appreciate how important my childhood had been. If I had been a typical healthy kid, I would have been too busy playing sports to bother spending time on writing. And I probably wouldn't have tried so hard to build a life for myself outside of the Grand Concourse. I had finally discovered a profession I could do if I was sick in bed, suffering from an allergy attack or a toothache. Writing was the best medicine a doctor ever could have prescribed for me. It not only brought me great happiness, it also improved my health.

Garry K. Marshall

8

A WRITER'S LIFE

*W*riting is easy; all you do is sit staring at a
blank sheet of paper until little drops of
blood form on your forehead.

Gene Fowler

Still Standing

All good writing is swimming under water and holding your breath.

F. Scott Fitzgerald

"Antioxidants!" I said as we walked off the tennis court.

My opponent tossed his racquet onto the grass, and we sat down at the courtside table. "I beg your pardon?"

"I take an antioxidant—a nature health pill—all the rage these days. Works like a charm. It keeps the swelling down in my ankle from an old ski injury."

"The Olympics?"

I smiled. "No, hardly."

He was referring to my long career as a participatory journalist for *Sports Illustrated*—that perhaps I had ventured out onto an Olympic ski slope.

"Did you ever get hurt playing on any of those assignments?" he asked.

"On occasion," I said, enigmatically.

I am often asked how I survived quarterbacking for the Detroit Lions, playing "power" forward for the Boston Celtics, boxing with light-heavyweight champion Archie

Moore, playing goalie for the Boston Bruins, and so on—
without showing some physical evidence of what I have
been through.

"You seem unmarked," my friend said. "You should
affect a limp or something."

"What I have suffered is mostly psychic damage," I
replied. "A bruised ego."

I explained that in each of my athletic confrontations, I
had been humiliated . . . losing 29 yards in five plays as
quarterback, being busted about in the boxing ring, giving
up record-length home runs in Yankee Stadium. The life of
a participatory journalist is not an easy one—the "dark
side of the moon of Walter Mitty," as Ernest Hemingway
described it.

"Surely you got hurt in the ring," he said.

I nodded. Our bout—a three-round exhibition—had
taken place in New York City's Stillman's Gym. I am not
built for the ring—a string bean with a long neck and
spindly legs, and I suffer from "sympathetic response,"
which means that when I'm hit, I weep. Nor do I have a
nose suited for prizefighting. It is long and thin and tapers
to a point, like an anteater's.

After just a few seconds, Archie Moore took one look at
it and bopped it lightly. A flow of blood appeared, along
with some heavy tearing. I think it startled him—to think
just a jab could produce such a result, an opponent both
weeping and bleeding.

"How long did you last?"

"Two-and-a-half rounds," I replied. "My trainer rang the
bell before three minutes were up. He wasn't sure how
Archie intended to finish the exhibition and thought it
best to conclude matters before Moore made up his mind."

"Was your nose all right?"

"For a few days it looked like a red light bulb."

Afterward, I asked Archie how quickly he could have

effected more serious damage, say a small contusion, or worse, an extermination. He was a cultured man. He paused briefly to find an appropriate analogy. "About as long," he finally said, "as it would take you to feel the nip of the guillotine."

"So from boxing we have a bent nose. What else?"

I told him that perhaps the oddest injury I ever sustained was when I performed in the Clyde Beatty-Cole Bros. Circus as an aerialist for the Flying Apollos. I tried for hours to complete a simple maneuver called a "feet across" in which the flyer hops off his platform, swings the length of the circus ring to the arms of the "catcher"— the largest member of the troupe, huge-armed, and wearing a tattoo on one of his biceps (a schooner, as I recall)—and then is released to soar back up to his original perch. In the course of practicing, dark bruises appeared on both of my shoulder blades—deeply colored patches caused, I was told, because my arms were literally being pulled out of their sockets as day after day I dangled from the trapeze bar. My fellow Apollos nicknamed me "The Flying Telephone Pole." I finally performed the feat in a public performance, but I wore the bruises for more than a month afterwards.

"What about hockey?" he asked.

"That was interesting," I said. "Something happened there that I was actually grateful for."

"What was that?"

One of the curious benefits of being damaged, I told him, was that it tends to cement one's relationship with the other players.

The incident occurred during a routine scrimmage with the Boston Bruins. I was in goal, protected by almost thirty pounds of equipment. One of the Bruins took a slap shot toward the right corner of the net. Rather than deflect the puck with my blocking pad, I turned it over and *caught* the puck in my glove—an ill-advised choice since the glove was a lightweight model not unlike a golf glove. The puck zipped in and opened up a jagged L-shaped wound on the end of my little finger. Blood seeped through the glove and dropped in surprising volume onto the ice. The players were delighted. They skated up to take a look. "Not bad," one commented. "Though a tooth would have been better."

From that point on, my relationship with the team improved enormously. I was one of them. I had bled for them—a blood brother.

"I'm almost afraid to ask about football," my friend said. "Surely you got banged up doing that."

I replied that nothing happened that I could remember from playing with the Detroit Lions, but when I played with the Baltimore Colts during the filming of the television special *Plimpton: The Great Quarterback Sneak,* I made the mistake of trying to find out what it would be like to be a running back.

"That wasn't very clever."

I agreed. The second time I carried the ball in a scrimmage, Ray May, the Colts' middle linebacker, picked me up and threw me into the ground rather in the trajectory of hurling a spear. The first point of impact was my right thumb, and my weight bearing down on it drove it back into my hand. I left the practice field for the local hospital. May came up afterwards and apologized. He looked at my thumb. "Hey man, didn't mean to jack you up."

I thought it was an odd and rather nice way of putting it—a garage phrase, as if I were up on a hoist for repairs. The damaged thumb, incidentally, was on my throwing hand, which meant that the arc of my passes getting ready for the "Big Game" resembled those of a shot-putter.

The "Big Game" was against my old team, the Lions. I ran onto the field at Ann Arbor, Michigan, in front of

106,000 puzzled fans to quarterback four plays in a scrimmage before the regular game. While in there, a surprise even to me, I made eighteen yards—fifteen of them on a rushing-the-passer penalty.

My friend laughed.

"Some people still consider basketball a non-contact sport," he said. "What was your experience?"

I told him that at a Boston Celtics basketball camp, I bumped into a rookie during a drill. I have no idea who it was—one would hope for the sake of a good story that it had been one of the Celtic greats like Bill Russell or John Havlicek, but it wasn't. The head butt, which was accidental, opened up a large gash above an eyebrow. No damage to him. For me, another visit to the hospital. I wish I still had concrete evidence of that experience, but alas, it has disappeared. Sometimes, if I scrounge around in my right eyebrow, I can feel a minuscule protrusion. Now I understand why German officers in dueling days were delighted if their cheeks were slashed by a saber cut. Astringents were added to make sure the scar was permanent—the mark of a professional soldier.

"Surely you got through golf okay."

"Blisters, of course, and the ankle bone on my right leg." I explained that I had taken an angry, one-handed swipe at the ground after flubbing a two-iron shot during the Bing Crosby pro-am and missed, hitting myself a crippling blow to the ankle.

"You may think golf is a non-contact sport, too," I said, "but it isn't." I gave him some examples I had come up with researching my book. *The Bogey Man*—players who had cracked themselves in the head with their putter after missing a short putt, or of a gentleman named Moody Weaver who broke both his legs during a practice swing. After my book came out, I got a letter from Weaver's wife saying I had been in error—he had only broken one leg.

Golf, though, did teach me a good lesson, indeed a kind of therapy for getting over the ceaseless humiliations suffered as a participatory journalist. It happened on the first tee of the Dinah Shore pro-am. One of the players in our foursome was a prominent Greenwich, Connecticut, advertising executive. A large crowd had collected, many of them in a wooden stand in front of the clubhouse, and he was obviously agitated as he stepped up to hit his drive. We could even hear him take a deep breath to steady his nerves. It didn't work.

He took a quick, desperate scoop at the ball. The heel of the club just barely ticked the top of the ball, nudging it gently off the tee, whereupon it rolled back against the tee itself. He had made an astounding drive of less than an inch, far more difficult than missing the ball altogether! The large crowd was audibly amused.

There then followed a discussion as to whether the tee could be removed before he hit his second shot. The professional determined that the tee constituted a "loose impediment" and could be removed. The executive bent down and carefully plucked out the tee, lined up his second shot, and promptly hooked his drive into the parking lot. He hung his head, a picture of dejection. But as we walked off the tee, I overheard the professional say to him, "I guarantee, after you get over it, that of all the shots you hit over the years, that little one will be the one you will treasure."

Some years later I ran into the executive at a cocktail party. I couldn't resist. "How many times have you told the story of your one-inch drive?"

He brightened. "About a hundred, at least!" He guided me to a corner. "Let me set the scene. It was the first tee. The ball was a Titleist 2 . . ."

My friend laughed. "So there's always a bright side to humiliation."

"Absolutely."

"What about physical pain?"

"The important thing to remember about pain is that once it's gone, it leaves no residual feeling—that is to say, you can't memorize pain the way you can a song or a poem. You can always say, 'Oh, it was just awful,' but there's no sensation, no actual physical twinge, that accompanies saying such a thing."

My friend asked, "So you're saying you'd go through it again."

"Yes, but this time I'd take along a bottle of antioxidants."

He wanted to know more about them. I told him about my skiing accident (compound fracture of the lower leg) when I was on vacation in the Alps from my studies at Cambridge. Increasingly, it had become a problem over the years.

Invariably, after a strenuous game of tennis or squash or Frisbee, the ankle would swell up, balloon-like, and it was hard to fit a sock over it. I had tried any number of therapeutic measures over the years, including acupuncture. The acupuncturist said I had a problem with my liver.

Then a friend had suggested an antioxidant. He said it would help, and indeed it has. "One of its properties is that it's an antiaging product," I said. "That's why I'm out here, twenty years older than you, giving you a run for your money."

He reached for his racquet. "Ready for another set, George?"

"Absolutely. This time I'm going to take it."

"Don't be so sure," he said. "Even a wonder pill won't help you there."

George Plimpton

A Man Called Charlie Black

He wasn't what you'd call a writer, exactly. He was more a reporter, a man who just wrote what he saw and heard and felt, put it down in simple words. Who, what, when, where. Rarely *why*. Why didn't so much concern him. His readers, moms, dads, wives and kids back in Columbus, Georgia—they knew why. They knew why their husbands, sons, and daddies were over in Vietnam: They were soldiers. Draftees, volunteers, privates, colonels, sergeants—soldiers all. In August of 1965, Lyndon Johnson had ordered them to go, and they went.

The families they left behind were from Illinois, Texas, California, New York and everyplace in between. And most of them stayed in Columbus because that's where they were when their men left to spend a year in Vietnam. They had an insatiable thirst to know how their men were faring. Even many that had gone back home for the year took out a mail subscription to the *Columbus Enquirer*. And Charlie Black told them what their men were doing in Vietnam.

Charlie told them in short sentences typed on a battered portable. Single-spaced, both sides of the page. Usually one of his friends in the Air Cav would put the copy in an envelope with a G.I.'s name for return address and scrawl "Free" on the upper right-hand corner and mail it through the APO back to the *Enquirer*, back to the world, back to where nearly every word Charlie wrote was printed for the families of the men in Vietnam. Charlie had to do things that way, because Charlie didn't have an expense account, to speak of.

He drew his regular salary, something less than a couple of hundred a week—and all that, every last dime after deductions went to his wife. Old Maynard Ashworth, a WW I colonel and the publisher of the *Enquirer*, gave Charlie $500 for expenses and a roundtrip ticket to the war. "Come back when you've spent your expense money, Charlie," he said. "Come back in a couple of weeks and tell us how it was."

Charlie couldn't tell it in just a couple of weeks. He'd been a Marine Recon type during WW II and in the Korean unpleasantness lost a brother to the Communists, killed in action, and Charlie couldn't tell the folks back in Columbus what this Air Cav war in Vietnam was like in a couple of weeks. So he lived in the field for weeks at a time. Longer than most of the grunts he went around with. In the field, Charlie could eat C rations, sleep on the ground, and he didn't have to spend any of that $500. And when he did come back to our base camp at An Khe for a bath and some rest and the leisure to write about what he'd seen and heard and felt, the word got around pretty quickly among the troopers of the Cav: Charlie's money is no good. When he'd try to buy a beer for the guys he'd been sharing the mean end of a dirty war with, they wouldn't let him. Because when the $500 was gone, so was Charlie. And nobody wrote about the war like he did. Nobody.

Eventually the $500 was gone. It took months. So Charlie cashed in his plane ticket and went out into the boonies to watch and learn and listen and write it all down and send it back to Columbus. When the plane fare money was gone, and he was totally and absolutely broke, he hitched a ride back on a Georgia Air National Guard plane. The pilot, a weekend warrior with a wife and a good civilian job, braved an Air Force court-martial for having an unauthorized civilian passenger on an intercontinental flight. But that's the way everybody felt about Charlie, who had to borrow a dime from the pilot to call his wife to come pick him up from someplace near Warner-Robins, Georgia.

In Vietnam, Charlie sometimes disappeared for weeks. More than once he was reported killed. And more than once he was reported missing in action. One time he was out of touch for nearly a month, last seen with a squad that had been mauled in the firefight near one of those unpronounceable hamlets, someplace near Binh Dinh. But every time he'd shown up again, gray under his grimy gaunt face, worn out, near collapse. And he'd say something like, "Hell no, I ain't dead yet." And he'd look for some place to lay his head for a few hours so he could think clearly while he filled in all those single-spaced lines on the old portable.

I first met Charlie at Camp Swampy, which was what everyone who'd ever been there called Ft. Stewart, Georgia. I was twenty-three and had bluffed my way into the photographer's slot with the Second Infantry Division PIO, and almost my first job was to drive a Jeep and meet some guy named Black at a crossroads, grid coordinates such-and-such at first light. When I showed on time, the only one more surprised than I was Charlie. He'd never met a PIO private who could read a map and sort-of drive a four-wheel Jeep.

We got rid of the Jeep soon thereafter because what Charlie wanted to see that morning was a combat river crossing exercise. "Can't cover a war from the road," he told me. So we walked, this old man of forty-two and me, and I learned about the engineers and being quiet in the woods and how to make coffee by kicking a hole in the mushy earth and feeding a few dried pine needles to a tiny fire in it, then mixing C-Ration instant into iodined water in a blackened steel canteen cup until it was lukewarm.

And I learned how a reporter works. Charlie had an interviewing technique that's never been bettered. It was how he covered an exercise at Camp Swampy, and how he covered the Vietnam War. Mostly he didn't say much of anything. Mostly he listened, and nodded his head, and wrote stuff down on a pad. Once in awhile he would ask a few questions. First names and hometowns and such. And they were the names of privates and buck sergeants and a topkick now and then. The names that no one from the *Washington Post* or the *New York* or *Los Angeles Times* or the *Chicago Tribune* or even the *Charlotte Observer* ever wrote down. The names of the guys who were fighting the war.

My phone rang late one October night and an old, familiar voice from my Air Cav PIO days told me that Charlie Black was dead at fifty-nine. Dead of a massive heart attack at his home near Auburn, Alabama. I can still see him, caked with mud, an M-16 slung casual-like over his shoulder, pushing aside the mosquito net and easing into our tent at An Khe. Someone would holler, "Heard you'd been greased, Charlie, where the hell you been?" And he'd cackle, "Hell no, I ain't dead yet."

Myself, I'm not so sure he won't turn up again some day.

Marvin J. Wolf

Mixed Blessings

In the gray light of early morning, the knob on my closed office door makes tiny clicking noises like the tumblers on a safe. But I'm lost at the computer, focusing hard on today's writing goal, prodded alert by a looming deadline.

The door scrapes open and breaks my concentration. I glance up and see a round, clear face fresh from sleep, framed by pale blond pillow-hair and lighted by the bluest eyes you've ever seen. Her smile shows perfect, seed-pearl teeth.

"Hi, Grammie!"

She whispers this, having been told downstairs that Grammie's working and shouldn't be disturbed. She's sure this doesn't apply to her, of course, but she's being quiet anyway. Her pink I-Dream-of-Jeannie pajamas are twisted at the tummy. One plump arm hooks the neck of a naked baby doll.

I don't speak, torn between the blue world of words and this three-year-old genie I don't see nearly often enough. Because she lives states away, her visits are rare—but last weeks at a time.

Reassured by my smile, Jessica reaches up to catch the doorknob again and push the door shut behind her. She grins conspiratorially. We're hiding from the rest of the family.

She runs the four steps to my chair, her eyes drawn to the lighted screen that looks like a TV. Still I say nothing, hoping somehow to sustain the magic world where I dwelled a moment ago. Jessica crawls into my spring-loaded chair and stands up behind me, pitching the baby doll overboard. My fingers go back to the keys. She peers over my shoulder at the few halting words that appear on the screen and whispers a question in my ear. I nod my head in answer.

Bored with the lack of action on the screen, she lifts my hair and pokes each mole on the back of my neck. Then, using both hands, she scoops my tousled hair completely over my head. When I turn to look at her, hair hangs over my eyes in a ragged curtain. She holds her breath a moment, eyes wide, then dissolves in giggles.

So do I, and that's the end of my writing session for today. Total production: two paragraphs, one unusable.

Funny how the things we love most require some tithe or sacrifice. Chocolate is full of fat and calories. Technology makes life easier but complicates it at the same time. Even the clean joy of physical work is tainted by fatigue and pain. I can't wait for my granddaughter and her family to visit, but when they do, I have to get up in the middle of the night to get my writing done.

And writing itself is a mixed blessing. We, who are addicted, berate ourselves and feel guilty when we don't write, at the same time put it off and hunt for diversions. Why? Because the thing that makes us happiest is also tedious, frustrating and hard. Writing makes us crazy; not writing, even crazier.

One of the few things I know that's more elusive than writing well is wisdom. And even wisdom, with all its benefits, exacts a price. We pay for it with long years of experience, and when we've finally earned a share and life begins to make more sense, we're jolted by a sudden understanding of its brevity.

But that very insight into the fleeting nature of time also bequeaths us an appreciation of every ticking moment. Each morning is a promise, each sunset not to be missed. New green on trees, clear running water, innocent faces fresh from sleep pierce the heart with intense poignancy. Wisdom teaches us to embrace our mixed blessing without mixed feelings, to savor both the pleasure and the pain.

Most of all, wisdom lets us grab life by the lapels and demand the most from it. I don't know about you, but I want it all. Perhaps I'll run out of time to experience everything, but I'm determined to try.

That's why right now I'll have to shut down this computer and sign off for the time being. Because there's a tiny, tumbler-like clicking at my office door, as the knob turns.

Marcia Preston

"Can it wait until Mommy's not in the middle of a vengeful, bloody, mob-related waterfront rub-out?"

Be Ready When Your Editor Calls

I started writing when I was seven, left hand tied behind my back because it was a sin to be left-handed . . . back then. Also, we didn't have 911 to call. I kept diaries, wrote words backward and sentences from right to left. I always knew how a story would end because that's where I would begin. I didn't know it then, but one day I would need an editor.

An editor is a long-suffering soul whose desk is landscaped with skyscrapers of manuscripts waiting to be read each morning. He prays a lot. Maybe, somewhere in those manila structures is the story he is looking for—one that hits him by surprise, takes chances and is told from the heart. Too busy to read them all at work, he takes dozens home in backpacks and wades through them at night.

If you have spell-checked, rewritten at least twenty times, followed guidelines, submitted to the appropriate market and spelled the editor's name correctly, you could be the lucky one to hear from him by phone. So, be ready for that editor's call. I wasn't.

We were still on the ranch the first time. I was filling the water tanks in my chicken coop with a hose when the jingle came from the barn—a fifty-yard dash. I bolted the door, latched it behind me, and eleven rings later grabbed the phone. "Hello!" I gasped.

"Hello," said the voice on the line. "Penny Porter? This is Philip Osborne from the *Reader's Digest*. We'd like to reprint your story that appeared in *Arizona* magazine."

"Oh wow!" My heart stopped. By the time I found Bill out on "the north forty," it was late afternoon, but I had to tell someone my news! That's when I remembered the hose. And my chickens! I dashed to the coop. No clucks. No squawks. No cackles. Nothing but an ominous trickle seeping from beneath the closed door. I lifted the latch. The door flew open and a four-foot tidal wave of straw, feathers, manure, chicken feed and half-drowned chickens flooded the barnyard. No eggs that month! But *Reader's Digest* bought my story.

Ever since, I've tried to be ready for my editor's call. Today, we have six telephones in our house—in my husband's office, our bedroom, the kitchen, by my computer, in the garage—and a "hotline" . . . next to the john!

A few years ago the phone rang. "Hi Penny. This is Phil Osborne. You sound sort of far away."

I'm in the garage. I wanted to add, *And it's 114 degrees in here,* but he beat me with, "Well, I've got just a few quick questions. Okay?"

"Sure!" I said. But my heart said, *After all, you're my editor. I'm actually talking to a living, breathing editor. I'd die of heat prostration before I'd ask you to wait while I ran inside to a phone where it's air-conditioned.* Ten minutes later I was drenched. I'd forgotten where it was I wanted to go, but *Reader's Digest* bought my story.

Then there's the time factor. Eight A.M. in New York is 5:00 A.M. in Arizona. The phone rang at 5:06. "Hi Penny. This is Phil Osborne." He knows I get up early to write, but just this one morning I'd rolled over . . . "Hi Phil!" Oops . . . I'm speaking into the wrong end. "I hope this isn't too early?" he says.

"Oh, no," I lie. "I was out walking the dog."

A few weeks ago our bathroom "hotline" put me to the real test. I was in the shower. The phone rang. I stepped out, grabbed the receiver and it fell in the john. I fished it out.

"Hi Penny. This is Phil."

I know who it is! "Hi Phil!" I tried to reach a towel but the cord wouldn't stretch that far.

"There's a buzz on your line," he said.

"Yes, something happened to my phone!"

"Oh well, I can hear you . . . just a few quick questions. Okay?"

I shivered. I wished I'd remembered to turn off the overhead fan. The puddle under my feet widened till water carved channels of its own between the Mexican tiles to the Berber carpeting, and I vowed never again to answer the phone when I'm in the shower. On second thought . . . *Reader's Digest* bought my story.

Penny Porter

Helen Help Us!

Opportunities are disguised by hard work, so most people don't recognize them.

Ann Landers

Mom was HELEN HELP US! That was the name of her nationally syndicated column. But often when she would show her ID in a store—invariably when her hair was in curlers, and she was in grubby jeans—someone would recognize the name and blurt out: "You're HELEN HELP US!" She would crumble in embarrassment.

When people read her advice, they felt her compassion, experienced her humor and were given hope.

Recently, when our local newspaper printed her final farewell on the front page of the Metro Section, letters flooded in from hundreds of people. Many we had never met, and many who never knew that Helen Bottel was our mother. They loved her even if they didn't know her personally.

She was a modest woman and never understood the impact she had on this nation as a newspaper advice columnist. She used to compare herself to Ann Landers and Dear Abby, by saying she was third in a market of two. She was printed in more than 200 newspapers nationally and eventually in Japan, receiving up to 100 letters a day from readers. She never employed a secretary and answered many of the letters herself, some days writing 5,000 or more words in personal letters.

Mom was truly incredible and always fun to be with. She would collect people wherever she went. No one was a stranger. This was most embarrassing when I was a teenager, but I have since grown to understand this as a gift, a gift she passed on to me, which I now witness in my own children. She taught us to respect all people, and not to prejudge.

Because Mom got to know so many interesting people, no one was immune from becoming material for her columns.

It started with Dad. She certainly married the right guy. Dad's unending dry sense of humor often appeared in the headlines of Mom's columns. She would be solicited often by manufacturers or book publishers wanting her to promote their products. I believe it was sometime during the '70s when Mom received the book *The Total Woman* in the mail. They wanted her to review it. The author explained in detail to married women how to completely serve her man. Mom always reeled at this. She would say, "If he's got two arms and two legs, he can serve himself!"

But one part of this book truly amazed her, so she shared it with Dad to get his opinion. The book suggested that a *good* wife might meet her husband at the door, after a long day at the office, wrapped in nothing but plastic wrap. She asked Dad, "Now, what would *you* think if I did *that?*"

Without hesitation he replied, "Well, I'd think: leftovers again."

That made it into the column. And it was eventually lifted by almost every comic in the entertainment industry.

Once a manufacturer sent a snore collar for Mom to test, hoping she would write wonderful things about it. She didn't have a problem with snoring, but Dad did. So she asked him if he would try it out. He was game for anything. For several nights he wore the contraption. Sure enough, he didn't snore, because every time he did, it would shock him awake! Mom loved it, and thought it worked great. She asked Dad for his opinion to be quoted in the column. He said, "I guess it works fine, but now, every time I drive up and down the street, electric garage doors open and close for no reason!"

She used that.

Mom always included us in her work. She felt strongly about being an available mother, so working out of her home made it easy to incorporate the whole family into this noble effort. We would open her mail, sort letters, even listen to her practice her speeches. We never knew at the time that she was lecturing us.

Mom and I wrote a column—Generation Rap—together for nearly nine years. I was only fifteen when we began the column. She would take the more liberal viewpoint, and I would take the more conservative side. That was not an act; we really did see life differently, but always respected each other's opinion. We agreed to disagree. She would tell people that I was the only teenager in America getting paid to argue with her mother.

Mom was a winner at whatever she did. In 1958, she was the editor of a small-town newspaper in Oregon. The four of us were born by then, and she worked from home, mostly. In fact, she often bragged that I was the one born into the newspaper business because she had to write my birth announcement from her hospital bed. She was practically the entire newspaper staff.

The story of her success in the national realm is really a Cinderella story. As she told it, my father was reading either Ann Landers or Dear Abby out loud to Mom one evening. He laughed at one of the replies written by the columnist and announced that she was quite good. "I could do better," she replied. To which Dad teased, "Then prove it."

So she did. She made up an advice column with problem letters from stories told to her by friends and sent it to the largest syndicate in the world, King Features Syndicate in New York. By now she was forty-four years old, and had no time to waste. Much to her and Dad's surprise, King wrote back and said they loved the column. "Send more," they said. But she had no more. So, she talked to more friends, listened in occasionally on the party line, and fabricated a few more columns. She sent them in, and they sent her a plane ticket to New York. She signed a contract that led to twenty-five years of syndication in more than 200 newspapers nationally. Our small town in Oregon gave her a party when she returned. There were banners at the airport and down Main Street where the high school band played. People took the day off work to honor one of their own.

At about the age of seventy, she quit King Features. Not to retire, but to syndicate herself internationally—to the *Yomiyuri Shinbaum*, the largest newspaper in the world, based in Tokyo, Japan. In the American and Japanese columns, she answered letters dealing with family issues, marriage and child rearing. There were times she became very close to her readers and wrote to many of them for years.

Mom recognized writing talent in many who wrote to her. One woman, who signed her letters EL FIN ("The End" in Spanish), told of a horrible childhood and an even worse adult life of neglect, abuse and even torture. Her letter was so beautifully written, Mom thought that she had, perhaps, been writing it as a college assignment. So,

Mom wrote back as if the letter were serious, ending it with a note that she was certain the letter was made up, but that this girl should become a writer. The girl wrote back. The letter was not a college assignment—but true. Mom wrote to her for ten more years, encouraging her to pursue a career in writing. Mom had a natural wisdom and deeply cared about her readers.

There is a blessing in having a mother who writes. We have millions of her words in print. Her opinions, thoughts, desires are all there for us to read whenever we wish. Several years ago, my sister and I wanted to write Mom's story. We asked her permission to write a book of her life. She was touched—and a bit embarrassed. It was still too hard to talk about her childhood, but she agreed to put all of her memories on audio tape. She did, then tucked them away and instructed us NOT to listen to the tapes until her death.

Mom died last month. The following week we found the tapes. We have not listened yet, but we will soon. We also found her diary. It was from her college days, when she met her first friends, ever. And, when she fell in love with our father. We have been reading her entries to him, and he is remembering the sweetness of her love . . . even in death.

Helen Bottel, our mother and a nationally known syndicated columnist, left us an invaluable gift: an appreciation of writing. Through her words and our memories, her legacy lives on.

Suzanne Peppers

A Bucket Full of Research

Many years ago, I read that James A. Michener, who did not publish until he was forty years of age, advised young writers to do extensive research before trying to write a novel. He visited the countries and areas he was interested in writing about, interviewing countless people as well as reading more than two hundred books for background material for each of his books—*Hawaii, Iberia, The Source, Texas, Poland, Alaska, Caribbean*—and for some forty other book projects, spanning a fifty-year writing career.

This careful research resulted in Michener winning the 1948 Pulitzer Prize for *Tales of the South Pacific,* his first novel, and other awards.

Michener believed a writer must know the country and experience an event to be able to write about it. I thought this was the right path to take, so I visited Spain, Australia (twice), Japan, China and other countries which, along with my library research, resulted in my publishing many hardbound books.

Such advice, however, can lead you astray—as in the research I did for a proposed book set in Hitler's Germany.

I read in a Paul Gallico book how the Nazis would put a tin bucket over a person's head and beat on it with a stick to drive the poor person crazy. I wondered if this were really true. Remembering Michener's advice on living the experience before you write about it, I decided to give it a try.

So I went out to my backyard and glanced around to make sure no one was watching. Then I put my scrub bucket over my head and beat on it with a broom handle. The noise was unbelievable and unbearable.

I banged the bucket a few more times to make sure I could write that scene for the book. With my ears still ringing, I quickly pushed back the bucket and found myself looking into the astonished, fearful face of my neighbor, staring out of her apartment window, located directly above the apartment my husband and I were renting.

We stared at each other for the longest time without saying a word. I know she thought I was crazy.

Within the week, the poor woman moved out!

Ethel Bangert

Making a 'Pottment

Words are clothes that thoughts wear.

Samuel Butler

I had bit into the hind end of a hippo. There's no question about it. As a mother, wife, homemaker for ten-plus years, and new writer, I had decided that I wanted a career as a home-based freelance writer. I began taking classes at the local community college, preparing the extra bedroom for use as an office, adjusting to a hectic pace, and studying how-to books for home-based businesses. I even taught my children to look at the sign on my door. If it said "working," they were to wait quietly until I addressed them. If it said "party," they were free to come in and be with Mom. I understood when I began this venture that the time and dedication required to get my business off the ground would be immense, but I was willing to sacrifice and work hard. I had faith in my abilities, and I knew I could succeed!

I was deep in thought, working on editing a draft, when my five-year-old son, Jake, came into my office. He waited patiently beside me . . . without saying a word. When I finished my thought, I glanced over at him. "Yes, Jake?" I asked. "What do you need, honey?"

"I want to make a 'pottment," he replied.

Confused and frustrated at being interrupted for the third time in an hour, I impatiently asked him "What do you mean—an appointment?"

His lips quivered, and his words gushed forth in a tide of emotion. "So you can talk to me, and write about me, and play with me, and make yellow sticky notes that say Jake on 'em . . . and so you won't ever forget me."

I was stunned. "Jake, honey, I could never forget you. I love you very much!" I exclaimed, but the words sounded hollow to us both. My actions had spoken for themselves. Standing in front of me was a sweet little boy, who missed his mommy. During all the long hours I had put in lately, I couldn't recall many spent with Jake. He didn't understand deadlines and query letters to editors. The mommy he knew, and wanted, made brownies for his kindergarten class, played in the mud when it was raining, and always had time to listen. Guilt and sorrow flooded over me in a wave.

As tears welled up in my eyes, I reached for my son and pulled him close to me. Struggling to talk beyond the lump in my throat, I whispered soothing words to him and hugged him tight. As I reached for a tissue, I turned off my monitor. Until that moment, my resolve to be an established writer had never wavered. I held him in a long, silent embrace, wanting to ease his fears, loneliness and frustration, as well as my own.

Long after he was tucked in bed that night, I turned on my monitor. I sat staring vacantly at the screen, wondering if I could make this all work. I finished the work I was editing and shut down the computer. As soon as I pushed the power button, I had an idea. Back on came the power, and I began immediately on a new project. A short picture book. This small book consisted of nothing more than photos, captions and a simple storyline, yet I could hardly contain my excitement. As the sun was rising, so was my enthusiasm for creating and writing. I could not wait for this book to reach its first reader!

Thankfully, I didn't have to wait long. I heard my son flip on the Saturday morning cartoons and called him in to me. He looked at the book (with its decorated card stock covers) and asked if I wrote it. He began flipping through the pages of photos, revealing special times we had shared together, as I read the words aloud. When we finished the story, his smile had curved up over his ears. "Wow!" Jake said, his eyes filled with awe. "You're a real writer, huh, Mom?"

Tickled, I said, "I guess so."

"I know what writers do," claimed Jake.

"What?" I asked.

He replied, "Writers make people feel good with words, that's cool!"

Exhausted and teary-eyed, I pulled my son to me. We held each other again, but with a new understanding.

Valerie Hutchins

Summertime, and the Writin's NOT Easy

. . . and so Matilda crouched in the sea chest, trying to still the pounding of her heart. She listened for the angry cry that would mean she had been seen seeking refuge on this unworthy vessel. But the night was blessedly silent. With trembling hands, she brushed back the waves of raven hair tumbling to her fragile shoulders and blinked back tears. The nuns had never prepared her for a world so cruel!

Soon Matilda felt the gentle sway of a boat in motion and rejoiced, for it meant she was free of her despised uncle and his ungentlemanly attentions. Her wild escape had led her (who longed only for a pious life at Mother Britain's bosom) to this boat and the unknown. At that moment the lid on her hiding place swung open and she looked up into the face of the Devil himself.

Eyes glazed in terror, Matilda opened up her mouth and screamed—

"Mommmmmy!"

"Don't listen to her, Mom. Nicole's just acting like a baby 'cause she doesn't want to clean under her bed."

"That's because *Tess* stuffed the clothes under there, and now she won't put them in the hamper!"

"Mom, tell her that she can't go to the swimming pool unless she cleans up her mess."

"She can't go to the pool unless she cleans the mess. Now, darlings, let me work. I've got to get this manuscript in the mail this afternoon, or I'll miss my deadline."

"I'm sick of having to share my bedroom with a slob."

"I'm not a slob. *You're* a slob! Mom, tell her that she's a slob."

"She's a slob. Now, scoot! It's summer vacation, and you should be outside playing."

"See? Even Mom says you're a slob!"

"She said it, but she doesn't really *think* it!"

"How do you know?"

"She doesn't think when she's writing."

"Out of this office! Now! One more word and—"

"You're grounded!" Matilda felt the gentle grate of the ship's bow against sand.

Captain Pierce Stone glared down at the delicate creature nestled in his sea chest. Grounded? Why, he'd sailed the Seven Seas and never beached a ship. He strode to the porthole. Damn! The ship had run aground on an uncharted island. He turned on the stow-away in fury.

The room spun and Matilda raised a limp hand to her pale brow. "Oh, why is everything swirling so?" she whispered. "Oh, dear me—"

"Help! Tess is pulling my hair."

"I'm just trying to comb it. If you did this more often, it wouldn't be so ratty."

"It's ratty 'cause we just went swimming—Mom, will you take us to the tennis courts now?"

"No."

"The library?"

"No."

"The park?"

"Go play and leave me alone. I can't work with all these interruptions! Every time I get on a roll one of you comes in here, and I lose my focus. It makes me feel like—"

"I'm going crazy." Matilda leaped from the sea chest. The cry of a mad woman ripped from her throat and spittle dripped from her mouth. She wiped it away with an arm as frail as a willow branch. Ever the gentleman, Stone offered forth his kerchief. The girl staggered forward but slipped on a puddle of spittle and fell, striking her head on a table.

"Ouch!" whispered Matilda feebly. "Get me some—"

"Water."

"No! I want another soda."

"Tess, put it back and have some milk! Oh, no! Is it really two o'clock? The mailman's going to be here in an hour and I'm—"

"I don't want to play with Nicole. She's a stinker."

"Stop the bickering! I have HAD it—"

"I am completely fed up." Matilda shoved aside the spoon filled with rich, coconut stew. Through Stone's valiant nursing, she had gained strength and the mad episodes had diminished.

Stone peered down at the convalescent. The sight of her voluptuous curves stirred his loins. This was the woman for a man like him—a man who feared to touch those brittle, skeletal females. This gal really knew how to pack away those coconuts.

"Kind sir," said Matilda with a ladylike belch and a blush. "As a maiden in your care, I really must tell you that—"

"I could just throw up."

"What?"

"I stepped in dog doo."

"Where?"

"In the back yard. Now, it's on the living room rug."

"That does it! You and your sister have been asking for it all day and now—"

"I'm going to give it to you." Matilda slowly swung dimpled knees over the side of the bed, allowing the coverlet to fall away.

Ever the gentleman, Stone wanted to resist her. He closed his eyes and shook his head, trying to remove the vision of the vixen. But it was for naught. With a groan, Stone strode to the bed, brushing away strands of raven hair to better see Matilda's smiling face.

"Oh, oh," said Matilda, sweeping her raven locks from her neck so Stone could apply kisses. "I feel like a hot tamale. But if you really want to toot my whistle you could—"

"Spit!"

"What are you two doing?"

"Having a contest. We need a judge."

"Not now! I'm in the home stretch and . . . is that the mail truck coming down the street? Run tell the carrier that I'll be right out with an envelope. Go on—"

"Move your butt."

Stone did. And it was good.

Matilda sighed. "Now, I'm in the mood for—"

"Quiet!"

"I am being quiet. It's turned way down. Besides, Mom doesn't hear when she's writing."

"I heard that."

"Mom? Will you—"

"NO! GO AWAY!"

"Where should we go?"

"GO TO . . . TO—"

"TIMBUCTOO," Matilda said. "Oh yes! I've always wanted to go there."

Stone lifted his satiated head and stared at Matilda. Life would never be dull with a wench like this!

The couple mounted the stairs to the deck. Wind blew Matilda's raven hair and whisked a bit of foam from the corner of her mouth. Lustful and bold, the couple faced a future filled with love.

Kerry Arquette

"'How I Spent My Summer Vacation,' by Lilia Anya, all rights reserved, which includes the right to reproduce this essay or portions thereof in any form whatsoever, including, but not limited to, novel, screenplay, musical, television miniseries, home video and interactive CD-ROM."

Marriage and Metaphors:
A Writer's Life On and Off the Pages

Yesterday, I overheard my neighbor, Bud, ask my husband, "What's it really like living with a writer?"

Craning my neck to look out the window, I watched my husband glance around the backyard and then toward the house. Confident he wasn't being taped, he sat back and let his words gush. He sounded relieved to share his nightmare.

"It's like living with Dr. Jekyll and Mrs. Hyde," he began. "There are more ups and downs than in the astronaut program."

Bud sat transfixed. "Go on," he urged, quaffing a beer and scratching his nether-regions, all without taking his eyes off my husband. From my perch inside the house, I marveled at Bud's coordination.

"When my wife is writing," my husband continued, "she's up. When she's finished, she's down. When she gets a rejection letter, she's up or down—it's confusing but sometimes she gets a *personal* rejection letter." He fluttered a phantom letter in Bud's face. "Isn't this wonderful?" he mimicked. "Someone took the time to personally reject me!"

My husband shook his head. "I don't understand that one. I guess you have to be a writer." Bud shuddered, drained his beer and belched his agreement.

As they sat on the deck, bonding and scratching over the mysteries surrounding women and writers, I sat at my desk and pondered my husband's words.

For the past four years, I've devoted my time to writing, and my husband has devoted his time to learning how to live with a writer. Both of us think the other has the easier job.

When I write a first draft, I'm reckless with words. I let them cascade helter-skelter onto the page, mixing metaphors and strangling syntax. My husband, however, chooses his words carefully; they may appear in a book someday.

I now read in bed and scribble notes into the wee hours. He now sleeps with a mask covering his eyes, the light casting shadows across his forehead.

Hubby's unearthed a fascinating fact about writers: Most will do anything not to write. He knows when I'm suffering from deadline deferral—I iron.

Not only am I mechanically maladroit (once singeing my eyebrows lighting the gas barbecue), I've no idea what an iron looks like on a daily basis. It's an implement for steers and criminals, right? Yet, when I'm ignoring my muse, out comes the iron. We always have the smoothest underwear on the block.

Another way I avoid writing is to arrange the soup cans alphabetically. Or, I'll organize a year's worth of snapshots into albums, complete with sidebars. "Here's our son, Rambo," I explain to the stranger walking down my street. "He's six days old in this picture. His outfit was a gift from Aunt Zelda, before she keeled over from a kidney stone she couldn't pass."

A nightly gourmet feast is also one of the perks of not

writing. Where I find the time between going to the gym, having my legs waxed on the way home, then vacuuming the ceiling, is still a mystery to my husband.

The flip side of not writing for a living is writing for a living. Hubby now recognizes this phase and dares not ask, "Where's dinner?" He can find it in the freezer or in the cupboard, instead of his more-preferred locations like the oven or the table. Occasionally, I get his hopes up by saying, "Dinner's on the table." He looks and finds the phone number for "Pizza To Go."

When I'm on a roll, my husband says, "You're shameless. You write anywhere—restaurants, the car, parties. It's unnerving for people to watch you scrawl away, muttering, 'I just have to get this down.' Waiters have asked me, 'Is she going to report me for forgetting your ketchup?'"

Be glad I'm writing novels instead of checks, I think.

He comments on my writing-phase appearance. "Your legs resemble a bear in hibernation, you wear the same coffee-stained sweatshirt for weeks, and you have ink marks on your face," he whines. "No point trying to talk to you—the phone's off the hook."

I make a mental note to greet him at the door wearing only plastic wrap—just as soon as I finish this article, two short stories and flesh out my characters for a mystery novel.

We both struggle to understand some writing-life oddities. I have trouble with magazines that promise, "Pays on acceptance." Is that acceptance of my manuscript or of the theory that SASE really means "Seldom Acknowledges Submissions Expeditiously"? He has trouble recognizing what phase I'm in when I say, "Talk to me, I'm writing." He swears it's a ruse.

Something my husband didn't need to learn was how to respond when asked, "How does it look?" He's memorized that answer since my pre-writing days, when I modeled a new outfit and asked, "How does it look?" These days, I thrust a manuscript under his nose and ask, "How does it look?" The answer is the same now as it was then. "Good."

To be fair, he answered differently once. I showed him a story and insisted he couldn't just pronounce it good. I watched him as he read; he began sucking his teeth, his lips curled and his eyebrows shot up to join his hairline.

"So, how does it look?" I asked.

"It's hard to express in words," he mumbled, his face the color of algae.

"Try retching sounds," I snapped, grabbing the story. I went back to my office, and he went back to *good*.

It's not that my husband doesn't write; he's an aerospace engineer, so presumably that entails some writing, although no spelling. But he writes things like, *To increase cruise efficiency, transfer cg aft to reduce lift-induced drag from the tail download"* while I write things like, *Bernard was going out of his mind, so he packed light, knowing it would be a short trip.* See, we do have something in common; we both write about travel.

Bud's voice interrupts my thoughts, and I peek through the window to see the guys still on the deck, Bud literally on the deck. "How come you've stuck around so long?" he slurs from his sprawled position.

I know the answer to this one. "She promised to buy me an airplane—a real one," my husband says. "She tells me about famous authors and their humble beginnings. Did you know Stephen King was rejected a hundred times before he sold a thing? By my count, only forty-four rejections to go and the plane is mine!

"It could be worse," he continued. "I could be married to a psychiatrist and become paranoid overnight. *Oh God, my tie is a millimetre off-centre; she'll say I don't love her. How does she know I'm left-brained; yesterday she said I was brainless.* And I doubt she'd promise me a plane."

I smile as I turn back to my work, knowing my husband understands a little about this writing life. After all, he's a nineties kind of guy and can take care of himself. He knows where to find the cream of broccoli soup.

It's right next to the cream of chicken.

Judith A. Chance

9

THE
POWER OF
PERSEVERANCE

Few things are impossible to diligence and skill . . . great works are performed not by strength but perseverance.

Dr. Samuel Johnson

A Strange Thing Happened on the Way to OK

Rejection letters aren't the worst thing you can get. Bedbug letters are worse.

A story is told that once upon a time, in the Steam Age, the president of a mainline railroad got a letter from a VIP passenger:

> *I was appalled to discover that my berth on your highly-acclaimed sleeper car was full of bedbugs. I shall not again require the services of your railway company and request the return of my fare.*

The railroad company president replied:

> *Dear Mr. Smith:*
>
> *It was with the greatest concern that I read your letter of April 9 and, thereby, learned of your unpleasant experience in discovering an insect in your bedclothing. I assure you, this unfortunate event has never happened before on our railroad system. Our sleeping accommodations are kept immaculate to serve the needs of our patrons, of whom you are one of the most valued. We are*

tireless in the preservation of our reputation as one of the foremost railroads in the land. I am at a loss to explain this unprecedented unpleasantry, and you may be assured such as this shall not happen again. We shall gladly refund your fare and beg you, Sir, to continue using our premier services for your traveling pleasure. With kindest personal regards, I remain respectfully yours, JP, President.

The VIP passenger calmed a degree at the presidential reassurance until he noted an interoffice memo which had adhered, most certainly by accident, to the correspondence. It instructed: "Lillian: Send him the bedbug letter. JP"

We got a bedbug letter once. From a VIP publisher. *We* means my husband and myself, coauthors. We had sent a book manuscript to this particular VIP publisher, having been introduced by our good friend the late Bishop James Pike, who had written for many publishers, lest you are guessing which VIP publisher is the subject of this discourse.

We were glowing with first-book-submission optimism, knew the material was good, and waited happily for a reply. It came in three weeks. They turned us down. Nicely. It was a real letter, not just a pink slip. It even had an erasure, kind of homey, this all having been before the Selectric II, or correcting tape rectangles even, and way before the just-as-if-I-never-ever-made-a-typo-in-my-life computer. The publisher said their editorial committee had considered our manuscript very carefully but determined it was not suitable for their readership . . . but thanks for allowing them the privilege of reading it."

Darn, said we. Our *darn* took on new spelling when we saw the inadvertently attached "bedbug letter," an interoffice memo:

*This is a strange but interesting ms. Wait three
weeks, then write them that our 'editorial committee'
[quotation marks theirs] does not consider this suitable
for our readership.*

Three years and many other close encounters of the
worst kind (ten rewrites minimum and self-publication
twice, which entailed the collating of 300 copies of 500
pages each equaling 150,000 lick-reach-and-grabs by kids
and kind neighbors who happened by) were to pass
before another even more VIP publisher, Harper & Row,
phoned to say a contract was on its way. And so were we.
And so was our book *I'm OK—You're OK*. It has been found
suitable, reportedly, for about twenty million readers in
twenty-five languages.

We consisted of the book's stated author and primary
source, my dear late husband Tom—Thomas A. Harris,
M.D. a psychiatrist—and myself, Amy, a writer by training and occupation. Tom died five years ago, but his contribution to millions of people goes on. Its most recent
translation, into the Chinese language, will open doors to
millions of new readers. I recently asked a clerk in a major
bookstore in my hometown how sales were going. "It's
one of our steadiest sellers," he said. Twenty-nine years
since its publication!

Check your rejections for bedbug letters or other pusil-
lanimous enclosures. Editors, "editorial committees," even
VIP publishers aren't always right. If you believe *you* are,
and *you believe in what you write*, then believe in yourself!
Rewrite until your fingers break, lick stamps until your
tongue sticks to your teeth, stay passionate, and never,
never, never give up.

Amy B. Harris

Nothing Comes Easy

My entrance into the world of writing began when my wife, Barbara, took a job at the local police department as a clerk and dispatcher working nights. After driving home through freeway traffic fifty-five miles from Los Angeles to our home in Costa Mesa, California, I'd fix dinner for our three children and then put them to bed by 8:30 P.M. With nobody to talk to the rest of the evening, I thought, *Why not write a book?*

Not having the great American novel burning inside of me, I thought it would be fun to create a paperback adventure series. Coming out of advertising and marketing, I launched a research campaign, studying all the great authors who wrote stories with continuing heroes. I read them all from Sherlock Holmes to Phillip Marlowe to Mike Hammer to James Bond. Then I wondered, what can I do that's different? So I decided to place my hero in and around water and write an underwater adventure series.

My series hero and his buddies were created on a small portable typewriter at a desk in my son's bedroom in a little tract house. Since he was named Dirk, I used the same name for my protagonist who became Dirk Pitt.

Although I had been sport-diving for fifteen years, I left

my prestigious job as creative director for a big national advertising agency writing and producing radio and TV commercials and took a position as a clerk in a dive shop to get a better understanding of advanced diving techniques and to study the latest state-of-the-art equipment. Financially, it was a struggle. My wife's salary from the police department helped, but my additional four hundred dollars a month selling diving equipment barely kept us out of debt.

One evening the writing was not going well. I began to think it was an exercise in futility. I was crazy to ditch a good-paying, prestigious job to be a book author. Disillusioned, I took my first unfinished manuscript, threw it in the wastebasket and went to bed. The next day, I fished it out and struggled on. On a Girl Scout calendar dated March 13, 1966, I made a notation. "Almost gave up today." I saved that page and still have it.

Seeing me struggling evenings and weekends at the typewriter, my wife said, "Don't get your hopes up. Nothing will ever come of it." Her words made me so mad, I plunged on.

I connected with a terrific agent who became my best friend. Peter Lampack and I have been together thirty years. Our only contract was a handshake. Four years after I began to write and three years after I became Peter's client at William Morris Agency, he was unable to get me published. His bosses said, "Dump Cussler. He's obviously not going anywhere."

Peter, bless his heart, resisted throwing in the towel. Editors who rejected my manuscripts said, "You're banging your head against a wall. Adventure doesn't sell." Still stubborn, I kept writing.

Finally, the first book became published. Then the second. Both sold minimal copies, but are now valuable as collectibles. Then *Raise the Titanic.* My publisher turned it down as just not a story anybody would want to read. I pushed on writing despite the criticisms. After the manuscript bounced around several editors, Viking finally bought it for seventy-five hundred dollars, but with great trepidation. One editor thought it was a stupid buy. Everyone in publishing circles knew that a series hero never sells.

Fortunately for the Cussler family, the book became a classic and great success, and I could now write full time and Barbara could quit her job and stay home. We celebrated by buying a used Fiat sports car and a new refrigerator.

When people came up and said, "Congratulations on your overnight success," I used to smile and say, "Yeah, eleven years."

Which all goes to prove, as my friends were fond of remarking, "If Cussler can do it, anybody can do it."

They neglected to consider the determination, endurance and obstinacy of a hardheaded character who ignored the cynics and pessimists and who refused to give up. I always took comfort in wishfully thinking that John Paul Jones and I had something in common.

Clive Cussler

The Courage of
the Long-Distance Writer

*In America only the successful writer is impor-
tant, in France all writers are important, in
England no writer is important, in Australia
you have to explain what a writer is.*

Geoffrey Cotterell

At the age of fifty-five, I became an "overnight" success.
My first novel *Power of One* was sold for a million dollars
and printed in eleven languages. I was featured on the
front page of a national newspaper as the first Australian
ever to receive a million dollars for a novel.

The media was wrong of course. Colleen McCullough,
the brilliant Australian author of *The Thorn Birds,* received
more money and sold more copies of her first novel in
more languages. They were also wrong about my being
an overnight success. I had written seriously as a writer
every day of my life since the age of eleven. Instead of
being an overnight success, I was, in effect, a pathetically
slow learner.

But I got there in the end, and you will, too. It has been my observation that success is not about being the most brilliant, educated or talented, it is about being the most determined, about hanging on the longest and never giving up.

Four years ago, I was invited to run in the Boston Marathon. The Boston is every marathon runner's dream, for it is the granddaddy of all marathons, and this time, it was celebrating its 100th anniversary.

While I have run some forty marathons, Boston is special, not only because it is the world's oldest continuously run foot race, but also, within the past year, in order to qualify you had to have run a stipulated time in your age group in a previous marathon. I hadn't done so, and, anyway, I wasn't running the kind of times that would qualify me for Boston. To have been invited was too good to be true, and I saw it as a brilliant conclusion to a far-from-spectacular running career.

I accepted with alacrity, even though I knew I had no chance of preparing adequately for the race. I had two book tours ahead of me where the only serious training I would do would be adjusting a jumbo jet seat and masticating through endless rubber chicken literary lunches.

In Boston, I arrived at the starting line overweight and underprepared, and it soon began to show. At around the eighteen-mile mark (30 kilometres), I knew that I'd finally run out of puff, my blood sugar was used up, and my muscles were beginning to eat themselves. In marathon terms, this is the equivalent of trying to keep a car going with no petrol in the tank. I was about to hit the wall.

However, I told myself, I'd been here before and knew that it is the mind and not the body that gets one through in times such as this. In order to get my mind off the terrible pain, I needed to find a victim, someone who like myself was all but spent, where the slightest disruption would send him crashing into the proverbial wall. This was, after all, survival time, when mercy or any sense of morality is forsaken for the great good of self. It was kill or be killed. The simple arithmetic of survival.

I must choose someone so close to the edge that the doubtful power of my personality would cause him to throw in the towel, force him to quit; then I would comfort myself with the thought that I was stronger than he was. This would hopefully be sufficient to get me through the race. Humans have been doing this since time began. I'd done it once before—to a Japanese runner in the Honolulu Marathon—where my persistent yabbering in the language he couldn't understand had finally taken him out. How much easier, I thought it would be, practiced on someone who spoke my native tongue.

I found my victim soon enough, a man of about fifty, balding, a little overweight, short legs, with a stocky frame, the whole put together quite wrong for a marathon runner. He was doing it real hard. I lightened my step to appear outwardly as though I hadn't a care in the world, or, in a marathon parlance, I was dancing on daisies.

"Hi, lovely day for a marathon, isn't it?" I asked.

No reply.

"Having a good time?"

No reply.

"You look great. Almost there. Only six miles to go. Should do it in another hour and a half, eh? Nothing to it, old son."

No reply, but I could feel the heat from the radiating hate.

"I'm from Australia, I've run thirty-nine marathons, this is going to be my best yet." I cheerfully lied, the cramp in my quads threatening to bring me undone.

A look of white-hot apathy, but still no reply. As they say in the vernacular, I was doing great, it was time to put in the clincher, the left/right combo, the old biff, bang, the whammo kazoo!

"What do you do for a living?" I said ingenuously. This is the one question no member of the human race has ever been able to refuse to answer.

"I'm a writer," he gasped.

I glanced up towards heaven, thank you, thank you, God! I had my man. I would now ask him the one question every successful author gets asked, which simply drives him or her nuts. The one question that will bring a grown writer to his or her knees every single occasion.

"A writer, eh? Well, well, well, what a wonderful coincidence. I'm writing a book myself." I waited for the full impact of what I'd said to hit him. This was going to be money for jam. "I wonder if you could tell me what you believe to be the single most important element in the success of the contemporary novel? You know, the secret of writing a bestseller?" I waited for his knees to buckle. Put down your glasses, my victim was as good as off the track, a DNF (did not finish), the glory of running Boston never to be his to own, to cherish and to brag about when he sat his grandchildren on his knee.

"Bum glue!" he said, spitting out the words.

"Huh?"

"Bum glue!"

"Bum glue?"

And then I got it.

Bum glue—glue your bum to a chair and keep going, and never give up. Writing is about time spent with words until eventually they become your friends and begin to cooperate with your gifted storyteller's mind.

Writing is about time and practice; it takes six years to become a physician, a task infinitely easier than learning to write. Until you've put the first six years into learning your craft, six years where you write at least three hours

a day, or fifteen hours a working week, you will not suffi-
ciently master the craft of words in order to be effective as
a writer. It is only then that you can begin to be a storyteller. Bum glue is the single most important ingredient in
becoming a published author.

Well, we helped each other get through the next six
miles, and we crossed the finishing line supporting each
other, not sure who was carrying whom. But I know one
thing for certain: It was bum glue that carried us through
the pain and the uncertainty and the running on empty.
And if you have the courage to be a long-distance writer,
it will do the same for you.

Bryce Courtenay

So He Must Be Right, Huh?

The small ad almost leaped off the page in Sunday's *Houston Chronicle* back in 1978. It said, "Literary agent moving to Houston—out of New York—to be where the writers are. Call . . ." and it gave a phone number. I called promptly at 8:00 A.M. the next morning. The receptionist answered. "An appointment? Well, Mr. Hudson is extremely busy—I'm afraid it'll be at least three weeks before he can even see you."

"No problem," I assured her. Three weeks, three months—what was three weeks to wait to be in the presence of an honest-to-goodness literary agent.

That Monday three weeks later, I pushed open the door to his suite in a Houston high-rise at exactly the appointed hour. Tall, good-looking, impeccably dressed Mr. Paul Hudson himself greeted me. Gesturing toward the empty receptionist's desk, he said, "I'm sorry, you caught everyone at lunch. Please come on back to my office—if you don't mind waiting until I finish a phone call."

I followed him back, trying to glimpse the names of all the books and authors lining the walls, so I'd know who my peers would be as one of his clients. Once back in his office, he picked up the waiting line. "Thank you for waiting, Jack. Listen, let me just put it to you directly. My author's not going to take less than a million-dollar advance. And if you can't come up with that by tomorrow, I'll just take the manuscript to another house. Yeah ... yeah. Okay, fine. Tomorrow at noon."

He turned back to me and started to say something, but the other line rang. "Sorry," he apologized again graciously. "No problem," I said. Actually, I was trying to soak up the atmosphere. While he took the next call, I noted the picture of him and Truman Capote arm-in-arm and read the caption about *In Cold Blood*. Then there was another photo on his credenza with Michener, as they seemed to be having a tug-of-war over a sizable advance check.

I tuned in once again to the phone conversation. "Listen, Barb, we've got to auction this book—I'm going to set up the auction with a floor of $300,000. It's going to be big. . . . Call you tomorrow."

Finally, he turned back to me. "So, tell me a little about yourself." I obliged, starting back in third grade, including an overview of my current novel, and ending with my intention not to be a one-book author. "You're just the kind of author I like to take on," he said finally. "And your novel sounds fascinating. I'm planning to go to New York on Friday to hand-deliver a manuscript for another author, and I'll just plan to read yours before I go. Maybe I can come back with two advance checks."

I stopped breathing for a short moment. Shouting would not be cool, I told myself. Was he ... Was he really that interested in the novel? Well, obviously, he knew what would sell, didn't he? Hadn't I just heard him trying to negotiate big bucks on the phone? Two full years of scraping and bowing around agents—and not even well-known agents at that—and never had I generated that much interest so fast in the novel premise. A real, honest-to-goodness agent was saying to me that I had what it took!

"One other thing I want to ask . . ." I struggled to get out this last question because his answer was the only thing that kept me from plunging over into ecstasy. "Uh, you don't charge any reading fees or an upfront payment of any sort, do you? Because I've read that the good agents just take you on if your stuff is good enough to sell."

He smiled, "No, no, no. You're absolutely right. No money upfront—we just don't have time to take on authors who can't write." That was the last tidbit I needed to hear. I floated out of his office and on to my university classroom the next day, where I was teaching a class on creative writing. And, of course, I just happened to drop his name and the fact that he would probably be hand-delivering my manuscript to New York publishers shortly.

Three weeks passed, and I phoned his office. "He's just so busy," the receptionist said. "He said to tell you that he didn't have an answer yet, but he's still working on it."

"No problem," I said. "Working on it" sounded good to me. Six weeks passed. I called his office again. This time the receptionist was straightforward. "Mr. Hudson said to tell you that you could come pick up your manuscript. He says it doesn't quite have the . . . potential . . . he's looking for."

I never mentioned the agent again to my creative writing class, nor my friends nor my family. They could tell that I was obviously embarrassed, and they all kindly let the matter drop. But I brooded. "No potential." "No potential." The phrase gnawed at me. Why had I ever tried? I scolded myself for even thinking I had the ability to write a novel. What made me think I could do something creative like that? And then I remembered the years in graduate school studying creative writing while trying to parent two children and work part-time. Wasted time. Wasted effort. Wasted money. No potential—why was I fighting it? I might as well get back to real life. I put the novel away and applied for a teaching fellowship in graduate school.

About two months later one Sunday afternoon I sat thumbing through the *Houston Chronicle,* when I saw a large photograph that looked very familiar. I zeroed in on the caption. "Mark Johnson, alias Paul Hudson, alias Jack Zimple, Posing as Literary Agent Bilks Would-Be Authors of Millions." The story that followed detailed the scam as he had moved from state to state, collecting retainer fees from would-be authors "to hand-deliver their manu-scripts to big-time New York editors."

The scene resurfaced in my mind. The mysteriously empty desks. The one-sided phone conversations. The obviously bogus photos. My comment about my unwill-ingness to pay upfront fees. And the best memory of all—an unmarketed, high-potential manuscript collecting dust in my file drawer! Ready to be marketed to a real agent. Sheer energy shot through my veins. I needed to proof that manuscript just one more time before getting it into the mail. . . .

Many years and thirty-seven published books later, I still recall the value of this experience: (1) All that you see and hear about publishing may not be what it seems. (2) Don't ever let somebody else tell you the value of your work. (3) Get ready for an emotional roller-coaster ride if you intend to publish a book.

No doubt about it, if you are serious about a writing career, then you, too, will face ups and downs along the way. But if you keep your eyes wide open and persevere, you'll find the journey is well worth it.

Dianna Booher

Mommy, Please Write a Book for Me

Hurrying to finish an assignment for a deadline, I felt my typewriter suddenly stop. I looked over to see that my six-year-old son had turned it off. He had correctly discovered that it was an immediate way to get my full attention. "Jeff, did you want something?"

"Uh huh," he replied. "Mommy, when are you gonna be a writer?"

Now this was a question for which I was absolutely not prepared. I was writing and being published regularly. In fact, I had even won several awards for my writing, so I had no idea what my son meant. I proceeded cautiously. "Uh, Jeffrey, what does Mommy have to do to be a writer?"

He smiled. "Write a book for me and my friends instead of all that boring stuff I can't even read. Will you do that Mommy? Will you write a book for me and my friends?"

Never having written for young children, I tried to divert his attention by suggesting some good children's books that were already available, but my son was having none of my tactics. "Mommy, please, please, please—"

"Okay, I'll try," I said, figuring he would soon forget about the whole idea.

Jeff grinned and went off to play. I got back to the article I was writing, and I confess that I pretty well forgot about our conversation until Jeff got home from school the next day. "Guess what," he said bounding into the house. "I told everybody at school that you were going to write a book for me, and we could put it in the library this Friday."

I gasped. "Jeff, you didn't?"

"I did!" he assured me, and his lower lip stuck out. "Aren't you going to write my book?"

Suddenly, I realized that his project was not going to go away, and although I knew there was no way I was going to get a book written by that Friday, I also knew that I better begin.

I wrote the book. I rewrote the book, and I rewrote the book again before I submitted it.

Two years passed. Other things were getting published regularly, but my children's book was only getting rejections. My son had long ago given up being excited. In fact, he'd even passed getting discouraged and was now just plain mad. He was sure that I wasn't trying hard enough, and he took my failure as a personal affront to himself.

I redoubled my efforts. Rejection continued. Finally, after four years and numerous rewrites, the book was accepted. Jeff was the first person I told, and he said, "Great, how soon will my book be in our school library?"

Unfortunately, the answer was not very. We waited two more years for the book to actually be published. By that time, Jeff was in sixth grade. He was older than the book's protagonist, and he was now reading more complex material. Nonetheless, the book's dedication read, "To Jeff Fields who always believed this book would come to be."

I handed him a copy, figuring that by now, he was too old to care about the book's appearance in his school library, but at least, he could see I'd kept my promise. Book in hand, Jeff looked at me. "Only one copy? I need another one for the school library."

And so five years after that day Jeff had first requested a book, we had an official ceremony in the school library. The librarian announced that this truly was a special day, for while she had had books signed by authors previously, never before had she had a book signed by the person to whom it was dedicated. It was Jeff whom she called forward to sign the library copy, and as he did so, he grinned at me and winked.

Jeff is now in college, but the lesson he taught me remains. A writer can face many pressures. A short deadline, an impossible editor, even writer's block. But there is no pressure greater than that of a child who believes in a parent, and no writing prize or reward is greater than fulfilling that belief.

Terri Fields

No One Faces Rejection More Often than an Author

Those who believe that they are exclusively in the right are generally those who achieve something.

Aldous Huxley

Why do so many books get their start being published by the author? Rejection! The explanation is simple and let us not blame the publisher for failing to recognize good writing. Publishers cannot be experts in every type of fiction and nonfiction. Let's face it, publishers specialize or, at least, they have a record of accomplishment with certain types of books.

When your manuscript is rejected by a publisher, that is not a bad grade for your work. That simply means that the publisher does not get it! If a publisher specializes in travel books and you send a manuscript on vegetarian eating or parenting, that publisher will not know whether your work is good and will not know where to sell it. You do not want that publisher. To find the right publisher for your work, do your homework and match your manuscript to the publisher.

Alternatively, to make more money, get to press sooner and keep control of your work, publish yourself. Self-publishing is legitimate, an early-American tradition. In the early days of the New World, the person with the printing press was often the author, publisher, printer and bookshop. Some people think that most of those who self-publish do so because several publishers have turned them down. That is occasionally true.

However, most people today weigh the advantages and disadvantages of selling out to a publisher and make an educated decision to publish themselves. The big New York publishers publish only 22 percent of the books. The rest come from small (mom and pop) publishers and single-title self-publishers.

Self-publishing should not be confused with "Vanity" publishing where an author pays (an exorbitant price to) a publisher to turn his or her manuscript into a book.

Here is a partial list of self-published books. Some are still sold by the author, some authors have sold out and some books have started successful publishing companies.

- *What Color Is Your Parachute* by Episcopal clergyman Richard Nelson Bolles. 22 editions, 5 copies and 288 weeks on the *New York Times* bestseller list. Now published by Ten Speed Press.
- *The Beanie Baby Handbook* by Lee and Sue Fox sold 3 million copies in two years and made #2 on the *New York Times* bestseller list.
- *In Search of Excellence* by Tom Peters. Over 25,000 copies were sold directly to consumers in its first year. Then it was sold to Warner and the publisher sold 10 million more.
- *Real Peace* by Richard Nixon in 1983.
- *The Celestine Prophecy* by James Redfield. His manuscript made the rounds of the mainstream houses,

and then he decided to publish himself. He started by selling copies out of the trunk of his Honda—more than 100,000 of them. He subsequently sold out to Warner Books for $800,000. The number-one bestseller in 1996, it spent 165 weeks on the *New York Times* bestseller list. Over 5.5 million copies have been sold.

- *The One-Minute Manager* by Ken Blanchard and Spencer Johnson sold over 20,000 copies locally before they sold out to William Morrow. It has now sold more than 12 million copies since 1982 and is in 25 languages.
- *Fifty Simple Things You Can Do to Save the Earth* spent seven months on the *New York Times* bestseller list and sold 4.5 million copies in its original and premium editions.
- *The Elements of Style* by William Strunk, Jr. (and his student E. B. White) as originally self-published for Strunk's classes at Cornell University in 1918.
- *A Time to Kill* by John Grisham. He sold his first work out of the trunk of his car.
- *The Joy of Cooking* by Irma Rombauer was self-published in 1931 as a project of the First Unitarian Women's Alliance in St. Louis. Today Scribners sells more than 100,000 copies each year.
- *How to Keep Your Volkswagen Alive* by John Muir sold more than 2 million copies and led to the establishment of a publishing company.
- *Leadership Secrets of Attila the Hun* by Wess Roberts sold 486,000 copies before selling out to Warner Books.
- *Embraced by the Light* by Betty J. Eadie spent 76 weeks on the *New York Times* Hardcover Bestseller List, 123 weeks on the Paperback List and was sold to Bantam Books for $1.5 million. The audio rights brought in another $100,000. Then she established Onjinjinkta Publishing to publish her future projects.

- *Sugar Busters!* by four Louisiana doctors and a former CEO sold 165,000 copies regionally in just a year and a half. Then they sold out to Ballantine Books.
- *The Wealthy Barber* by David Chilton has sold more than a million copies in Canada (second only to the Bible in Canada) and 2 million in the US.
- *When I Am an Old Woman I Shall Wear Purple* has been through the press forty-two times for 1.5 million in print. It allowed Sandra Haldeman Martz to build Paper Mâché Press.
- *Mary Ellen's Best of Helpful Hints* by Mary Ellen Pinkham became a bestseller and then she sold out to Warner Books.
- *The Macintosh Bible* by Arthur Naiman has become the bestselling book on Apple products with over 900,000 sold.
- *Dianetics* by L. Ron Hubbard has been in print more than forty-five years, 20 million copies are in print, and it has been translated into twenty-two languages. The book started a movement and later a church.
- *Mutant Message Down Under* by Marlo Morgan sold 370,000 copies before it was sold to HarperCollins for $1.7 million. It was sold to two book clubs, and the foreign rights were sold to fourteen countries.
- *Feed Me, I'm Yours* by Vicky Lansky sold 300,000 copies. She sold out to Bantam, and they sold 8 million more.
- *The Encyclopedia of Associations* by Frederick Ruffner led to the establishment of Gale Research Company with 500 employees.
- *The Lazy Man's Way to Riches.* Joe Karbo never sold out and never courted bookstores. He sold millions of his books via full-page ads in newspapers and magazines.
- *The Christmas Box* by Richard Paul Evans. The eighty-seven-page book took him six weeks to write. He published it and promoted it himself. It did so well he sold

out to Simon & Schuster for $4.2 million. It hit the top of the *Publishers Weekly* bestseller list and was translated into thirteen languages.

- *Twelve Golden Threads* by Aliske Webb was rejected by 150 publishers. After self-publishing and selling 25,000 copies, she signed a four-book contract with HarperCollins.
- *Life's Little Instruction Book* was initially self-published by H. Jackson Brown. Then it was purchased by Rutledge Hill Press. It made the top of the *New York Times* bestseller list in hardcover and soft at the same time. More than 5 million copies were sold.
- *The Jester Has Lost His Jingle* by Barbara Salzman was turned down by eight publishers. The glossy hardcover book made it to the *New York Times* bestsellers list.
- *Let's Cook Microwave* by Barbara Harris sold over 700,000 copies.
- *Juggling for the Complete Klutz* by John Cassidy has sold over 2 million copies and lead to the establishment of Klutz Press with more than 50 award-winning books.
- Ben Dominitz published *Travel Free* and then founded Prima Publishing. Prima now has 1,500 titles, 140 employees and does $60 million a year.
- *How to Flatten Your Stomach* by Jim Everrode was self-published before he sold out to Price/Stern/Sloan. Since then, the book has sold more than 2 million copies.
- *The Self-Publishing Manual* by Dan Poynter has 143,000 copies in print after twelve revised editions since 1979. The publisher is Para Publishing (Dan Poynter). Because of this book, Poynter has been called "the godfather to thousands of books."

Other well-known self-publishers include: Deepak Chopra, Louise Hay, Mark Twain, Ken Keyes, Jr., Gertrude Stein, Zane Grey, Upton Sinclair, Carl Sandburg, James

Joyce, D. H. Lawrence, Ezra Pound, Edgar Rice Burroughs, Stephen Crane, Mary Baker Eddy, George Bernard Shaw, Anaïs Nin, Thomas Paine, Virginia Wolff, e. e. cummings, William Blake, Edgar Allen Poe, Rudyard Kipling, Henry David Thoreau, Benjamin Franklin, Walt Whitman, Alexandre Dumas, William E.B. DuBois and Robert Ringer.

Dan Poynter

Learning from Rejection

I got another one of those darned letters the other day. You know the type. The "Dear-Contributor-we're-sorry-but-due-to-the-enormous-volume-of-unsolicited-manu-scripts-we-receive-every-ten-minutes-a-personal-reply-is-simply-not-possible-so-why-don't-you-just-take-a-sledgehammer-to-your-computer-and-go-get-an-MBA" type of letter.

Ah, rejection. Will there ever be a time when we no longer know each other so intimately? After all these years as a writer, I still feel the same way when I open that thin self-addressed, stamped envelope.

I once told a friend that I kept every rejection letter I ever received. "Throw them away!" she howled. But I can't. I keep them in a file labeled *rejections*, next to a file labeled *contracts*, a handy little metaphor that I can con-template on a daily basis.

And I must say, I've got plenty to contemplate. I have a nice collection of those little postcards with a form reply stamped on the back. I also have an impressive sampling of the slightly more encouraging form letters with per-sonal notes that say, "Keep trying us." I've even received some personally written rejections that were downright sweet, sort of like letters from long lost friends or from the telephone company.

My absolute favorite rejection letter came from an editor with whom I actually had a contract. I was assigned to cover a spectacular Christmas pageant called Las Posadas, held every winter along the River Walk in San Antonio, Texas. I wrote the story, sent the manuscript to the editor and smugly awaited my check.

The editor's reply began like this:

Dear Ms. Rosenblum:

Well, your article needs a lot of work. Our staff believes it should be rewritten. One of the editors wonders whether you really witnessed the event.

He waited until the second paragraph to tell me what he *really* thought:

Most of the quotes are inane. Do not begin sentences with 'it is,' 'there is,' or 'there were.' Check your verbs to be sure that most of them are active.

I think his parting words were meant to cheer me up. "Be not discouraged. Please try to return the article by the middle of March."

Be not discouraged? Me? Don't be silly! Where's the nearest cliff?

After I nursed my bruised ego for a day or two, I rewrote the manuscript and returned it with a cover letter that read, in part:

Dear Editor:

I must admit that I was deeply disappointed to find that my first manuscript displeased you as much as it did. As a freelancer, I realize the importance of delivering the goods on

*time and in excellent condition. Please let me know soon how
I fared this time around.*

I should probably have ended it there. You know, the
mature writer graciously accepting the inevitable pitfalls
that come with the territory. But I couldn't help myself.
"*Incidentally,*" I continued, "*please pass on to the editor who
wondered whether I witnessed Las Posadas that yes, indeed, I was
there and the evening will be one of my fondest memories of San
Antonio. And please add that the next time I am in San Antonio, I
would like to invite her to lunch on the river—and push her in.*"

His reply was prompt.

Dear Ms. Rosenblum:
   *All right, that's more like it. I knew you could do it. Our
surly staff is really happy with the rewrite. I don't know why
you seemed so upset about my returning the article. We do it
all the time with veteran writers. Did you ever read many
Hemingway books or short stories? Some of his things
should never have been published. Sometimes a writer just
misses the mark. But professionals accept criticism with a
shrug and go on.*
   *About the editor you want to push into the San Antonio
River . . . Ol' Rosie is pretty mean. But she likes your second
version.*

When the magazine arrived with my rewritten article, I
felt incredibly proud. It *was* better than my original draft.
But I felt more than proud. I felt overwhelming gratitude
to that editor, who took the time to make me do—and
help me do—what I should have done all along.
   After rereading the editor's words yesterday, I stared at
my most recent rejection letter, which is for a short story
I've been trying to sell. And I took his advice. I shrugged

my shoulders and got down to the gritty task of rewriting it for the thousandth time.

Someday this short story will find a home. And when it does, I'll smile a little and add the invoice to my contract file. Maybe I'll even take the rest of the day off to, say, edit a few chapters of a Hemingway novel.

Gail Rosenblum

Consider This

The marvelous richness of human experience would lose something of rewarding joy if there were not limitations to overcome. The hilltop hour would not be half so wonderful if there were no dark valleys to traverse.

Helen Keller

- Richard Hooker worked for seven years on his humorous war novel, *M*A*S*H*, only to have it rejected by twenty-one publishers before Morrow decided to publish it. It became a runaway bestseller, spawning a blockbuster movie and a highly successful television series.
- Richard Bach completed only one year of college, then trained to become an Air Force jet-fighter pilot. Twenty months after earning his wings, he resigned. Then he became an editor of an aviation magazine that went bankrupt. Life became one failure after another. Even when he wrote *Jonathan Livingston Seagull,* he couldn't think of an ending. The 10,000-word manuscript lay dormant for eight years before he decided

how to finish it—only to have eighteen publishers reject it before it was finally published by Macmillan. However, once it was published, the book went on to sell more than 7 million copies in numerous languages and make Richard Bach an internationally known and respected author.

- Louis L'Amour, successful author of more than 100 western novels with more than 200 million copies in print, received 350 rejections before he made his first sale. He later became the first American novelist to receive a special congressional gold medal in recognition of his distinguished career as an author and contributor to the nation through his historically based books.
- British Writer John Creasy received 774 rejections before selling his first story. He went on to write 564 books, using fourteen different names.
- In 1953, Julia Child and her two collaborators signed a publishing contract to produce a book tentatively titled *French Cooking for the American Kitchen*. Julia and her colleagues worked on the book for five years. The publisher rejected the 850-page manuscript. Child and her partners worked for another year totally revising the manuscript. Again the publisher rejected it. But Julia Child did not give up. She and her collaborators went back to work again, found a new publisher, and in 1961—eight years after beginning—they published *Mastering the Art of French Cooking*, which has sold more than one million copies. In 1966, *Time* magazine featured Julia Child on its cover. Julia Child is still at the top of her field thirty years later.
- Dr. Seuss' first children's book, *And to Think That I Saw It on Mulberry Street*, was rejected by twenty-seven publishers. The twenty-eighth publisher, Vanguard Press, sold six million copies of the book. All of his children's books went on to sell a total of more than 100 million copies.
- The author William Kennedy had written several

manuscripts, all of them rejected by numerous publishers before his "sudden success" with his novel *Ironweed*, which was rejected by thirteen publishers before it was finally accepted for publication.

- Pearl Buck's *The Good Earth* was rejected fourteen times and went on to win a Pulitzer Prize.
- *The Naked and the Dead* by Norman Mailer was rejected twelve times.
- Margaret Mitchell's classic *Gone with the Wind* was turned down by more than twenty-five publishers.
- Mary Higgins Clark was rejected forty times before selling her first story. More than 30 million copies of her books are now in print.
- Robert Pirsig's classic, *Zen and the Art of Motorcycle Maintenance*, was rejected by 121 publishers before being published.
- Fifteen publishers and thirty agents turned down John Grisham's first novel, *A Time to Kill*. More than 60 million copies of his novels are now in print.
- Jack London received 600 rejection slips before he sold his first story.
- Eight years after his novel *Steps* won the National Book Award, Jerzy Kosinski permitted a writer to change his name and the title and send a manuscript of the novel to thirteen agents and fourteen publishers to test the plight of new writers. They all rejected it, including Random House, which had published it.
- When we completed the first *Chicken Soup for the Soul* book, it was turned down by thirty-three publishers in New York and another ninety at the American Booksellers Association convention in Anaheim, California, before Health Communications, Inc., finally agreed to publish it. All the major New York publishers said, "It is too nicey-nice" and "Nobody wants to read a book of short little stories." Since that time more than 8 million copies of the original *Chicken*

Soup for the Soul book have been sold. The series, which has grown to thirty-two titles, in thirty-one languages, has sold more than 53 million copies.

- Alex Haley received a rejection letter once a week for four years as a budding writer. Later in his career, Alex was ready to give up on the book *Roots* and himself. After nine years on the project, he felt inadequate to the task and was ready to throw himself off a freighter in the middle of the Pacific Ocean. As he was standing at the back of the freighter, looking at the wake and preparing to jump into the ocean, he heard the voices of all his ancestors saying, "You go do what you got to do because they are all up there watching. Don't give up. You can do it. We're counting on you!" In the subsequent weeks, the final draft of *Roots* poured out of him.

- The movie *Star Wars* was rejected by every movie studio in Hollywood before 20th-Century Fox finally produced it. It went on to be one of the largest-grossing movies in film history.

- *E.T., Forrest Gump, Home Alone, Speed* and *Pulp Fiction* were all rejected by major studios before they finally found a studio willing to produce them.

- In 1902, the poetry editor of the *Atlantic Monthly* returned the poems of a twenty-eight-year-old poet with the following note: "Our magazine has no room for your vigorous verse." The poet was Robert Browning.

- In 1889, Rudyard Kipling received the following rejection letter from the *San Francisco Examiner:* "I'm sorry, Mr. Kipling, but you just don't know how to use the English language."

- Louisa May Alcott, the author of *Little Women,* was encouraged to find work as a servant or seamstress by her family.

- Leo Tolstoy, author of *War and Peace,* flunked out of college. He was described as "both unable and unwilling to learn."

- Woody Allen—Academy Award-winning writer, producer and director—flunked motion picture production at New York University and the City College of New York. He also failed English at New York University.
- Leon Uris, author of the bestseller *Exodus,* failed high school English three times.
- Malcolm Forbes, the late editor-in-chief of *Forbes* magazine, one of the most successful business publications in the world, failed to make the staff of the school newspaper when he was an undergraduate at Princeton University.
- After Thomas Carlyle lent the manuscript of *The French Revolution* to a friend whose servant carelessly used it to kindle a fire, he calmly went to work and rewrote it.
- John Bunyan wrote *Pilgram's Progress* while confined to a Bedford Prison cell for his views on religion; Sir Walter Raleigh wrote the *History of the World* during a thirteen-year imprisonment; and Martin Luther translated the Bible while confined in the Castle of Wartburg.
- Novelist Carson McCullers endured three strokes before she was twenty-nine. While she was crippled, partially paralyzed and in constant pain, she suffered the profound shock of her husband's suicide. Others may have surrendered to such afflictions, but she settled for writing no less than a page a day. On that unrelenting schedule, she turned out many distinguished novels, including *Member of the Wedding, The Ballad of the Sad Cafe* and *The Heart Is a Lonely Hunter.*

Jack Canfield, Mark Victor Hansen and Bud Gardner

Some People Just Can't Take a Hint

Other authors write many stories. I write the same story many times. Take "The Gift," for instance. You might say the story began several decades ago when I was a student in college. In the class where I did my student teaching was a plain-looking, shabbily-dressed little girl named Elizabeth. (That was in an era before it was fashionable to be shabbily dressed.) Elizabeth was, even at the age of eight, a loser—what we educators refer to as a "social isolate." I was intrigued by the knowledge that Elizabeth's mother, a divorcee, was a well-known artist and a very glamorous one at that. Why would someone like that have a daughter so drab and lacking in self-concept?

Elizabeth and those unanswered questions were shoved aside in the attic of my mind and not remembered again until twenty years later when I first decided I was a writer. (This decision was based on the sale of a 200-word story to a Sunday School paper, for which I received $1.35.)

The first time I wrote the story of Elizabeth, the manuscript emerged as a "thing"—a character sketch, possibly —which was rejected by all the first-class magazines and women's magazines.

In the second writing, I changed Elizabeth's name to Lisa on account it was easier to type. I also had learned by that time that a story needs a theme, so my message was that a child can drown in a family where the parents' personalities are overpowering. The story was rejected by all the first-class magazines, women's magazines and religious publications.

Meantime I had joined a writers' circle, where we read aloud and critiqued one another's manuscripts. What my story needed, the writers told me, was a romantic angle, so I went into the third version of the story. This time I gave Lisa a father instead of a divorced mother, and had the father in love with Lisa's teacher. At this point the story was entitled "The Listening Heart." "Listening Heart" was rejected by all the first-class magazines, other-class magazines, religious publications and education journals. Many of the rejections specified that the editors had "similar material on hand." What I needed, the writers' circle decided, was a unique theme.

So okay. Now Lisa got her glamorous mother back, and the divorced father got taken out of the story. My new message was that a parent has something to give a child which no one else can give, even when the parent doesn't know how to be a parent. I liked this theme so much that I used it for all the subsequent revisions and rewritings. The story's new title was "The Gift." I liked that title because of its symbolism. The gift was a book which Selma, Lisa's mother, wrote for her daughter. (In the last dozen or so versions of the story, Selma was an author instead of an artist.) Besides its obvious connotation, "the gift" referred to the quality of parenthood.

The story was still being rejected by all the first-class magazines, other-class magazines, religious publications, education journals and a newly discovered category, the "little" magazines.

By then, however, I was getting some editorial comments on the manuscript: "Readable, but I'm afraid I don't know what your point is." "Beautiful story, but not for us." "Touching. Try us again." "Well-written, but might be stronger if your point was that poor parents destroy their children." "Sorry!" (I didn't know whether that meant the editorial staff was sorry, or the story was.) "Skillful writing. Send us something, but not this."

Meantime, changes were taking place among the members of the writers' circle—more bunions and varicose veins, more reading glasses, more children and grandchildren. We were even learning how to write and to sell what we wrote. I sold a number of articles, a couple of mediocre poems, some teenage novels and three pamphlets. The most unchanging feature about the group was that I always had a version of "The Gift" to read. This became a standing joke, and every meeting opened with some remark such as: "Does anyone have something to read? Besides 'The Gift,' that is. "What magazine didn't want 'The Gift' this week, Meg?" "If anybody needs a title, there's always 'The Gift.'"

I became so self-conscious about my story that I got an emotional block whenever the word "gift" came into my conversations, and I always said "present" instead.

"Which version of 'The Gift' do we have tonight?" someone would invariably ask at the writers' circle. Then everyone would bray with mirth for several minutes. I would join in the merriment, all the while thinking, "Wait till the slobs see it in print!"

It became an obsession with me that my story must appear in print, mostly on account of the writers' circle, but also because "The Gift" was costing me so much in postage, twenty-pound typing paper, large manila envelopes, typewriter ribbon and trips to the post office. I had long since run out of markets and started over on the list. An editor commented, "We didn't want this last year, and we haven't changed our minds."

One editor did change his mind, however. On its 124th trip out, "The Gift" found a home with a magazine that had rejected it a couple of times before. Ironically, I experienced a stab of loneliness. "The Gift" was rather like a spinster daughter who is around the house for years. The parents are afraid they'll never unload her, but when they finally do, there's a hole in the household. I didn't wish my spinster daughter back, however!

Now instead of affording merriment, "The Gift" and I were being taken seriously. I was introduced to people as "the writer who had sold a manuscript after 123 rejections." I was invited to talk at a writer's conference about marketing. I was a record-breaker! This must be how those guys at the Olympics feel when they run a mile in forty-six seconds, or whatever it is they run it in.

One thing I am sure—however long I continue to write and however many words I manage to sell, there will never be another triumph quite as rewarding as the sale of "The Gift."

Meg Hill

PEANUTS. *Reprinted by permission of United Feature Syndicate, Inc.*

How I Want to Be Remembered

If my doctor told me I had only six months to live, I wouldn't brood. I'd type faster.

Isaac Asimov

I was once asked by the Americans to write how, when I die, I want to be remembered.

After more than ninety-seven years of life, this was quite an undertaking because so many things have happened during those years.

I have been ecstatically happy, very miserable and deeply saddened, especially when I lost my father, Captain Bertram Cartland, in May of 1918, during World War I, then both my brothers at Dunkirk in 1940—Anthony on May 29, and Ronald on May 30—in World War II.

I have been shown great kindness. I have endured a certain amount of teasing and sometimes ridicule by the press. At the same time, they have helped and supported wholeheartedly my often very controversial *crusades*.

I would like to be remembered for my books, especially for my novels, through which I have tried to give morality, beauty and love to the world.

I have written at the moment 704 books all together and have sold approximately 750 million. *The Guinness Book of World Records* says that I am the "Best Selling Author in the World," and I hold the world's record for writing and publishing twenty-three or more books a year for twenty-one years straight. And it delights me to think that I am now published in every country.

Journalists who come to interview me always start by saying:

"When did you start writing, Dame Barbara?"

"When I was five years old," I reply, and they do not believe me.

I did, however, write a book for my mother when I was that age. I illustrated it and bound it with some pieces of wallpaper. My mother was delighted. I called it *The Little Slide Maker.*

My mother, Mary Hamilton Scobell, was heartbroken when my father was killed. She was left with me, aged seventeen, and my two brothers—Ronald and Anthony—who were still at school at Charterhouse, where my father had also been educated.

We had very little money, and my mother asked where I would like to live. I said: "London," and we moved there. But my mother said we would have to go to the country on school holidays.

I was bored in the country, and once when my brother told me to be quiet because he had to write an essay, I replied: "Then I will write a book."

Everyone said I would never finish it because I was out dancing all night. However, I did finish it, and I called it *Jigsaw.* This was my first novel, published in 1923. It was a huge success, going into six editions and being published in five languages.

After that, I began to write seriously to make money.

I was asked by a friend who had just come out of the

Navy, who was working for a new newspaper called *The Daily Express,* if I would give him a paragraph for his newspaper in the morning after I had *danced all night,* and he would pay me five shillings.

This was the first time I had written for a newspaper, and I thought it would be rather fun.

After a few weeks, the owner of the newspaper, Lord Beaverbrook, sent for me. He said I wrote very well, but he wished to correct my contribution every night before it went to the newspaper. He taught me to write as a journalist, which has been a tremendous help to me all my life.

Lord Beaverbrook sent a car for me every week, and I went to his house for dinner where I met his friends.

They were Lord Birkenhead, who was a great judge at the time; Winston Churchill, who had just lost his seat in Parliament; Viscount Castlerosse, the greatest wit of the time; the Duke of Sutherland, whose ancestral home Dunrobin Castle in Scotland was like a fairy palace with its turrets and towers; and Sir James Dunn, who was very rich and a Canadian like Lord Beaverbrook.

Later, in 1935, my brother Ronald, who was working in the Conservative Central Office, told me that the Constituency of Kings Norton in Birmingham had come into the market, and he would love to stand. But, unfortunately, he could not afford it, as in those days a candidate had to pay the cost to run which came to about £1,000. The first time, I began to write 10,000 words a day. I paid Ronald's expenses and helped him by speaking every night to win the seat of Kings Norton, Birmingham.

When World War II came in 1939, Ronald joined the Worchestershire Regiment and went out to France.

Sir Winston Churchill, then the Prime Minister, said that if he returned from Dunkirk, he intended to make him a Minister. He did not return, and after Ronald's death, I wrote his biography; Sir Winston Churchill wrote the preface.

I am very thrilled by what I have achieved in my life, and I hope I have helped a great number of people to find love. What really matters, however, is that I do bring happiness to people, for the simple reason that my heroines are the sweet, loving, genuine women who were first portrayed by Shakespeare in *Romeo and Juliet* and whose example has been copied by all classical authors.

It is they who evoke in a man the real love that is both spiritual and physical, and it is the woman in a marriage who stands for Morality, Compassion, Sympathy and Love. I finish all my books with:

"They found Love. Real Love, which comes from God, is part of God, and is theirs for Eternity."

Dame Barbara Cartland

10

INSIGHTS AND LESSONS

There are three rules for writing the novel. Unfortunately, no one knows what they are.

W. Somerset Maugham

The House on Phoenix Circle

There are depths in mankind that go to the lowest hell, and reach the highest heaven, for are not both heaven and hell made out of him, everlasting miracle and mystery that he is?

Thomas Carlyle

I suppose every writer reaches a point in his career where it seems that the well has gone dry. That putting sentences on paper is like chiseling each word out of solid rock.

I might have been less discouraged if I had been writing for years, but I had only just begun. My writing credits consisted of two novels sold to a minor publisher, two years worth of newspaper columns and a couple dozen articles published in national magazines. Was it enough to have justified giving up a successful career as an artist, a painter of murals and seascapes? The questions in my head could no longer be dismissed.

My husband loved my paintings. On the rare occasions when I worked in the evenings, he would stand behind me, awestruck by the way a stone fence slowly emerged from a few blobs of umber and ocher and gray, or the way a hint of cerulean blue made sunlight glitter through the transparent crest of a breaking wave.

He hated the thought that I was becoming seduced by the written word. That writing threatened to take over my life.

But old yearnings can be hard to lay to rest. From the time I first discovered books, I wanted to be a writer, but they said you must write about what you know. For me, this would have covered about three pages. It seemed hopeless.

I had spent a fruitless morning becoming more aware by the moment of the growing pile of crumpled beginnings of a new novel. Desperate, I picked up my sketchpad and began walking through my neighborhood. On impulse I turned a corner that led into a cul de sac. We had lived in the area for only a few months. This was the first time I saw the house at the end of Phoenix Circle.

It was of old Spanish design, painted stucco faded to a pearly mauve that in places peeled away like thick makeup worn too long in the hot summer sun. Patches of dusky green moss and lichen freckled the coves and niches shaded by an ancient olive tree. At the roof level, spreading eaves overhung hooded window openings; stone arches accentuated with ornately carved corbels at the terminus of the arches. Iron grillwork gave the impression of separateness, closing the house off from all intruders.

Where one wing joined the main section of the house, a vine-covered archway bore the inscription: *Esta es su casa.* This is your house.

I was enthralled. Here was something I could paint. I sat down on the curb and began to sketch. There was none of the usual hesitation . . . where to begin . . . where to put the horizon . . . perspective . . . light, shadow. It was all there, I just had to get it down.

I worked frantically, unaware of the passage of time when suddenly a long shadow spread across the sketchbook.

"Good afternoon, my dear, I was worried about you. You've been sitting in the hot sun for over an hour."

I looked up to see a woman in a pale blue floor-length dress, banded at the hem with a wide border of scarlet, black and white. Her hair was grayed, shot with silver streaks and tucked into a fat braid that hung well below her waist.

"I've startled you," she said. Infinitely fine wrinkles spiderwebbed her face as if choreographed to move to the music of her voice. "Forgive me. May I offer you a glass of iced tea."

At first, I was too surprised to answer. A cautious upbringing told me to refuse, but an innate curiosity combined with a parched throat, drove me forward.

"That's very kind of you," I said. "Yes, I'd love some tea if it's not too much trouble."

"No trouble at all. I wanted to see your drawing of my house. And besides, I would enjoy the company."

She turned then and led me through the gated archway. For the first time I noticed her cane and how time had exacted its bounty on her stooped shoulders. I guessed her to be in her late eighties.

We entered the enclosed patio, a garden of flowers surrounded by the house, and in the center, a murmuring fountain sprayed mists of dew upon mossy paving stones. The sun was brilliant. She directed me to a round table set with white linen and fine crystal sheltered by a galleria that ran the length of the center wing. Wind chimes, driven by the spray of water, played a soft counterpoint to the whisper of the fountain on the motionless air.

We sat there for perhaps an hour, sipping tea and talking. That is, I did most of the talking, because for some reason, she was able to draw from me all the insecurities I had kept so carefully hidden during the past two years. She listened, never interrupting, never passing judgment, either by expression or by spoken word.

Exhausted, drained dry, I laughed shakily. "I can't imagine why I burdened you with my problems. I'm so sorry. It must be this exquisite house."

"You love it, don't you," she said. "I can see it in the way you've depicted it in your drawing. You have a rather nice touch with the pen."

"I think it's the most wonderful house I've ever seen," I said, trying to ignore the less than enthusiastic comment about my sketch. "I love houses and trees and gardens. There's something so welcoming about this house. So warm and inviting."

"Oh, it's not the house. It's the people." She laughed then, a thin papery sound, old, fragile, but entirely pleasing to the ear. "That's not to say I meant myself. But it's people who make life fascinating. People leave their imprint on old houses like these. People in all their complexities with all their goodness and all their sins." Her eyes twinkled. "My dear, you must know that a place is nothing until you have people to dance to its music."

I couldn't help but smile. "And what kind of people have danced in this beautiful old house," I wondered aloud.

"Child, you couldn't begin to imagine."

Her face was transformed as she settled back in her chair. Her delicately blue-veined hands linked together by gnarled fingers, she closed her eyes and began her story of how the house came to be built.

In Mexico, her grandmother, Elena, was forced into marriage to Carlos Vandera, a famous fighter of bulls. He treated her cruelly and refused to release her from their marriage. A high-spirited woman, Elena escaped from her husband, only to be denied refuge in her father's house.

While being pursued by her husband, Elena was lost in the desert and rescued by a handsome bandito, named Alejandro Cordillera. Seeing that she suffered from exposure, Alejandro gave her sanctuary in his mountain hideout. When Elena's husband discovered where she was, he came after her and tried to take her back, but the bandit shot him and two of his followers. The rest fled.

The bandit, fearing for their safety, fled with Elena across the border to California where he bought a piece of land, built this house, and because of his love for Elena, became a peaceable, law-abiding citizen and respected businessman.

My hostess sighed and closed her eyes as if reliving some special moment.

"There you have it, my dear. That is what this house is all about. The people. Generations of families who by their mere existence, left their mark on the world. From the congressman to the priest, to Sara, the beautiful prostitute who died giving birth . . . to me." Her eyes clouded, then brightened.

"Not all of them good, mind you, but these people had character, character to be reckoned with. They were people who were driven to meet their destinies, be it heaven or the darker kingdom. Just like in your books, I rather imagine."

I stood suddenly and paced the floor. "No! Not like in my books." An uncontrollable surge of joy flowed through me. "And that's what's been wrong. I see it now. My people aren't driven. They have hardly begun to breathe." Sinking once again into the chair, I noticed that my hands were shaking.

It was as if a door just opened for me, and I could see dawn on the other side. Oh, my characters were nice enough. Maybe they were too good, too uncomplicated. I had become so obsessed with plot that I forgot to create a history for my players, solid reasons for them to love and hate . . . and to triumph.

I leaned forward, babbling, but unable to stop myself. She listened, nodding encouragingly until I was finally purged of all the doubt that had plagued me.

"I can write," I vowed. "I know I can."

She raised an eyebrow. "And what will your husband say, if you give up your painting?"

"He will understand," I said. "I know he will. Above all, he wants me to find my own way."

"Ah, one of the good people." She tapped her chest. "And you will be happy. I feel it here in my heart."

I thanked her then and said my good-bye with the hope to see her again. As I walked down the street toward home, I turned once and looked back, half expecting the house to disappear mirage-like in the waves of heat rising up from the pavement. But she stood there in the archway leaning into her cane and waving a Queen Elizabeth salute.

The last time I saw her alive was when she was guest of honor at a party to celebrate the success of my first bestseller, *The Sleeping Heiress.*

My husband was at my side, as he was for the publication of my next seventeen books. She was right. People make a difference.

Phyllis Taylor Pianka

Nothing Unconnected Lasts

The Marine who lived on the ground floor next to us was just back from Vietnam. We heard him slowly climb the stairs and knock on the door of the apartment directly above him. The young Southern couple who had recently moved in opened the door together. They faced the Marine side-by-side: silent, righteous and united. They thought he had come to discuss their grievance, but they were wrong.

"Do you see those stairs?" he said without blinking.

"And do you see this knife?" He had a double-edged switchblade in his hand and he flipped it open.

"If you ever pour water through the floor again when I'm doing my music— I don't care if it's two, three, four in the morning—I will cut your white throats, and I will drag your bodies down those stairs."

He looked at them in silence, then said, "They will go bump, bump, bump, as I drag them. Do I make myself clear?"

The couple nodded quietly and shut the door.

It was 1968 and Gayle and I were living in a quadruplex on 8th Avenue in Berkeley. Berkeley was the place, and the sixties, the time of supposed Cultural Revolution. But the Southern couple did not know the realities of this movement. They, like us, thought they were there to save "the people": oppressed women, blacks, the poor of all races, and young men being shipped to Vietnam. They naively believed that "the people" welcomed their presence and wanted to be saved. Like so many who place themselves in the position of savior, they thought they were elegant human beings.

Being unwanted and disliked by those we were there to fight for was just one of countless ironies and conflicts Gayle and I had encountered since moving to Berkeley. There were also questions about how to react to the call to take hard drugs, to have open sex and to hate the establishment. And, for us there was the more pressing question, of my failure to get anything published in the two years since Gayle began supporting us.

Gayle had a secretarial job in San Francisco that paid the rent and kept food on the table. She was also the only person left who still supported my decision to become a writer. Both our families were openly disdainful of what I was attempting and increasingly lobbied for me to "get a real job." And now, this incident that I had witnessed between the Marine and the Southern couple seemed to signal the end of our experiment. Financially and emotionally, I knew that my time as a wanna-be writer was about up.

In my turmoil, I began writing out on yellow pads my questions and confusions about the last two years. For me, these jottings were merely a personal exploration and had nothing to do with real writing. Real writing is found in novels, poetry journals, and "serious" magazines. It is an act of intelligence and ample creativity. Thus real writing earns you respect, recognition and needed income. Yet push this envelope just a little and real writing, at least potentially, brings you fame, importance, wealth, and other forms of separateness—nothing any hippie in the sixties would have admitted wanting. Yet I could see now that this was the driving force behind everything I had written to that point.

The one ingredient that the writing I was doing strictly *for myself,* contained—and that my writing for publication had lacked—was truthfulness. By truthfulness, I don't mean the kind of surface honesty that is so often touted today—a mere spewing forth of the ego layer of our mind—but rather a quiet vision that goes to the core of our beliefs and values. Ego honesty answers the question, "What are my momentary opinions and emotions about the people around me—the reactions that will change within seconds of the time I give them voice?" Truthfulness answers the question, "What kind of person do I want to be toward those around me; what kind of person do I want to see that I have been when I look back at the end of my life?" One question accesses the agitated and separate; the other accesses the quiet and connected.

One day, during this period of self-examination, I wandered into Cody's bookstore off Telegraph Avenue. I picked up a book entitled *Person to Person* and on the first page was a solicitation for manuscripts. The only material I had that had not already been rejected was this stack of yellow pads. I guess you could call it a diary or journal, but it didn't look like much. More or less in desperation, I cleaned it up, entitled it what it was *Notes to Myself* and rather hopelessly sent it to the address given in the solicitation. Two days later, I got a letter of acceptance.

Although the company, Real People Press, had published only two other books, ran no ads and had no sales reps, my little journal of sorts went on to sell five million copies, and today, thirty years later, is still selling pretty well.

It is significant that the first three pages of the manuscript (the introduction was added later) were about my love for Gayle. If truthfulness distinguished this writing from my earlier attempts, my sense of oneness with another person—the first committed relationship in my life—was what *allowed* me to be truthful. Gayle and I have been married thirty-four years, and the fifteen books we have written since *Notes to Myself* all come from our deep bond, and later, from the broader unity that extended to our children.

The prerequisite to being truthful to yourself is to feel connection with another. This was a dawning realization for me even in the late sixties. It has been such a constant in my life as a writer since then that I can't grasp what so many authors mean when they speak of the inherent loneliness and isolation of the writing process. I certainly don't deny the validity of their experience, but I want you to know that I, personally, could not have written anything meaningful except out of my connection and calm sense of oneness with another person. My worst work has always come when I was feeling separate or judgmental of Gayle. The Cultural Revolution of the sixties did not last because it did not unite. And I know in my heart that my career would have gone nowhere if it had not contained a wellspring of empathy. For me, writing a book is like giving birth to a child—it is a creation of love, and love has its origins in unity.

Hugh Prather

Lesson of a Lifetime

The stuff of which masterpieces are made drifts about the world waiting to be clothed in words.
Thornton Wilder

After many years in publishing—a writer at *Business Week, Time* and CBS, assistant managing editor at *Reader's Digest*—I've come away with one single golden rule of writing. This is simply that there's a writer in every one of us, because there's a story in every one of us. In fact, there are many stories, because some of the best writing—the kind that readers readily identify with—comes out of all the little happenings in our daily lives. These are also the easiest stories to write, as author E. B. White noted. The only kind of writing he could accomplish with minimum effort, White once said, was about the small things in his day.

Martha Sweeney discovered this a few years ago. One afternoon, she was in a coin laundry outside her hometown of Stonewall, Texas, when half a dozen young motorcyclists suddenly roared up to the gas station next door. They were all a boisterous, rough-looking lot, and one of them—younger than the others, no more than seventeen—was the loudest and roughest-acting of the bunch. With several of his friends, the boy entered the laundry, and then something happened when he looked around at this small, rural town—and, especially, when he noticed this older woman observing him. In one of those revealing moments we've all lived through, Martha made eye contact with the boy and saw him hesitate.

Later, after his friends had gassed up their cycles, he told them his starter was on the blink and to go on without him. He said he'd catch up. After the others went roaring off, the boy brought some dirty clothes into the laundry. "His shoulders sagged as if he were terribly weary," Martha later wrote. "Dust and grease and sweat stained his shirt and jeans. A beginning beard faintly shadowed his chin and lean cheeks. He turned, and briefly our eyes met again. Emotion flickered across his face—doubt, longing, pain?"

Moments later the boy ran his clothes through the washer and dryer, then disappeared into the men's room. When he emerged ten minutes later, he was wearing clean pants and shirt, and he had shaved his scraggly beard, scrubbed his hands and face, and even combed his hair. He now grinned in Martha's direction and, jumping on his motorcycle, zoomed away. Not following the others, but going back the way he'd come—back toward home. From this small, moving experience, Martha wrote an article that was later published in *Reader's Digest*.

Good stories are all around us. The trick is developing an active curiosity about them—the way a child does. "Long before I wrote stories, I *listened* for stories," Eudora Welty recalls in *One Writer's Beginnings*. "Listening *for* them is something more acute than listening *to* them. I suppose it's an early form of participation in what goes on. Listening children know stories are *there*. When their elders sit and begin, children are just waiting and hoping for one to come out, like a mouse from its hole."

In her *Reader's Digest* article, "You Must Go Home Again," Ardis Whitman listened hard and heard a story that grew out of a trip she made to Nova Scotia, where she visited the house she'd grown up in many years before. Ardis emphasizes that this trip proved much more than a routine sentimental journey. It was a pilgrimage of spirit, reaffirming who she really was and giving her back again the blessed peace of belonging that we all—every one of us—need.

As Ardis writes: "Contrary to Thomas Wolfe's famous lament, 'You can't go home again,' we *must* all go home again—in reality or memory. When we don't, our lives lose their structure. Nostalgia is not simply a wistful exercise in sentiment. Rather, it is an illumination of the present; an invitation to reexamine oneself; to know the nature of the seed that started the tree; yes, and to remember what it was to be a child. Even if the past was not kind to you, turn it to account, to understanding."

I believe strongly in these simple, everyday stories that we all experience, and in the same way, I feel strongly that they should be written in the simple, everyday language that we all use. Among most writers, there's a natural tendency to get too exquisite and ornamental in their prose. Such writers spend all their time, as someone once put it, trying to pound the pig iron of language "into the bright toys and gleaming blades of literature." They ignore the fact that the best stories deal with the small concerns and verities of life—and you don't need fancy words for that.

So think more in terms of creating a small, delicate watercolor, rather than a giant oil painting. You want sentiment that stops short of sentimentality—simple words and simple construction for what should basically be a simple theme. Winston Churchill phrased it well: "I find the short words good, and the old, short words best of all."

Moreover, you want words that convey what I like to call "sensory detail." You want the reader to taste, touch, smell and feel the very experience you're sharing. As E. L. Doctorow once noted: "Good writing is supposed to evoke a sensation in the reader—not the fact that it's raining, but the *feeling* of being rained upon."

Jean George, a New York writer, is a master at this kind of sensory writing. After a winter storm several years ago, Jean was asked to check a friend's Long Island beach house while the friend was away. Jean expected to find a "dreary scene—an abandoned cottage set among pines, stirred by mournful winds." But the instant she climbed from her car, she found a world of harsh beauty, discovery and sensory delight.

"The air smelled clean as I looked out on a brilliant landscape," she wrote in an article for *Reader's Digest*. "The sea was a violet blue, the sky turquoise, and the beach, which last summer had sloped gently, was now steep, scooped out and luminous. Crabs scurried for burrows and gulls spiraled down on them, like paper airplanes against the sky. At the water's edge, empty shells that whisper when summer waves turn them now made shrill, whistling sounds."

Teased and tempted by what she found, Jean started thinking more and more about winter beaches—and soon, like any good writer, she decided to get her experience on paper. Jean's article glories in the many moods and sensory drama that she's observed on winter beaches: "I saw a couple walking hand-in-hand. The man leaned down and wrote something in the sand. I smiled at his age-old act, the epitome of transience: romantic declarations written and so quickly erased by the sea. Not so. When I came upon his sand message—one word only, his companion's name—the erosive winter waves were sweeping it, etching the letters more sharply and deeply until they fairly shouted their permanence. They will be there forever, I thought . . . or at least until the next high tide."

Ultimately, the key to such personal-experience stories is change. Where our personal lives are concerned, in fact, change is probably the biggest single challenge we all face and share. That's why the best personal stories explore our transitions in life—if only to encourage us to accept ourselves in some new context, or as we're becoming. Such transition or change is vital to storytelling, since it's bound up with the overall message that underscores any good story—and yet, too often, writers fail in this one key area of change and, especially, the message that comes out of it. Without a message, a story is like an egg without a shell. Why do so many writers neglect this fundamental requirement? Why are they content to wander through the garden and sniff every flower without ever picking one?

In "Lessons from Aunt Grace," which appeared in *Reader's Digest*, Nardi Reeder Campion delivers an experience and a message that any reader would benefit from. Nardi's story describes a time in her life when she was down in the dumps, and then discovered a diary that had been kept more than forty years before by a maiden aunt who had gone through some bad times herself. Aunt Grace had been poor, frail and forced to live with relatives. "I know I must be cheerful, living in this large family upon whom I am dependent," Aunt Grace wrote. "Yet gloom haunts me. Clearly my situation is not going to change; therefore, I shall have to change."

To help hold her fragile world together, Aunt Grace resolved to do six things every day: (1) something for someone else, (2) something for herself, (3) something she didn't want to do that needed doing, (4) a physical exercise, (5) a mental exercise, and (6) an original prayer that always included counting her blessings. From there, the article explores how these six steps helped change Nardi's life, just as they had helped change Aunt Grace's life many years before.

"Can life be lived by a formula?" Nardi asks in her article. "All I know is that since I started to live by those six precepts, I've become more involved with others and, hence, less 'buried' in myself. Instead of wallowing in self-pity, I have adopted Aunt Grace's motto, 'Bloom where you are planted.'"

Better than anything else, that probably summarizes what these personal stories are all about and what they tell us about the diversity and story-worthiness of ordinary people. They speak to our sense of closeness—and, above all, to our spacious sense of possibility. As columnist George Will once put it so succinctly: "It is extraordinary how extraordinary the ordinary person is." And even more extraordinary is the number of stories they're carrying around—waiting to be written.

Philip Barry Osborne

The Flop Artist Writer

I'd written over forty thousand radio commercials during my career as a copywriter. But when station management moved my workspace to the noisiest room in the building, I decided forty thousand were enough for one lifetime.

Armed with nothing more than a twenty-five-year-old bachelor of arts degree in English, I had to face the fact that at age forty-seven the only skill, talent or training I had was that of a writer. In addition to radio and television commercials, I'd written promotional material, newsletters, speeches, brochures, videos, policy manuals and catalogs for numerous advertisers over the years. But I was tired of all that advertising writing. Convincing people to buy things they probably didn't need, and perhaps couldn't afford, did not seem to be the most noble thing I could do with the writing skills God gave me.

So in September, 1992, I left the job that had been paying me a respectable salary to live on my savings while I got serious about the kind of writing I really wanted to do—inspirational articles, books and columns. I decided to become a full-time freelance writer, working in my home.

It was wonderful! I enjoyed leisurely cups of tea in the morning while I watched the *Today* show. I soon realized that I didn't even have to get dressed. I could slop around in my sweatshirt and baggy red pajama bottoms all day if I wanted to.

"What's this?" I said aloud to myself as I flipped TV channels. "A talk show? I love talk shows!" The topics were shocking. Women in their thirties and forties who married teenage boys; men having sex change operations; women murderers; children being indoctrinated into the Ku Klux Klan; women who married prisoners on death row; people who physically abused their elderly parents; fourteen- and fifteen-year-olds who demanded to be allowed to smoke, drink, do drugs and have sex in their own homes. The shows depressed me, but I kept watching, intrigued by real people who would tell all on national TV.

After the talk shows I'd have another cup of tea. Then I'd begin some serious putzing. Water the plants. Paint another sweatshirt for my Christmas gift collection. Talk to my unemployed nurse friend on the phone for an hour. Put a load of clothes in the washer. Feed the birds. Make spaghetti sauce. Run errands.

"Whoa, lunch time already?" Time for another TV talk show. More phone calls. Well, you get the picture. Very often I didn't get to my writing room until 3:00 P.M., and more often than not I didn't get there at all. But I was having a ball. After Christmas I took up cross-country skiing. Mother Nature cooperated with more snow than we'd had in years.

That winter I also welcomed hosts of out-of-town friends and relatives and spent days doing "white glove inspection" cleaning before my houseguests arrived.

After weeks of not setting foot inside my writing room or even turning on my computer, I started to feel like a slug. But I kept busy running errands, cleaning house, watching more TV talk shows and, yes, I even started taking mid-afternoon naps.

One day at the drug store I picked up three candy bars, favorites of my thirteen-year-old son Andrew, my only child still at home. My other three were all full-time college students, living away from home, so mothering Andrew had become my sole occupation from 4:00 P.M. until 8:00 A.M. the next morning. When I got home I sat down at the kitchen counter, flipped on the TV and decided it would be fun to send Andrew on a treasure hunt for his candy. I cut a sheet of paper into eight pieces. On the first I wrote, "There's a tasty prize for you at the end of the Mama Lorenz treasure hunt. The first clue is at the place that rhymes with bears."

Taped to one of the upper stairs was the next clue. "Clue number three is not on this floor. But it is near the door. Look up!" Andrew ran upstairs and down looking for and finding his clues, laughing all the way. He was having as much fun on his treasure hunt as I had writing and hiding the clues.

Clue number eight said, "You're tired, right? Go to bed. Hug your pillow. Dream sweet dreams and enjoy your prize. I love you, Mom." He found the candy inside his pillow.

After a big hug and giant "Thanks, Mom!" Andrew stood next to the kitchen counter where I was sitting watching *Oprah* on the kitchen TV. My son put his arm around my shoulders, held out the eight slips of paper with the treasure hunt clues, and paused for a moment before he said, "So, Mom, is this what you do now instead of earning money?"

His simple question hit me hard. The eight clues I'd written for Andrew's little treasure hunt were the first words I'd actually written in months. I'd found every excuse imaginable to avoid real writing, the kind of writing that could help me earn an income.

I walked to the bathroom and looked at myself in the

mirror. I was a single woman, flop artist. I'd gained fifteen pounds since I'd quit my job. I felt brain dead. I knew that writing silly little treasure hunt clues for my seventh-grader was not what the good Lord had in mind when He gave me the ability to write.

I knew I had to get back in shape physically, mentally, spiritually and professionally. On the white message board next to the front door, I wrote five lines in bold, black marker:

FIVE MILES, FIVE DAYS
FIVE GLASSES OF WATER
FIVE MINUTES OF SCRIPTURE
FIVE ARTICLES TO READ A DAY
FIVE ARTICLES MAILED EACH WEEK

It was my prescription for my new career and my new life. I would ride my exercise bike five miles a day, Monday through Friday. I would drink at least five glasses of water a day to flush out all the sugary foods I'd been eating and to help get my body back in shape. I would start each morning with five minutes of scripture or prayer. I'd been meaning to read the Psalms, one by one, for years. Now I would do it. If I kept the Bible on the kitchen counter, I knew I'd pick it up and start reading each morning.

I needed to catch up on reading and turn off the TV. Books, magazines and newspapers were stacked on my coffee table, abandoned in favor of those ridiculous TV talk shows. My new promises to myself included reading at least five articles or chapters each day, especially the ones in my professional writer's magazines.

And finally, five manuscripts in the mail each week meant that I had to get busy in my writing room every single day. I had to write. I had to rewrite and rework articles, stories and essays that I'd written in previous years and get them in shape to send to editors. My goal was to rewrite old pieces or write new ones to the tune of at least five a week and then put them in the mail to editors.

By the end of the next week I'd put a dozen manuscripts in the mail, some newly written, some I was trying to sell as reprints. I started writing more and searching for new markets on a daily basis.

I even started dressing for work. My new routine consisted of breakfast, reading and finishing my second cup of tea by 9:00 A.M., riding my exercise bike at least five miles (and often seven or eight) a day, showering, getting dressed (no pajamas allowed at work!) and being on the job in my writing room by 10:00 A.M. each weekday morning.

I still had time for a treasure hunt with Andrew every once in a while, but my five-step plan taught me that I had a lot more to share with him when he came in the door at 4:00 P.M. than silly treasure hunt clues. My own treasure hunt for more structured, more successful, work-at-home writing so far has reaped six books, dozens of newly published articles and stories, a syndicated column and a speaking career to boot. But the best part of all is the knowledge that who I am is truly based on what I do with the talent God has given me. And what I do is write. Every day.

Patricia Lorenz

The Miraculous Link

I didn't realize Beijing would be so cold in November. The ubiquitous smell of sulphury coal rides on freezing gusts that snake their way through the cracks in my tiny room. This concrete cubicle dormitory, without carpet, without heat, without water, is still a gift from the Universe and I am grateful. Illuminated by the same buzzing fluorescent light fixture that everyone here in the city uses, I am reminded of my connection to each person in this city . . . a city that is absorbing me into its embrace.

Though twice as old as most here, I am a student once again . . . as if the learning in life ever stops. On the brink of the twenty-first century, *yuan fen,* the Mandarin word for destiny, has brought me together with twenty-five Chinese students. Ranging in age from fourteen to twenty-one, these young souls have come from all over their country to learn the ancient healing art of Qigong (pronounced "chee gung"). This is our common tie, as I, too, am here to learn. It may be our only link as we don't share a common culture, a common generation or even a common language.

Yet each time my eyes locked with my beautiful fellow students, I was clearly reminded that the differences were illusion.

With one student I felt an instant affinity. I fell into her catlike gaze that lasted only brief moments, swept away by the cultural rules governing interaction with strangers. We would laugh at the certain knowledge that we shared, a common feeling in our encounters. We would look at a flower together and then nod in agreement about how we felt about it. All this took place without words. As Qigong is a healthcare modality that works with energy, we were somewhat accustomed to exploring the realms beyond the intellect. Even so, that drive to communicate with words is innately human and holds us in its clutches. Our passion to be alive overflows our emotional reservoirs and floods our mind, driving us to share what we feel. My new friend and I were at that precipice, yet without a common language to build a bridge of communication.

I went to my dorm and began teaching myself Chinese characters. If I could at least copy the ones I needed, I would be able to write my friend a note. This daunting task brought me face-to-face with even more challenges as the Chinese grammar and language structure are completely different from our romance roots. There are no plurals, no genders, no sense of past-present-future. To top that, each character is more of a "concept" or a story than a mere word. How am I to write even a short note facing the task of mastering this?

The gift of the written word is something we take for granted. It's that miraculous link between our inner and outer worlds. I sat in my dorm room, pen in hand, and I was stumped. I've always loved to write, watching the words flow like nectar, surprising me as they appeared on the page, emerging from my pen like gossamer from a spider. At that moment, I was trapped in a web spun from my feelings of separation.

But I'm not one to give up easily. I trust that intention carries us beyond the form something takes . . . and in this case, beyond the Chinese characters that I would select. It was a chance to release my need to be eloquent. It was my opportunity to not worry about coming across as intelligent or worldly. I had a feeling in my heart I wanted to convey and if what I purported to believe was true, that desire would ride on my intention like clouds on the wind.

I set about to draw four characters, *wo, gaoxing, ni, pengyou*. This translates to "I happy you friend." That's what I wanted to say after all. I drew these over a small painting I did of a bamboo branch with a mountain in the background to symbolize growth and stability.

That evening at around eleven o'clock, like each night for the past month, we met in the Institute's courtyard. With studies and duties behind us, these few moments in the shadows were our time to laugh and share the experiences of the day . . . all without words . . . except for tonight. I revealed the note I had so carefully worked on that afternoon and handed it to my young friend. She took it, covering her mouth to muffle her laughter. As it was too dark to read, she simply put it in her pocket, said good night, and turned to walk away. Within two steps, she turned back toward me and with an extended hand, offered me a piece of paper. I accepted it and she ran into the darkened dormitory.

Smiling, I held my gift and returned to my room, warm with joy and anticipation. I dared not turn on that ghastly fluorescent light, so I walked over to the single window to read this little note by the moonlight pouring in. Unfolding the delicate paper that was folded origami-style into a swan, I made out four roughly hewn words. They read, "I happy you friend."

I covered the note to guard it from falling tears.

Garri Garripoli

Power Lounging

I used to think of Sisyphus as the patron saint of worka-holics, one of whom I provisionally consider myself to be, though more out of economic necessity than compulsion. That is, freelance writing is a heavy stone, and demands a steady labor to keep it rolling.

Lately, though, I feel I've been overlooking the true instruction of Sisyphus' life which is that each time his great grindstone rolls to the bottom of the mountain, he is granted a rest while he walks back down to retrieve it. Though he must work for all time, according to the myth, he does not work all the time.

Nor, I decided recently, should I.

Having completed a book that took me fifteen months of twelve-hour days, I suddenly hit a wall I had never hit as a working man and a freelance writer—burnout. The thought of doing another day's work on anything even remotely related to the machinations of career-building, income-producing or generally "getting ahead" was nearly enough to buckle me at the knees. As it was, in the waning days of the book project, I pulled myself up to my desk each morning as if to a chin-up bar.

After such an intemperance of work, no trip seemed too

extravagant or protracted, no binge too vulgar, no amount of goofing off too unreasonable.

So I decided to take a break. In fact, I decided to extend the spirit of Sabbath to outlandish proportions—by taking four months off, living off savings and for a brief period here in the middle of my work life, seeing what it would feel like to simply not work, to make time for the kind of creative idleness that an acquaintance of mine calls "power lounging." For someone who had just finished a book about how to survive as a freelancer, taking a break of such duration seemed contrary to my own advice, but I simply had to do it.

Toward the end of the book project, in fact, I discovered that writers have their own patron saint, Saint Francis de Sales, who exhorts his flock to practice "simplicity, simplicity, simplicity." And I felt that when the disparity between my work ethic and my desire for simplicity and balance grows too large, as it had during that year spent writing the book, then I begin to feel like a man with one foot on the dock and other foot on a boat that is slowly drifting out to sea.

What I needed was what people so obliquely refer to as space, a distance from what was pressing in on me, a penetrating quiet inside. And I needed to hold that silence up to my ears, like an empty shell, and listen to the roar of my own life. I needed time to reacquaint myself with some nonwork modes of expression, to open myself to some of the things that gave me joy as a child, to savor the benediction of play, to read a novel again—and to await further instructions.

And I wanted time, unencumbered by economic concerns, to experiment with my writing—a luxury I rarely grant myself when on the treadmill of earning a living—and by doing so to make out what direction my writing wanted to take next, and where I was willing to be led.

When I told a colleague what I planned to do now that the book was done, he asked, "What are you, rich?"

"No," I replied. "Desperate."

The first phase of my vocational celibacy was marked by the postpartum depression that followed the delivery of the book. A big project, to say nothing of a lifetime of working, generates a tremendous momentum that doesn't end just because the work ends. It's a bit like a head-on collision. The car stops, but the passenger doesn't.

This seemed to set the tone for my entire sabbatical: a delicious and bewildering freedom marked by a maddening restlessness that routinely propelled me back into my office as if in a trance, despite my policy statements to the contrary. There I would sit for sometimes hours, twisting slowly back and forth on my chair and pulling anxiously at my lower lip, listening to the blathering traffic of noises in my head, while my legs vibrated like tuning forks.

"This is what it must be like when men retire," my partner Robin declared after a morning of watching me pace around the house aimlessly, opening the refrigerator half a dozen times.

The pull of work, the rhythm of the nine-to-five world, exerts a force that is nearly tidal in its irresistibility. Cut off from it, I felt adrift. This was exacerbated by being in a profession in which there is such a thin, porous line between life and work. Simply to be a writer is to always be at work. Vacations turn into assignments, lunches with friends become interviews. I study movies instead of just enjoying them, and my office is at home. As a writer, to be is to do, and without a clear sense of where one leaves off and the other begins, it is almost impossible to punch out.

Thus, unconsciously and instinctively, I began reestablishing order, ebb and flow, routine. Before I knew it, I had managed to fill half my time with busyness that looked suspiciously like business: sending manuscripts out to magazines, doing market research, feeling behind, worrying about what would happen when the four months were up. I felt as though I were cheating on a fast, or taking my briefcase with me on vacation.

What I began to realize with crackling clarity is that I come from a long line of doers, starting with a workaholic family that hardwired me to excel, to stay on top of things, to expect that hard work and material wealth would put me in line to receive the key to the cosmic washroom. On his deathbed, my grandfather asked my mother what day it was. "Tuesday," she said.

"Pay the gardener," he instructed her.

His obituary was like most others, betraying the compulsive preoccupation with work, and helping me to understand why I had such a devil of a time not working. Obituaries are little more than posthumous résumés, lists of accomplishments: books authored, titles held, military ranks attained, degrees earned. They are summary statements of our lives, testaments to what we hold in esteem, and there are no hallelujahs for idleness, for time spent with family, for afternoons given over to long, dreamy walks.

Droning away in the boiler room of the culture is a juggernaut of a machine, one that heaves out a message strong enough to pump cement through my veins: Work! Value adheres to what I produce, so I'm constantly doing. And when I'm busy doing, I don't have to be busy feeling—feeling that maybe I'm burned out, that I need a change, or that my work, which normally offers me a sense of control over my life, has instead made my life feel like a parody of being in control, like I'm frantically trying to shovel coal into a furnace that's burning it up faster and faster.

About a month into my leave of absence from writing, I had a dream that was to prove pivotal. A Zen monk gave me a large block of wood to sand down to nothing. As I neared the end, and began to look forward to the project's completion, the monk came back and took my sandpaper away, telling me to use only my fingernails. The point, he said, was the process, not the goal. Every life ends the same way, I understood him to be implying—the hero always dies—so why be in such a hurry to get to the finish line.

With that dream, something shifted inside me, and I became determined to not only take the full time off, but to use it well—to return the *free* to freelancing. Although it was a tremendous discipline to not be disciplined and goal-oriented, to stop looking for work, to stop feeling like I was wasting time (when really it is time that is wasting me), I slowly began immersing myself in the kind of activities I had originally intended for my sabbatical.

The day after the dream, I succumbed to the lazy lure of a spring afternoon spent in my own backyard, watching the shadows of clouds bend in the folds of the hills, the hawks and vultures sweep into view on long, slow arcs, the tomcats stalk birds in the low branches of the fig. And for a brief spell I was released from being pinned to the ground by the gravity of my endeavors.

Over the next three months, as the days flicked by like white lines on the freeway, I took great long walks by the sea and in the forests, lost myself in epic novels, wrote poetry again, traveled, and stopped postponing jury duty. I went surfing, joined a men's group, got to know my friends better, and even did my exercises with greater observance, not so grimly and perfunctorily. I felt expansive and that life was full of possibilities.

I not only discovered that I can stop work for months at a time and my life doesn't crumble, but that having my nose to the grindstone, my ear to the ground, and my shoulder to the wheel is, for long periods of time, not the most comfortable position. Sometimes lying in the bathtub is.

As my time off drew to a close, and I prepared to re-enter the world of work, to start writing in earnest again, I felt as I usually do at the end of vacations: not ready to come back, but renewed nonetheless. And though I saw that I'm not quite the master of my fate that I claim to be, I also realized that my life utterly belongs to me, and that it is meant to be savored and not just worked at.

Gregg Levoy

The Gift

I just don't want to get there and find out it stinks.

William Goldman

June, 1985. I'm standing in the West Village, in New York. One of those street corners with a late night news-stand where you can go to get tomorrow's papers ahead of time. I had just ducked out of the cast party of an off-Broadway show I'd written, and this was our opening night. With me was a guy I'd known since college, and together we were going to see if the reviews had come out yet. I was the writer, and my friend was the producer. We had a lot riding on this.

Two hours before that, I was back at the theater. The show was over, and almost everyone else had cleared out by then. Some family and friends were hanging around, out among the seats, and I was still backstage, watching them through the gaps in the scenery and wondering how I was going to walk out there and say hi, and how I was going to deal with them saying hi to me.

But before I did that, I took a minute. I went up to the second floor of this two-story set—my two-story set—

and I stood behind the door that was supposed to lead to a master bedroom. And I thought to myself: In two hours, I'll know. If they say it's great, we're a hit. If they say it stinks, we have to close. If they say something in the middle, then we'll see. We'll have a meeting in the morning, and we'll figure out what to do.

Something came to me then—a comment that the mother of one of the actors had made, back during rehearsals. Her son was nine years old, and played a paperboy with a mean streak. Since he was so young, his mother sat in on most of the rehearsals, because that's what stage mothers do. During one of the breaks, I was standing in the aisle, near where she was sitting and reading a book. Up on the stage, there was hammering going on, set walls getting placed, and furniture getting put into position, with people and technicians going back and forth in all directions—exactly the picture of a young playwright standing in the theater while his dream came together.

The stage mother could see that, and she looked up from her book and said something to me that I never forgot. "You must be so excited," she said. I looked at her, and forced a smile, and said something back that *I* never forgot. "Yeah," I said. "I must be." And right away, I knew that something was going on, that I was going to have to pay attention to someday.

So, on opening night here I was standing behind the door, getting ready to make my *entrance,* and thinking about that stage mother and what we'd said to each other. Because the truth was, I *wasn't* excited. I knew I wasn't back then, and I knew that my answer puzzled her. It puzzled me, too. Because all I could think, with two hours to go before a handful of newspaper critics could decide my fate, was this:

I don't care what they say. I just want to go home.

Clearly, there was something very wrong with that. Because I was miserable, and I shouldn't have been. All I knew was that after two years of writing, and rewriting, and planning, and having plans fall apart and maneuvering, and struggling with every aspect of putting this show on, of dodging and weaving every possible obstacle that can come your way when you decide to open a production in New York—all that effort and work had only added up to one tired and miserable and disillusioned writer, standing at the top of a fake set of stairs, afraid to go out and take his place among people who loved him, because *he knew in his heart that he had gotten it wrong.* Because if all this didn't excite him, the way that lady assumed it would, then he had goofed. Big time. And *that* was worth examining.

Back in the Village. We opened the first paper. The *Times.* It wasn't good. We opened the second paper. Either the *Post,* or the *Daily News,* I can't remember the order. I just know they didn't get any better. One was so downright vicious, as if I had personally insulted the critic by writing the thing at all, that I wouldn't have been surprised if the cops drove up at that moment and hauled me away for the crime of having been born. I think the critic had even suggested as much.

"This isn't good," my partner said.

"I know."

All I had wanted when we started this whole thing, was to see what it would be like to have my work in front of an audience. I had been writing all my life and had always gotten good responses and feedback. I had written movie scripts that had "almost there" written all over them—but they didn't get bought, and they didn't get made. While I hadn't yet figured out how to hit the right combination of story and storytelling, I felt like I was on the right track.

But I wasn't a kid out of college anymore. I was thirty years old, married with a four-month-old daughter, and if this wasn't going to work, I was going to have to finally face up to it somehow, and figure out what to do with my life instead. And now, supposedly, I knew. In cold print. They couldn't have put it any plainer than that.

Go home.

We started back to the restaurant where the party was. Farther uptown, my wife and daughter were in our hotel room, sleeping. My wife didn't know yet, and I wasn't going to call her; the news would be the same in the morning. For the moment, it was just me and my partner. My college buddy. I knew he felt terrible about all this. He had wanted it to be a much better experience than it was. And the amazing thing was, that at that moment he didn't have a selfish bone in his body. More than himself, he was hurting for me. So I figured I should say something to him. So I did.

"This is a gift," I said.

"What?"

I said, "It's a gift."

"How in the world is this a gift?" he said. "We have to close the show down. We have to let everybody go. These are some of the worst reviews in the world. There's no possible way we can wiggle out of this."

"I don't know how it's a gift," I said. "And I don't know what the hell kind of gift it is. I just know it's a gift. Otherwise, I'm going to go crazy. So, let me think of it this way. It's a gift."

"Okay," he said. Then we walked the rest of the way in silence. While walking, I thought about where and how I had messed the thing up. I came to the conclusion, pretty fast, that it wasn't the play, and it wasn't the writing. It was me. It was the writer. There was something wrong with me, and that needed addressing. *I* needed addressing. By *me*. At the thirty-year mark, I wasn't happy with the person I had turned out to be—and I needed a hard

core look at how that had happened, at some of the deci-
sions I had made along the way, and I needed to trace it all
back to where I had started being miserable. That's where
I would have to begin. Because if experiences like this
were really *character builders,* the way people are always
saying, then I was going to damn well have to build some
serious character. Using me as the raw material and with a
better me as the end product. It was pretty sobering. But I
knew it was true, and I knew it had to be done.

When we got to the door of the restaurant, I turned to
my friend. "Here's how it's a gift," I said. "Because in order
for any of this to make sense, I'm going to have to come
up with something that leads to an evening that is so
much better than this, that it all evens out. Because
tonight is only one half of a coin—and it's up to me to create the other half. It'll probably take a while, because I'll
be starting from so far behind. And that's okay—let it take
as long as it takes. But next time, I'm going to enjoy every
minute of it, every inning of the game. And when it's over,
I'll be happy no matter what happens—not miserable.
And that'll be the gift."

Summer, 1993. Eight years later, to the week. I was in
New York again, within a few blocks from that same
newsstand. *Sleepless in Seattle* had opened the week before,
and it was already a hit. Up until then, no romantic comedy in history had made as much money in its opening
weekend than our little movie did. I was in town because
I had been asked to speak to a film class, headed by Dr.
Richard Brown, who was pretty well known in New York
but a complete stranger to me. I said I would love to come,
and figured on about twenty people sitting on wooden
chairs on a bare floor, in bad fluorescent light.

I was wrong.

It was a major auditorium, packed with over five hundred people, and when Richard brought me out, they all

clapped like I had never heard before. And for the next two hours, I sat up there and answered Richard's questions, and their questions, about the movie: how I had come to think of it, and how crazy the whole thing was in the first place, that you could write a modern movie love story where the two main characters don't even meet until the very last scene. No guns, no violence, no sex, no car chase, no bad language and no villain. We had broken every rule, and people were coming in droves.

The evening was a love fest. It was one of the most wonderful nights of my life—and the beauty of it was, I knew it at the time. I was aware of it. Because it never left my mind, not for one minute, that *this moment right here was the other half of that coin, from eight years ago.* And that I had done exactly what I'd promised myself I was going to do.

I gave myself a gift.

Jeff Arch

How to Be Madder than Captain Ahab

How does one go about becoming a writer?

Well, you might as well ask, how do you go about becoming human, whatever *that* is!

I suppose you fall in love, early, with all kinds of things.

I fell in love with books when I was five or six, especially the way books looked and smelled.

I have been a library jackdaw all of my life, which means I have never gone into that lovely holy place with a book list, but only with my beady bright eyes and my curious paws, monkey-climbing the stacks over among the children's, and then again where I was not allowed, burrowing among the adult's mysterious books.

I would take home, at the age of ten, eight books at a time, from eight different categories, and rub my nose in them and all but lie down and roll on them like a frolicsome springtime dog. *Popular Mechanics* and *The Boy Mechanic* were my bibles. The encyclopedia was my open meadow-field where I rambled and muttered: "curiouser and curiouser!" and lay down with Jules Verne's robot pups only to arise with Edgar Rice Burroughs' Martian fleas.

I have run amuck ever since in libraries and bookstores, with fevers and deliriums.

Hysteria must be your way of life, then, if you wish, any of you, to become writers. Or, for that matter, painters or actors or any other crazy, lovely things!

If I emphasize libraries it is because school itself is only a beginning, and writing itself is a continuation. But the meat must be found and fed on in every library you can jump into and every bookstore you can pole-vault through.

Even as I did not prowl there with preconceived lists, so I do not send you there with nice dry tame indexes of my taste crushing you with an iron anvil dropped from a building.

Once started, the library is the biggest blasted Cracker Jack factory in the world.

The more you eat, the more you want!

And the more you read, the more the ideas begin to explode around inside your head, run riot, meet head-on in beautiful collisions so that when you go to bed at night the damned visions color the ceiling and light the walls with huge exploits and wonderful discoveries.

I still use libraries and bookstores in the same fashion, forty years later. I spend as much time in child's country as I do over the corseted adults'.

And what I take home and browse and munch through each evening should give you a relaxing view of a writer tumultuous just this side of madness.

I may start a night's read with a James Bond novel, move on to Shakespeare for half an hour, dip into Dylan Thomas for five minutes, make a fast turnabout and fasten on Fu Manchu, that great and evil Oriental doctor, ancestor of Dr. No, then pick up Emily Dickinson, and end my evening with Ross MacDonald, the detective novelist, or Robert Frost, that crusty poet of the American rural spirit.

The fact should be plain now: I am an amiable compost heap. My mind is full of moron plus brilliant trash, shoved in my eyes and sticking out of my ears and elbows. For I learned early on, that in order to grow myself excellent, I had to start myself in plain old farmyard blood manure. From such heaps of mediocre or angelic words, I fever myself up to grow fine stories, or roses, if you prefer.

I am a junkyard, then, of all the libraries and bookstores I ever fell into or leaned upon, and am proud that I never developed such a rare taste that I could not go back and jog with Tarzan or hit the Yellow Brick Road with Dorothy, both characters and their books banned for fifty years by all librarians and most educators. I have had my own loves, and gone my own way to become my own self.

I highly recommend you do the same. However crazy your desire, however wild your need, however dumb your taste may seem to others . . . follow it!

When I was nine, I collected Buck Rogers comic strips. People made fun. I tore them up. Two months later, I said to myself: "Hold on! What's this all about? These people are trying to starve me. They have cut me off from my vitamins! And the greatest food in my life, right now, is Buck Rogers! Everyone, outa the way! Git! Runty Ray is going to starting collecting comic strips again!"

And I did. For I have the great secret!

Everyone else was wrong. I was right. For me anyway.

What if I hadn't done as I have done?

Would I ever have grown up to become a writer of science fictions or, for that matter, any kind of writer at all?

No. Never.

If I had listened to all taste-mongers and fools and critics, I would have played a safe game, never jumped the fence, and become a nonentity whose name would not be known to you now.

So it was I learned to run and leap into an empty swimming pool, hoping to sweat enough liquid into it on the way down to make a soft landing.

Or, to change metaphors, I dropped myself off the edges of cliffs, daring to build myself wings while falling, so as not to break myself on the rocks below.

To sum it all up, if you want to write, if you want to create, you must be the most sublime fool that God ever turned out and sent rambling.

You must write every single day of your life.

You must read dreadful dumb books and glorious books, and let them wrestle in beautiful fights inside your head, vulgar one moment, brilliant the next.

You must lurk in libraries and climb the stacks like ladders to snuff books like perfumes and wear books like hats upon your crazy heads.

I wish for you a wrestling match with your Creative Muse that will last a lifetime.

I wish craziness and foolishness and madness upon you.

May you live with hysteria, and out of it make fine stories.

Which finally means, may you be in love every day for the next 20,000 days. And out of that love, remake a world.

Ray Bradbury

Supporting Writers of the World

In the spirit of supporting writers everywhere, we have selected the **Maui Writers Foundation** as our charity of choice. We are donating a portion of the proceeds from *Chicken Soup for the Writer's Soul* to the **Maui Writers Foundation**, a nonprofit organization formed to create and operate the Maui Writers Conference and the Maui Writers School and Retreat.

Held each year over the Labor Day Weekend in September, the **Maui Writers Conference** offers seminars and workshops in the craft of fiction, nonfiction, screenplays, poetry, playwriting, children's books, cookbooks and many other genres and subjects pertaining to writing and the writing life. The Conference also offers writers the invaluable opportunity to meet one-on-one with many of the most influential editors, agents and executives in publishing and film.

The **Maui Writers Retreat** is an intensive, six-day writing school in which students who qualify work one-on-one in study groups and in seminars with bestselling authors and the country's finest writing instructors.

In eight years, the **Maui Writers Conference and Retreat** has attracted more than 10,000 writers, helping thousands to find editors, agents and film executives for their books and screenplays.

For information, please call, write or e-mail:
Maui Writers Conference and Retreat
P.O. Box 1118
Kihei, HI 96753
phone: 808-879-0061
fax: 808-879-6233
e-mail: *writers@maui.net*
Web site: *www.mauiwriters.com*

More Chicken Soup?

Many of the stories and poems that you have read in this book were submitted by readers like you who have read other *Chicken Soup for the Soul* books. We would love to have you contribute a story, poem, quote or cartoon to future editions of *Chicken Soup for the Writer's Soul*.

Feel free to send us stories you write yourself, or even ones that you clip out of your local newspaper or a magazine. It could also be your favorite quotation you've put on your refrigerator door or a personal experience that has touched you deeply. If you find something in another book or off the Internet that you think others would enjoy, send them to us as well. Just make sure to send us as much information as possible about where it came from.

Chicken Soup for the Writer's Soul
P.O. Box 936
Pacific Palisades, CA 90272
fax: 310-573-3657
e-mail: *stories@writerschickensoup.com*

You can submit a story or send an e-mail by visiting our Web site at:

www.chickensoup.com

Who Is Jack Canfield?

Jack Canfield is a bestselling author and one of America's leading experts in the development of human potential. He is both a dynamic and entertaining speaker and a highly sought-after trainer with a wonderful ability to inform and inspire audiences to open their hearts, love more openly, and boldly pursue their dreams.

Jack spent his teenage years growing up in Martins Ferry, Ohio, and Wheeling, West Virginia, with his sister Kimberly (Kirberger) and his two brothers, Rick and Taylor. Jack won a scholarship to attend Harvard University, where he majored in Chinese history. Jack played intramural football and was a member of the Harvard rugby team. He was also a member of the SAE fraternity, where he was the social chairman and later the vice president of the chapter.

After graduating from Harvard, Jack pursued a masters degree and a doctorate in education at the University of Chicago and the University of Massachusetts. He taught undergraduate and graduate classes at U Mass, Hampshire College and the School for International Training. He later developed a graduate-education program for Beacon College in Massachusetts.

In recent years, Jack has focused most of his efforts on the empowerment of adult learners in both educational and corporate settings.

For further information about Jack's books, tapes and trainings or to schedule him for a presentation, please contact:

The Canfield Training Group
P.O. Box 30880 • Santa Barbara, CA 93130
phone: 805-563-2935 • fax: 805-563-2945
e-mail: *theresa@canfieldgroup.com*
Web site: *www.chickensoup.com*

Who Is Mark Victor Hansen?

Mark Victor Hansen wants to "Change the World, One Story at a Time" through the *Chicken Soup for the Soul* series.

As a professional speaker he wants to talk to people who care about things that matter and make a difference in listeners' lives now and forever. He has spoken live to over 2 million people in forty countries at over 2,500 speaking engagements.

As a businessman/entrepreneur he wants to save lives, fortunes and futures. He's actively involved in many business interests—dedicated to feeding the hungry, housing the homeless and reforesting our planet with 18 billion trees.

Mark attended Southern Illinois University (SIU) and was a research assistant to the "Leonardo da Vinci of our time" Dr. R. Buckminster Fuller. Dr. Fuller finished Einstein's "Unified Field Theory," called *Synergetic Mathematics*. Dr. Fuller patented two thousand inventions, including Geodesic Domes, wrote forty books and created World Games. World Games is a simulated model to "Make the World Work for 100 percent of Humanity." Mark loved working with Dr. Fuller and his fellow research assistants on World Games.

Mark has coauthored thirty-two *Chicken Soup for the Soul* books, *Dare to Win,* and *The Aladdin Factor.* Additionally, Mark Victor Hansen has authored *Future Diary, Miracle of Tithing, How to Achieve Total Prosperity*, and is busy at work on several new titles.

An autobiographical video called *The Real Me* has been created and highlights Mark's lifetime of achievements.

Mark's audio programs include *Sell Yourself Rich; Visualizing Is Realizing; How to Build Your Speaking and Writing Empire* and *Living Your Dreams.*

Mark has worked tirelessly to help the *Chicken Soup for the Soul* series be the first series to sell one billion copies.

For further information about Mark contact:

Mark Victor Hansen & Associates
P.O. Box 7665
Newport Beach, CA 92658
phone: (949) 759-9304 or (800) 433-2314
fax: (949) 722-6912

Who Is Bud Gardner?

Bud Gardner is a published writer, professional speaker, business-writing consultant, award-winning teacher, Jack London Award Winner, Sacramento Hall of Fame Coach, and former host of his own Writing for Publication TV class.

Bud wrote and sold 60 articles before taking over the writing for publication program at American River College, Sacramento, California, in 1977. To date, his students have sold more than 3,000 articles and 110 books, earning more than $3,000,000 from their writing, reaching an estimated 500 million readers worldwide.

Bud, with twenty-four of his top students, wrote a motivational book titled *Write to $1,000,000—Turn Your Dreams into Dollars,* which was published by Carol O'Hara's Cat*Tale Press and became a best-seller in northern California.

A California Governor, the California Joint Legislature, and the Superintendent of Public Instruction wrote resolutions, all praising Bud for his outstanding teaching accomplishments.

In May 1992, The American Society of Journalists and Authors (ASJA)—one of the most influential and prestigious writing organizations in the country—named Bud the first-ever Robert C. Anderson Memorial Award winner, distinguishing him as the most inspirational writing teacher in America.

Bud served as co-captain, along with Dan Poynter, of the Maui Writers Nonfiction Retreat and conducts seminars at the annual Maui Writer's Conference each Labor Day weekend.

A member of the National Speakers Association, Bud is an acclaimed motivational speaker for organizations, conferences and schools, and is available for speaking engagements.

To contact him:

Bud Gardner and Associates
5098 Foothills Blvd. #3
PMB #383
Roseville, CA 95747
fax: 916-781-8128
e-mail: *bgardner@calweb.com*
Web site: *www.bud-gardner.com*

Contributors

Although most of the stories in this book are original, some were taken from previously published sources such as books, magazines and newspapers. These sources are acknowledged in the permissions section. These stories were written by professional writers, celebrity authors, speakers, seminar presenters and readers like yourself, who responded to our request for stories. If you'd like to contact the writers for information or to hire them, you can reach them at the addresses and phone numbers provided below.

Steve Allen, star of the critically acclaimed NBC series *The Steve Allen Comedy Hour,* has authored 52 published books, including the 1998 publications of *Murder in Hawaii, Die Laughing* and *Dumbth.* Mr. Allen has also written and published 8,000 songs (even though he doesn't read music), including "This Could Be the Start of Something Big," "Picnic," "Impossible," and "Pretend You Don't See Her." In 1999, he published *Steve Allen's 100 Song Lyrics.* He created, wrote and hosted the Emmy award-winning PBS-TV series *Meeting of Minds.*

Jeff Arch went from anonymous writer to Oscar nominee with the 1993 release of *Sleepless in Seattle,* made from his original screenplay. He co-wrote Disney's *Iron Will,* and wrote and co-produced the CBS telefilm *Sealed with a Kiss.* In addition to active projects in feature films and for television series, Jeff's first novel, *The Bell Tower,* is scheduled to be published in 2001.

Kerry Arquette, an exhausted mother of three, has written for national and regional magazines, including *Good Housekeeping, Ladies' Home Journal, Seventeen, Woman's Day, Parenting* and *American Baby.* She is the author of *Daddy Promises, Scrapbooking with Memory Makers, Punch Your Art Out* and *What Did You Do Today?*

Ethel Bangert has been writing and teaching for fifty years. She has written and published thirty books and more than 400 magazine articles. She taught creative writing in local colleges for nearly thirty years. Her second syndicated column "Collectibles" about antiques ran for twenty-three years. She received the Life-Time Achievement Award from the Romance Writers of America and from the Outdoor Writers of America.

Hal Zina Bennett is the author of twenty-five-plus books. His titles include two novels: *Spirit Circle* and *White Mountain Blues.* His book *Write from the Heart: Unleashing the Power of Your Creativity* is on creative writing. In addition he has written three novels for young teens. Mr. Bennett's e-mail: *Writer@Saber.Net.*

Lawrence Block has two instructional books for writers, *Telling Lies for Fun & Profit* and *Spider, Spin Me a Web*. His novels range from the urban noir of Matthew Scudder (*Everybody Dies*) to the urbane effervescence of Bernie Rhodenbarr (*The Burglar in the Rye*). His articles and short fiction have appeared in *American Heritage, Redbook, Playboy, GQ* and *The New York Times*, and he has brought out three collections of short stories. He is a Mystery Writers of America Grand Master, and a multiple winner of the Edgar, Shamus and Maltese Falcon awards. He can be reached at *Lawbloc@aol.com*.

Dianna Booher has published thirty-seven books, including *Communicate with Confidence, Worth of a Woman's Words* and *Well Connected*. Several have been book club selections. Her works have been translated into seven languages and several software, video and audio series. Booher Consultants offers keynotes and training on life balance/productivity and communication (written, oral, interpersonal, gender). Contact information: *www.booherconsultants.com* or call 817-868-1200.

Ray Bradbury is the author of more than thirty books. Among his best known works are *The Martian Chronicles, Fahrenheit 451, The Illustrated Man* and *Something Wicked This Way Comes*. He wrote the screenplay for John Houston's film *Moby Dick* and has been nominated for an Academy Award. He adapted sixty-five of his short stories for TV on *Ray Bradbury's Theater* and won an Emmy for his teleplay of *The Halloween Tree*. In 1998, Avon published his latest book *Ahmed and the Oblivion Machines*.

Catharine Bramkamp lives in the wine country in northern California. She has a background in video and radio production, and experience as an on-air radio personality. She has published more than 300 newspaper and magazine articles, and lectures on fundraising on the Internet and Web design for non-profit organizations. Despite the title, her Web site *www.missbehaved.com* does not capitalize on the #1 content found on the Web.

Kate M. Brausen has written news features, essays and fiction for various newspapers and magazines, and coauthored two business management books. She and her brother were diagnosed with muscular dystrophy as young children. Kate pursued an active business management career in publishing prior to her current writing profession.

Claire Braz-Valentine lives in Capitola, CA. She works with incarcerated writers through the Arts-in-Correction Program. She is a widely published poet, playwright and columnist. Her plays on Frida Kahlo, Susan B. Anthony and Amelia Earhart have been produced worldwide. She can be reached at *Cbrazvalen@.aol.com*.

Gordon Burgett has had eighteen books and 1,600-plus articles published, and twenty-five audio cassette programs produced. He currently speaks nationwide about the topic of his latest book, *How to Create Your Own Super Second Life: What Are You Going to Do with Your Extra 30 Years?* He hides at *sops@fix.net* and *www.age-masters.com*.

John Caldwell describes his cartoons as anthrobioclastic without being portofagious. He says they are best enjoyed by the person who likes to make up words for no good reason. He lives in upstate New York with a confused grin, a lovely wife and an elderly dog. His cartoons have appeared in books, magazines, greeting cards, newspapers and on that passing craze that kids like to call the Internet.

Dame Barbara Cartland, D.B.E. D.St.J., has written and published 704 books which have sold 750 million copies. *The Guinness Book of World Records* named her the "Best Selling Author in the World." She holds the world's record for having published twenty-three books a year for twenty-one years straight. She has been published in every country of the world. She has been called the world's best-known author of romantic fiction.

Judith A. Chance is a full-time writer who lives in Alberta, Canada, with her husband, Larry, and two children, Joseph and Hailey. Author of three humorous middle-grade fiction novels, she is writing a humorous adult nonfiction book. She would like to grow up to be a combination of Erma Bombeck and Dave Barry; considering that she is forty-two and female, she has her work cut out for her. You can contact Judith by e-mail at *jchance@telusplanet.net*.

Christine Clifford is CEO/President of The Cancer Club, a company marketing humorous and helpful products for people with cancer. Author of two award-winning books, *Not Now . . . I'm Having a No Hair Day!* and *Our Family Has Cancer Too!*, Christine's work has been featured on *CNN Live, Leeza,* Lifetime Television, and in or on more than 500 magazines, newspapers and radio stations. She can be reached at 800-586-9062; 6533 Limerick Drive, Edina, MN 55439; or by e-mail at *canclub@primenet.com* or her web site at *www.cancerclub.com*.

Barnaby Conrad, an O. Henry Prize short story winner, has authored twenty-seven books, including *Matador, Hemingway's Spain, The Complete Guide to Writing Fiction* and *Name Dropping!*, the story of his San Francisco saloon. He wrote a *Playhouse 90* script for John Frankenheimer, the screenplay for John Steinbeck's *Flight* and a Broadway play from his novel, *Dangerfield*. New books are: *Learning to Write Fiction from the Masters* and *The World of Herb Caen*. He is the founder and director of the Santa Barbara Writers Conference.

Bryce Courtenay, an Australian novelist, exploded on the literary scene with his international bestseller *The Power of One,* which was translated into eleven languages and became a successful movie. His other novels *Tandia, April Fool's Day, The Potato Factory* (now a miniseries), *Tommo & Hawk* and his latest, *Jessica,* were also bestsellers. To reach Bryce, contact Bob Sessions, Penguin Books, 487 Maroondah Highway, Ringwod Victoria 3134, Australia. Phone: 03 9871 2400; fax: 03 9879 2791; e-mail: *robert.sessions@penguin.com.au*.

Chet Cunningham was born in Nebraska, blown out of the dust bowl, and moved to Oregon, where he was graduated from Pacific University. After two years in the army, he received his M.S. degree in Journalism from Columbia University in New York. As a freelance writer, he is closing in on 300 published novels. He married Rose Marie Wilhoit and has a grown son and daughter. He now lives in San Diego where he writes seven days a week.

Clive Cussler, acclaimed as America's grandmaster of adventure, has eighteen international bestsellers to his credit, including *Raise the Titanic* and his latest *Atlantis Found*. He has sold more than 100 million books in forty languages in more than 110 countries. All have made the *New York Times* list as well as other bestseller lists around the world.

Lois Duncan is the award-winning author of numerous magazine articles and forty-five books. Several of her teenage suspense novels, including *I Know What You Did Last Summer,* were made into movies. She is also the author of *Who Killed My Daughter?,* the true story of the murder of Kaitlyn Arquette, the youngest of Duncan's five children.

Elizabeth Engstrom is the author of six books and more than seventy short stories, articles and essays, editor of two anthologies and publisher of two works of fiction. She is a sought-after instructor and speaker, teaching fiction since 1987. She is the coordinator of the Maui Writers Retreat and Director of their Continuing Education program.

Richard Paul Evans is the bestselling author of *The Christmas Box, Timepiece* and *The Letter* which complete *The Christmas Box Trilogy*. His other bestsellers include *The Locket* and *The Looking Glass* as well as two children's books, *The Dance* and *The Christmas Candle,* which received the 1998 American Mothers' Book Award. There are currently more than 10 million copies of his books in print.

Howard Fast, over a 67-year writing career, has produced more than seventy-five books, along with mystery novels (under the pseudonym E.V. Cunningham), science-fiction, innumerable newspaper and magazine articles, short stories, plays, screenplays and poetry. Among his best-known novels are *Spartacus, Citizen Tom Paine, Freedom Road, April Morning, The Last Frontier* and *Redemption*.

Terri Fields is a teacher and writer. She was named Arizona Teacher of the Year in 1986 and is part of the twenty-member 1999 All USA TODAY Teacher Team. She has written fifteen books, and her books have been nominated for awards in three states. Though her son Jeff is now grown up, his name still appears somewhere in each of the books she writes for children.

Barbara Jeanne Fisher, a prolific writer living in Fremont, Ohio, has been published in numerous magazines and in several *Chicken Soup for the Soul* books, including *Women's Soul, Single Soul, Writer's Soul,* and the upcoming *Sister's Soul*. Her first novel, *Stolen Moments,* was based upon her experience in dealing with lupus in her own life. Her writing goal is to reach out from her heart to touch the hearts of others.

Ernest J. Gaines has written eight novels, including *The Autobiography of Miss Jane Pittman, A Gathering of Old Men* and *A Lesson Before Dying,* which became an HBO movie, winning two Emmys for Best Drama and Best Script. He received a MacArthur Foundation Fellowship, was named a Chevalier de L'Ordre des Arts et des Lettres (France), and elected to The American Academy of Arts and Letters.

Pat Gallant has written for *The Saturday Evening Post, Writer's Digest, The New*

Press Literary Quarterly and *Poet Magazine*. A former columnist, she was a finalist in the 1991 PEN Syndicated Fiction Project and one of seven finalists to the grand prize in the 1999 William Faulkner Literary Competition. She can be reached at 212-886-1818 or by writing to P.O. Box 42, Cathedral Station, New York, NY 10025.

Garri Garripoli is the author of two books, including *Qigong: Essence of the Healing Dance,* and many television scripts. A Harley-riding producer, director, Qigong instructor, and entrepreneur, he is CEO of WellRing.com, which provides complementary healthcare programs, services and products via the Web, television, and wellness centers worldwide. He can be contacted at 2060 Queen Street East, Suite 10, Toronto, Ontario, Canada M4E 3V7; e-mail: *garri@wujiproductions.com* or *www.wellring.com.*

Mort Gerberg, from New York, is a cartoonist and author best known for his magazine cartoons, which have appeared regularly in publications such as *The New Yorker, Playboy, Harvard Business Review, Barron's* and *Publishers Weekly.* He has drawn several nationally-syndicated newspaper comic strips and has written and/or illustrated 36 books for adults and children. Mr. Gerberg can be reached online at *abcmort@aol.com.*

Sue Grafton entered the mystery field in 1982 with the publication of, *'A' Is for Alibi,* introducing female hard-boiled detective, Kinsey Millhone. The fifteenth novel, *'O' Is for Outlaw* appeared in 1999. At the current rate, she will complete the series in the year 2015, give or take a decade.

Reg Green is a former journalist, who worked for England's (Manchester) *Guardian, The* (London) *Times* and *The Daily Telegraph.* In the U.S., he was head of public information for the Investment Company Institute in Washington, D.C., then moved to Bodega Bay, California. He is author of the bestseller *The Nicholas Effect,* the story of his son's death and how loss and tragedy were transformed into acts of love and hope.

Frances Halpern, a seasoned print and broadcast journalist, hosts "Connections," a lively Saturday morning radio show in southern California, where authors, poets, editors, agents and screenwriters share their triumphs and failures. She is the author of *Writer's Guide to Publishing in the West* (Pinnacle). Her weekly column "Words & Images" ran for six years in the *Los Angeles Times.* She is currently working on a memoir.

Edmund Hansen retired after a thirty-one-year career at the University of Wisconsin—Oshkosh. He writes for a hobby while promoting AIDS awareness. Those affected by AIDS may want to read his book, *A Father's Story.* Contact him at 1011 Norfork Island Court, Sun City Center, Florida 33573 or at *www.aidskilledmyson.com.*

Amy B. Harris, with her late husband, psychiatrist Thomas A. Harris, M.D., coauthored *I'm OK—You're OK,* which sold more than 15 million copies and was translated into twenty-five languages. A sequel, *Staying OK,* was also published by Harper & Row. A former newspaper and magazine editor, columnist, reporter and a governor's press secretary, she continues her writing today at 1951 Empire Oaks Court, Gold River, CA 95670.

Johnny Hart created his comic strip, *B.C.*, in 1958. Today *B.C.*, distributed by Creator Syndicate, Inc., is featured in 1,300 newspapers worldwide, bringing laughter to more than 100 million readers. Hart has won numerous awards, including Best Humor Strip in America, The Reuben, and Cartoonist of the Year (National Cartoonists Society); and the Seger Award (King Features). Hart draws *B.C.* in his Endicott, N.Y., studio.

Frank Harvey wrote hundreds of magazine articles, many to the major magazines, and five books, four of them novels. A former war correspondent and world traveler, the late Mr. Harvey lived in Hackettstown, NJ and spent much of his free time flying—including advanced aerobatics.

Meg Hill is a wife, parent, teacher, school counselor and writer. She has written numerous articles, stories, poems, educational materials and teen novels. "Children and teenagers," she said, "don't let you grow old." The theme of all her writing is: "Let's get on with the business of living."

Dierdre W. Honnold is a teacher, artist, musician, orchestra conductor, tour guide, linguist—but finds parenting and writing the most rewarding. More than 100 of her articles and essays have been published on four continents. Her books, fiction and nonfiction, have won many awards. Write her at: *wordintl@calweb.com.*

Valerie Hutchins lives with her husband Mark and their two children, Kelly and Jake, in Sacramento, California. She is a freelance writer and illustrator. She is also an avid motorcyclist. She enjoys contact with readers and can be reached through her e-mail address at: *argus@inreach.com.*

Cheewa James is a master storyteller, writer, professional speaker and trainer. Throughout her keynote "Climb Off Dead Horses" and other presentations, she emphasizes finding balance in life and accepting change. Enrolled with the Modoc Tribe of Oklahoma, Cheewa often draws from Native American thought for illustration. Reach her at *www.cheewa.com* for her speaking topics, training subjects, books and articles.

Catherine Lanigan is the bestselling author of *Romancing the Stone, Jewel of the Nile, Tender Malice* and *Wings of Destiny*. She is the creator of the "evolving woman," a new breed of heroine, who makes choices that enrich her internally, and, as a result, enrich the world around her as well. Lanigan drew upon her own life experiences to create this amalgam, and she does so from a perspective that is as passionate as it is personal.

Gregg Levoy, author of *Callings: Finding and Following an Authentic Life* and *This Business of Writing,* is a former adjunct professor of journalism at the University of New Mexico, and former reporter for the *Cincinnati Enquirer* and *USA Today*. His writing has appeared in the *New York Times Magazine, Washington Post, Omni, Psychology Today, Reader's Digest* and others. E-mail him at *callings@gregglevoy.com.*

Art Linkletter, a television and radio star for more than sixty years, performed in two of the longest-running shows in broadcast history—*House Party*, which ran on daytime CBS TV and radio for twenty-five years, and *People Are Funny*, which ran on nighttime NBC TV and radio for nineteen years and won two Emmy Awards. *Kids Say the Darnest Things*—one of the top fourteen bestsellers in American publishing history and number one for two consecutive years—is one of twenty-three books Art has written. His most recent national best-seller is *Old Age Is Not for Sissies*.

Patricia Lorenz has stories in many *Chicken Soup for the Soul* books (*2nd Helping, 3rd Serving, 4th Course, 6th Bowl, Woman's Soul, Single Soul, Unsinkable Soul, Christian Family Soul* and *Writer's Soul*). She's the author of two books and more than 400 articles in such magazines as *Reader's Digest, Guideposts, Working Mother, Woman's World* and *Single-Parent Family.* She is a newspaper columnist and an inspirational speaker. You may contact her at 7457 S. Pennsylvania Avenue, Oak Creek, WI 53154. For speaking engagements contact Associated Speakers, Inc. at 800-437-7577.

Kris Mackay lives in Sacramento, CA. She claims her middle name is "Try Something New." She has served as an editorial steno with the *Sacramento Bee*, a stewardess with United Airlines and secretary of Mitchell Junior High. She is the author of five books and countless articles. She and her late husband Ed traveled extensively, living in Switzerland twice. She can be contacted at *KMackay525@aol.com.*

Garry K. Marshall is a writer, producer, director and actor. In the four decades since his career began, he has produced fourteen television series, directed eleven feature films, including *Runaway Bride,* and written three produced plays. His autobiography *Wake Me When It's Funny,* released in 1995 by Adams Publishing, was written with his daughter Lori.

Jennifer Martin is a writer, speaker, educator and television producer living in Roseville, California. Along with Rosemary Dean, she is the coauthor of *The Angels Speak: Secrets from the Other Side.* She is working on her first novel. E-mail: *bgardner@calweb.com.*

Michael Maslin is a cartoonist for *The New Yorker* magazine. His cartoons have also appeared in *Mother Jones, Omni, The Saturday Evening Post, Changing Times, New Woman* and *The New York Times Book Review.* He has published several car-toon collections.

Terry McMillan published two novels, *MAMA* and *Disappearing Acts* before compiling an anthology of contemporary African-American fiction titled *Breaking Ice.* She then wrote two novels that hit the *New York Times* bestseller list: *Waiting to Exhale* (Viking, 1992) staying for thirty-eight weeks, and *How Stella Got Her Groove Back* (Viking, 1996) for twenty-one weeks. She cowrote the screenplays for both movies. Her new novel, *A Day Late and a Dollar Short,* is scheduled for publication in the fall of 2000. She is also is a syndicated colum-nist for the *New York Times.*

Dan Millman is a former world trampoline champion, coach and college pro-fessor at Stanford, U.C. Berkeley and Oberlin. His eight books—including *Way of the Peaceful Warrior, The Life You Were Born to Live, The Laws of Spirit* and two children's books—have inspired millions of people in twenty-one languages worldwide and influenced leaders in the fields of health, psychology, education, the arts, business, politics, entertainment and sports. His newest book is *Everyday Enlightenment: The Twelve Gateways to Personal Growth*, published by Warner Books.

Ruben Navarrette Jr., a graduate of Harvard and the John F. Kennedy School of Government, has published more than 300 articles, editorials, and essays, hosted radio shows in three markets and lectured around the country. He is the author of *A Darker Shade of Crimson: Odyssey of a Harvard Chicano* (Bantam), a former columnist for the *Arizona Republic*, and a contributor to the *Los Angeles Times*. He can be reached at: *www.navarrette.com*.

Erik Olesen, a licensed psychotherapist and a BCIA certified biofeedback trainer, has spoken to or consulted for more than one hundred organizations throughout the United States. His award-winning book, *Mastering the Winds of Change*, a Book-of-the-Month selection, was published in foreign editions in Europe, Asia and South America. He has written many magazine articles and a picture book for children, *The Little Sailboat and the Big Storm*. He maintains an office in Auburn, CA. His phone: 530-885-2673.

Philip Barry Osborne—a former writer for *Time* magazine and CBS, a former Senior Writer for *Business Week*, author of *The War Business Must Win* (McGraw-Hill), a member of the Academy of American Poets and a published poet, and most recently, former Assistant Managing Editor at *Reader's Digest*—is now writing full time. He won a Loeb Award, two John Hancock Awards and a National Magazine Award. He lives with his wife Fran and their two rambunctious dogs in Chappaqua, NY.

Suzanne Peppers lives on a small ranch in Placerville, CA, with her husband, Sacramento Sheriff's Lt. Cliff Peppers. They have two grown sons. She co-authored a syndicated column "The Generation Rap" with her mother for nine years, worked in television for sixteen years and now owns Peppers Productions, a video production company.

Gene Perret is a three-time Emmy winner for his work on *The Carol Burnett Show* writing staff. Gene has also written for Bob Hope since 1969, several of those years as his head writer. He traveled with Hope on his military shows to Beirut, the Persian Gulf, Saudi Arabia and on his Final Tour around the world. Presently, Gene writes a monthly humor column for *Arizona Highways*. He has written more than twenty books on humor, including the top-selling book in the field, *Comedy Writing Step by Step*.

Phyllis Taylor Pianka, a bestselling author, has published twenty novels with twenty-two foreign translations. Her latest novel is *The Thackery Jewels* trilogy. She teaches writing classes on the Internet and lectures at colleges and meetings across the country. Her text, *How to Write Romances*, is in its eighth printing. Her e-mail: *ptpianka@aol.com*.

George Plimpton, the editor of the literary journal, *The Paris Review*, is the author of numerous books, many with a sports background, including *Out of My League, Paper Lion, The Bogey Man* and *Shadow Box*. His latest book is an oral biography on author *Truman Capote* and *The Writer's Chapbook*, a compendium of fact, opinion, wit and advice from the twentieth century's preeminent writers.

Gregory Poirier, raised by hippies on Maui, attended the USC School of Theatre and the UCLA film school. His screenwriting credits include Warner Brother's *Gossip* and *Rosewood* for which he won the Paul Selvin Award from the Writers Guild of America. He has done uncredited rewrites on such films as Disney's *Mission to Mars* and *Gone in 60 Seconds*. He will direct his first feature film this year. Mr. Poirier lives in Santa Monica, CA, with his wife, Jana, and his two sons, William and Joseph.

Penny Porter, a veteran freelancer for the *Reader's Digest*, has been published in *Arizona Highways, Nevada Magazine, Catholic Digest, Guideposts* and many other magazines. She has stories in five of the *Chicken Soup for the Soul* books with more scheduled. She is the author of five books including *The Keymaker*, a novel for grades 4 to 12, and *Heartstrings and Tail-Tuggers* (1999), her first illustrated collection of true stories. She is the current director of the Society of Southwestern Authors conference.

Cookie Potter, who writes mainly for *Guideposts, Angels on Earth, Reader's Digest* and the cat magazines, wrote her first book *Growing Up in My Childhood Paradise* while in her twenties. She was the garden editor for the *San Francisco Chronicle* and west coast editor of *Parents Magazine*. For years, she taught creative writing to eight-year-olds.

Dan Poynter, the author of eighty books including *The Self-Publishing Manual* now in its twelfth printing, is a frequent speaker, successful publisher and renowned book-publishing consultant. He is leading the book-writing revolution, revealing how writers can make more money, get to press sooner and keep control of their work. Contact him at *www.ParaPublishing.com*. He lives in Santa Barbara, CA.

Hugh Prather was called "an American Kahlil Gibran" by the *New York Times*. Although a minister, columnist and radio talk-show host, he is best known as the author of fifteen books. His latest—from Conari Press—is the *Little Book of Letting Go*. Hugh can be contacted at *www.prathernotes.com*.

Marcia Preston is editor and publisher of *ByLine*, a national magazine for writers (*www.bylinemag.com*). She writes a "Final Draft" column for *ByLine*. She is also an active freelancer and novelist, living in Oklahoma.

Marilyn Pribus has more than 725 sales of fiction and nonfiction to magazines and newspapers worldwide. A freelance editor, she has edited a number of successful books; some were sold to publishing houses, many were self-published. Her e-mail address is: *pribus@compuserve.com*.

Tom Prisk has been a published cartoonist and illustrator since 1977. He has been published in *The Saturday Evening Post* (including *The Best Cartoons*), *Woman's World, Reader's Digest, Yankee Magazine, Today's Christian Woman, Leadership* (including *Best Cartoons*), *Writer's Digest* and *ByLine* magazine.

Nora Profit is an investigative journalist and freelance writer whose articles have appeared in the *San Francisco Chronicle, San Jose Magazine* and PBS (Public Broadcasting Service). She is currently working on a book about the plight of the families of America's condemned—men who are incarcerated. She can be contacted at 5005 Arden Way, Paradise, CA 95969. Phone: 530-877-2292. E-mail: *noraprofitross@msn.com* or *noraprofit@journalist.com.*

Michele Bazan Reed is a public relations professional and writer of fiction, nonfiction and haiku. She dedicates "Cash Rewards" to her father, Bill Bazan, "one of the greatest storytellers and letter writers I have ever known." She and her husband, Bill Reed, have a son and daughter, Mike and Katie, and live in Oswego, NY. Michele can be reached at *bazanreed@hotmail.com.*

Ed Robertson is the author of *The Fugitive Recaptured, Maverick: Legend of the West,* and *This Is Jim Rockford/The Rockford Files,* and also coauthor of *The Ethics of Star Trek.* He has collaborated on projects ranging from professional memoirs to books on writing and technique. Read more about Ed's work at *www.edrobertson.com* or contact him at *edsweb@slip.net.*

Noel Phillip Rodriguez, a genuine troubadour, once took to collecting beaches the way most people might collect shells. He is a poet, novelist, painter, architect . . . prince, pauper, pirate and priest. He lived in Bali, Barbados and Baja, then spent years living with the Native Americans of Arizona. Now based in southern California, he has dedicated his story to the memory of Baron Munchausen, and all others who dare to think for themselves. E-mail him at *varunadas@yahoo.com.*

Gail Rosenblum is a journalist, essayist and public speaker. She is the mother of three young children. Her essay, "A Final Letter to a Father," appeared in *A Second Chicken Soup for the Woman's Soul.* To contact her for speaking engagements or to read more of her essays, visit her Web site: *www.dealingwith.com.*

Leigh Rubin created the cartoon panel, *Rubes,* in 1979. Distributed by Creators Syndicate, *Rubes* appears in more than 400 newspapers worldwide. U.S. newspapers include the *Philadelphia Daily News,* the *Seattle Post-Intelligencer,* the *Columbus Dispatch,* the *Rochester Democrat and Chronicle, Newsday* and the *Orlando Sentinel.*

Charles Schulz, the late cartoonist of the comic strip *PEANUTS,* made an inexorable contribution to our cultural landscape for fifty years, enthralling the world with his magical microcosmic world of a group of wise-beyond-their-years children and their beloved dog, Snoopy.

Connie Shelton authors the Charlie Parker mystery series, set in Albuquerque, NM. A commercial hot air balloon pilot, Shelton holds a women's world altitude record. She has been featured in *Who 's Who* and *The World Who's Who of Women.* Her short stories have won several awards. Web site: *www.connieshelton.com.*

Bob Thaves created the comic strip, *Frank & Ernest,* in 1972. The strip, winner of three Reuben awards from the National Cartoonists Society, appears in over 1,200 newspapers worldwide. Thaves, a former industrial psychologist, lives in California with his wife, Katie. You can see much more *Frank & Ernest* at *www.frankandernest.com.*

John Tullius is the Director of the Maui Writers Conference. He is the author of fourteen books including *I'd Rather Be a Yankee, The Science Digest Book of*

Halley's Comet, and *Once a Cowboy*, and is the coauthor of the national best-selling novels *Body of a Crime* and *Against the Law*. He has also written scores of articles for dozens of magazines including *Cosmopolitan, Playboy* and *Town and Country*, and was a contributing editor for *Tennis* magazine.

Irving Wallace, after writing political articles, biographical profiles, human-interest stories, and fiction for the leading national magazines, turned to writing bestsellers—sixteen novels and seventeen nonfiction works—which sold more than 250 million copies around the world. The notable books of the late Mr. Wallace include *The Chapman Report, The Prize, The Man, The Word, The R Document* and *The Plot*.

Dottie Walters—author, consultant, and international speaker—is president of Walter International Speakers Bureau, and editor/publisher of *Sharing Ideas* magazine for speakers, meeting planners and speakers' bureau owners. She is the founder of the Speakers Bureau Owners Association, IGAB, author with her daughter Lilly Walters of *Speak & Grow Rich* (Prentice Hall) and producer of audio albums. She can be contacted by phone 626-335-8069; fax 626-335-6127; or e-mail: *dottie@walters-intl.com*.

Naida West left careers in academia and lobbying to write history novels. Her *River of Red Gold*, according to *West American Literature Journal*, is "a gripping story firmly rooted in historical research, reads with the power of good fiction." Likewise, her second novel *Eye of the Bear*, out in 2000, tells another important, untold story of the West.

Larry Wilde is a motivational humorist whose unique background as a former stand-up comedian, television actor and author of fifty-three bestselling books shines through on the platform. He speaks at conferences and conventions demonstrating why a healthy sense of humor is essential to success in today's world. E-mail: *larrywilde@aol.com*. Web site: *www.larrywilde.com*.

Josie Willis's voice has sung in the whimsical: *Frog Pond* newsletter; the practical: *Florida Gardening*; and the serious in numerous national poetry publications. She is currently working on her life's goal, a book about child abuse. Write her at 2602 Seacrest Blvd., Delray Beach, FL 33444; e-mail: *josiewillis2000@yahoo.com*.

Tom Wilson launched his cartoon, *Ziggy*, America's lovable hapless hero, in 1971 in fifteen newspapers. *Ziggy* now appears in 600 newspapers, countless books and calendars, and in more than 50 million greeting cards purchased each year. The televised animation special, "Ziggy's Gift," won an Emmy for "Outstanding Animated Special."

Marvin J. Wolf was commissioned an infantry second lieutenant while serving with the First Air Cavalry Division in Vietnam, where he shot hundreds of people, mostly at 1/250@F11. His FBI file is said to be better reading than his nine books and hundreds of magazine articles. He can be reached at *http://come.to/marvwolf*.

Make Sure You Have the Latest Servings

Chicken Soup for the Christian Family Soul

Themes of forgiveness, faith, hope, charity and love will lift your spirits, deepen your faith and expand your awareness of how to practice Christian values in your daily life—at home, at work and in the community.

Code #7141 • Quality Paperback • $12.95

Chicken Soup for the Golden Soul

Celebrating the myriad joys of living and the wisdom that comes from having lived, this collection offers loving insights and wisdom—all centering on the prime of life. You will be sure to cherish these invaluable stories as a reminder that the soul of those young at heart is truly "golden."

Code #7257 • Quality Paperback • $12.95

Books For Life

Chicken Soup for the Teenage Soul III

The third volume in this bestselling series is here! Offering teens more stories on love, friendship, family, tough stuff, growing up, kindness, learning lessons and making a difference.

Code #7613 • Quality Paperback • $12.95

Collect them all!

Chicken Soup for the Teenage Soul
Code #4630 • Quality Paperback • $12.95

Chicken Soup for the Teenage Soul II
Code #6161 • Quality Paperback • $12.95

Chicken Soup for the Teenage Soul Journal
Code #6374 • Quality Paperback • $12.95

Chicken Soup for the College Soul
Code #7028 • Quality Paperback • $12.95

Selected titles are also available in hardcover, audiocassette and CD.

Available wherever books are sold.
To order direct: Phone — **800.441.5569** • Online — **www.hci-online.com**
Prices do not include shipping and handling. Your response code is **CCS**.

Nurture Your Spirit at Work and at Play

Chicken Soup for the Golfer's Soul

This inspiring collection of stories from professionals, caddies and amateur golfers shares the memorable moments of the game—when, despite all odds, an impossible shot lands in the perfect position; when a simple game of golf becomes a lesson in life.

Code #6587 • Quality Paperback • $12.95

Chicken Soup for the Soul at Work

This powerful book gives you new options, new ways to succeed and, above all, a new love and appreciation for yourself, your job and those around you. Share it with your mentor, coworkers or staff, and enjoy renewed joy and pleasure in your chosen vocation.

Code #424X • Quality Paperback • $12.95

More from the *Chicken Soup for the Soul*® Series

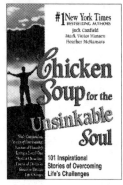